# An introduction to
# **CULTURAL THEORY**
# **and**
# **POPULAR CULTURE**

Second edition

**John Storey**

Published in the United States of America in 1998 by
The University of Georgia Press, Athens, Georgia 30602

Typeset in 10/12pt Baskerville
by Dorwyn Ltd, Rowlands Castle, Hants

05  04  03  02  01    P    7  6  5  4  3


First published in Great Britain in 1993 by Harvester Wheatsheaf

ISBN 0-8203-1960-0 (pbk.)

Library of Congress Cataloging in Publication Data available upon request

For Kate and Jenny

# CONTENTS

*Preface to first edition*  xi
*Preface to second edition*  xiii
*Acknowledgements*  xiv

**1  What is popular culture?**  **1**
Culture  2
Ideology  2
Popular culture  6
Popular culture as *other*  18
Further reading  19

**2  The 'culture and civilization' tradition**  **21**
Matthew Arnold  22
Leavisism  28
Mass culture in America: the post-war debate  35
The culture of other people  42
Further reading  44

**3  Culturalism**  **45**
Richard Hoggart: *The Uses of Literacy*  46
Raymond Williams: *The Long Revolution*  54
E. P. Thompson: *The Making of the English
    Working Class*  60
Stuart Hall and Paddy Whannel: *The Popular Arts*  63
The Centre for Contemporary Cultural Studies  70
Further reading  71

**4  Structuralism and post-structuralism**  **73**
Ferdinand de Saussure  73

Claude Lévi-Strauss, Will Wright and the
American Western 77
Roland Barthes: *Mythologies* 81
Post-structuralism 89
Jacques Derrida 90
Jacques Lacan 92
Discourse and power: Michel Foucault and
Edward Said 96
Further reading 100

**5 Marxism** **101**
Classical Marxism 101
The Frankfurt School 104
Althusserianism 115
Neo-Gramscian cultural studies 123
Popular culture as carnivalesque 130
Further reading 134

**6 Feminism** **135**
Feminisms 135
Cultural politics 136
Popular film, cine-psychoanalysis and cultural
studies 139
Janice Radway: *Reading the Romance* 146
Ien Ang: *Watching Dallas* 153
Janice Winship: *Inside Women's Magazines* 161
The other gender: men's studies and masculinity 165
Feminism as reading 166
Further reading 167

**7 Postmodernism** **169**
The postmodern condition 169
Postmodernism in the 1960s 170
Jean-François Lyotard 174
Jean Baudrillard 177
Fredric Jameson 182
Postmodern pop music 189
Postmodern television 193
Postmodernism and the pluralism of value 196
Further reading 200

**8 The politics of the popular** **202**
   A paradigm crisis in cultural studies 203
   The cultural field 206
   The economic field 219
   Hegemony revisited 225
   The ideology of mass culture 227
   Further reading 229

*Journals on cultural theory and popular culture* 230
*Notes* 231
*Index* 261

# PREFACE TO FIRST EDITION

As the title of this book indicates, my subject is the relationship between cultural theory and popular culture. But as the title also indicates, my study is intended as an *introduction* to the subject. This has entailed the adoption of a particular approach. I have not tried to write a history of the encounter between cultural theory and popular culture. Instead, I have chosen to focus on the theoretical and methodological implications and ramifications of specific moments in the history of the study of popular culture. In short, I have tended to treat cultural theory/popular culture as a discursive formation, and to focus less on historical provenance and more on how it functions ideologically in the present. To avoid misunderstanding and misrepresentation, I have allowed critics and theorists, when and where appropriate, to speak in their own words. In doing this, I am in agreement with the view expressed by the American literary historian Walter E. Houghton: 'Attitudes are elusive. Try to define them and you lose their essence, their special colour and tone. They have to be apprehended in their concrete and living formulation.'[1] Moreover, rather than simply survey the field, I have tried through quotation and detailed commentary to give the student of popular culture a 'taste' of the material. However, this book is not intended as a substitute for reading first hand the theorists and critics discussed here.[2] And, although each chapter ends with suggestions for further reading, these are intended to supplement the reading of the primary texts discussed in the individual chapters (details of which are located in the Notes at the end of the book).

Above all, the intention of this book is to provide an introduction to the academic study of popular culture. As I have already indicated, I am under no illusion that this is a *fully* adequate account, or the only possible way to map the conceptual landscape that is the subject of this study. My hope is that this version of the relationship between popular culture and cultural theory will encourage other students of popular culture to begin their own mapping of the field.

Finally, I hope I have written a book that can offer something to both those familiar with the subject and those to whom – as an academic subject at least – it is all very new.

# PREFACE TO SECOND EDITION

In writing the second edition I have sought to improve and to
expand the material in the first book. To achieve this I have revised
and rewritten. More specifically, I have added new sections on
Popular culture and the carnivalesque, and Postmodernism and
the pluralism of value. I have also extended five sections, Neo-
Gramscian cultural studies, Popular film, cine-psychoanalysis and
cultural studies, Feminism as reading, Postmodernism in the 1960s
and The cultural field.

# ACKNOWLEDGEMENTS

I would like to thank students on the 'Cultural Theory and Popular Culture' module (1990–97) on the BA (Hons) Communication Studies and BA (Hons) Media Studies degree programmes at the University of Sunderland, with whom I have rehearsed many of the ideas contained within this book. I would also like to thank colleagues in Media and Cultural Studies, and those at other institutions, for ideas and encouragement. I would like to thank Christina Wipf of Harvester Wheatsheaf for giving me the opportunity to write a second edition. But last, and most of all, I would like to thank Kate for help and support throughout the rewriting of this book; and Jenny, for again tolerating (more or less) my many absences.

For kind permission to reproduce copyright material I wish to thank the Department for Education.

# An introduction to
# CULTURAL THEORY
## and
# POPULAR CULTURE

# 1
# WHAT IS POPULAR CULTURE?

Before we consider in detail the different ways in which popular
culture has been defined and analyzed, I want to suggest some of
the general features of the debate which the study of popular
culture has generated. It is not my intention to pre-empt the specific findings and arguments which will be presented in the following chapters. Here I simply wish to map out the general
conceptual landscape of popular culture. This is, in many ways, a
daunting task. As Tony Bennett points out, 'as it stands, the concept of popular culture is virtually useless, a melting pot of confused and contradictory meanings capable of misdirecting inquiry
up any number of theoretical blind alleys.'[1] Part of the difficulty
stems from the implied *otherness* which is always absent/present
when we use the term popular culture. As we will see in the chapters that follow, popular culture is always defined, implicitly or
explicitly, in contrast to other conceptual categories: folk culture,
mass culture, dominant culture, working class culture, etc. A full
definition must always take this into account. Moreover, as we will
also see, whichever conceptual category is deployed as popular
culture's absent/present *other*, it will always powerfully affect the
connotations brought into play when we use the term popular
culture.

Therefore to study popular culture we must first confront the
difficulty posed by the term itself. That is, 'depending on how it is
used, quite different areas of inquiry and forms of theoretical definition and analytical focus are suggested.'[2] The main argument
which I suspect students will take from this book is that popular
culture is in effect an empty conceptual category, one that can be
filled in a wide variety of often conflicting ways depending on the
context of use.

## Culture

In order to define popular culture we first need to define the term culture. Raymond Williams calls culture 'one of the two or three most complicated words in the English language'.[3] Williams suggests three broad definitions. First of all, culture can be used to refer to 'a general process of intellectual, spiritual and aesthetic development'.[4] We could, for example, speak about the cultural development of Western Europe and be referring only to intellectual, spiritual and aesthetic factors – great philosophers, great artists and great poets. This would be a perfectly understandable formulation. A second use of the word culture might be to suggest 'a particular way of life, whether of a people, a period or a group'.[5] Using this definition, if we speak of the cultural development of Western Europe, we would have in mind not just intellectual and aesthetic factors, but the development of literacy, holidays, sport and religious festivals. Finally, Williams suggests that culture could be used to refer to 'the works and practices of intellectual and especially artistic activity'.[6] In other words, those texts and practices whose principal function is to signify, to produce or to be the occasion for the production of meaning. Culture in this third definition is synonymous with what structuralists and post-structuralists call 'signifying practices' (see Chapter 4). Using this definition, we would probably think of examples such as poetry, the novel, ballet, opera and fine art. To speak of popular culture usually means to mobilize the second and third meanings of the word culture. The second meaning – culture as a particular way of life – would allow us to speak of such practices as the seaside holiday, the celebration of Christmas and youth subcultures as examples of culture. These are usually referred to as lived cultures or cultural practices. The third meaning – culture as signifying practices – would allow us to speak of soap opera, pop music and comics as examples of culture. These are usually referred to as cultural texts. Few people would think of Williams's first definition when thinking about popular culture.

## Ideology

Before we turn to the different definitions of popular culture, there is another term we have to think about: ideology. Ideology is a

2

crucial concept in the study of popular culture. Graeme Turner calls it 'the most important conceptual category in cultural studies'.[7] James Carey has even suggested that 'British cultural studies could be described just as easily and perhaps more accurately as ideological studies.'[8] Like culture, ideology has many competing meanings. An understanding of this concept is often complicated by the fact that in much cultural analysis the concept is used interchangeably with culture itself, and especially popular culture. However, although ideology has been used to address the same terrain as culture and popular culture, the terms are not quite synonymous. As Stuart Hall suggests, 'Something is left over when one says "ideology" and something is not present when one says "culture".'[9] The conceptual space to which Hall refers is, of course, politics. The fact that ideology has been used to refer to the same conceptual terrain as culture and popular culture makes it an important term in any understanding of the nature of popular culture. What follows is a brief discussion of just five of the many meanings of the concept of ideology. We will consider only those meanings which have a bearing on the study of popular culture.

First of all, ideology can refer to a systematic body of ideas articulated by a particular group of people. For example, we could speak of 'professional ideology' to refer to the ideas which inform the practices of particular professional groups. We could also speak of the 'ideology of the Labour Party'. Here we would be referring to the collection of political, economic and social ideas which inform the aspirations and activities of the Party. A second definition suggests a certain masking, distortion, concealment. Ideology is used here to indicate how some cultural texts and practices present distorted images of reality. They produce what is called 'false consciousness'.[10] Such distortion, it is argued, works in the interests of the powerful against the interests of the powerless. Using this definition, we might speak of capitalist ideology. What would be intimated by this use would be the way in which ideology conceals the reality of domination from those in power: the dominant class do not see themselves as exploiters or oppressors. And, perhaps more importantly, the way in which ideology conceals the reality of subordination from those who are powerless: the subordinate classes do not see themselves as oppressed or exploited. This definition derives from certain assumptions about the circumstances of the production of cultural texts and practices. It is

3

argued that they are the superstructural reflections or expressions of the power relations of the economic base of society. This is one of the fundamental assumptions of classical Marxism. Here is Karl Marx's famous formulation:

> In the social production of their existence men enter into definite, necessary relations, which are independent of their will, namely, relations of production corresponding to a determinate stage of development of their material forces of production. The totality of these relations of production constitutes the economic structure of society, the real foundation on which there arises a legal and political superstructure and to which there correspond definite forms of social consciousness. The mode of production of material life conditions the social, political and intellectual life process in general. It is not the consciousness of men that determines their being, but on the contrary it is their social being that determines their consciousness.[11]

What Marx is suggesting is that the way a society organizes the means of its economic production will have a determining effect on the type of culture that society produces, or makes possible. The cultural products of this so-called base/superstructure relationship are deemed ideological to the extent that, as a result of this relationship, they implicitly or explicitly support the interests of the dominant groups who socially, politically, economically and culturally benefit from the economic organization of society. In Chapter 5, we will consider the modifications made by Marx and Frederick Engels themselves to this formulation, and the way in which subsequent Marxists have further modified what has come to be regarded by many cultural critics as a rather mechanistic account of what we might call the social relations of culture and popular culture. However, having said this, it is nevertheless the case that

> acceptance of the contention that the flow of causal traffic within society is unequally structured, such that the economy, in a privileged way, influences political and ideological relationships in ways that are not true in reverse, has usually been held to constitute a 'limit position' for Marxism. Abandon this claim, it is argued, and Marxism ceases to be Marxism.[12]

We can also use ideology in this general sense to refer to power relations outside those of class. For instance, feminists speak of the power of patriarchal ideology, and how it operates to conceal, mask and distort gender relations in our society. It is ideological not because it presents lies about gender relations, but because it presents partial truths as the whole truth. Its very power depends on its capacity to confuse any distinction between the two.

A third definition of ideology (closely related to, and in some ways dependent on, the second definition) uses the term to refer to 'ideological forms'.[13] This usage is intended to draw attention to the way in which texts (television fiction, pop songs, novels, feature films, etc.) always present a particular image of the world. This definition depends on a notion of society as conflictual rather than consensual. Texts are said to take sides, consciously or unconsciously, in this conflict. The German playwright Bertolt Brecht summarizes the point: 'Good or bad, a play always includes an image of the world. . . . There is no play and no theatrical performance which does not in some way affect the dispositions and conceptions of the audience. Art is never without consequences.'[14] Brecht's point can be generalized to apply to all cultural texts. Another way of saying this would be simply to argue that all texts are ultimately political. They offer competing ideological significations of the way the world is. Popular culture is thus, as Hall claims, a site where 'collective social understandings are created'. It is engaged in 'the politics of signification', the attempt to win readers to particular ways of seeing the world.[15]

A fourth definition is one that was very influential in the 1970s and early 1980s. It is the definition of ideology developed by the French Marxist philosopher Louis Althusser. We will discuss Althusser in more detail in Chapter 5. Here I will simply outline some key points about one of his definitions of ideology. Althusser's main contention is to see ideology not simply as a body of ideas, but as a material practice. What he means by this is that ideology is encountered in the practices of everyday life and not simply in certain ideas about everyday life. Principally, what Althusser has in mind is the way in which certain rituals and customs have the effect of binding us to the social order; a social order which is marked by enormous inequalities of wealth, status and power. Using this definition, we could describe the seaside holiday or the celebration of Christmas as examples of ideological practices. This would point to the way in which they offer pleasure and release from the usual demands of the social order, but that, ultimately, they return us to our places in the

5

social order, refreshed and ready to tolerate our exploitation and oppression until the next official break comes along. In this sense, ideology works to reproduce the social conditions and social relations necessary for the economic conditions and economic relations of capitalism to continue.

A fifth definition of ideology is one associated with the early work of the French cultural theorist Roland Barthes. Barthes argues that ideology operates mainly at the level of connotations, the secondary, often unconscious meanings, texts and practices carry, or can be made to carry. Ideology (or 'myth' as Barthes himself calls it) is the terrain on which takes place a hegemonic struggle to restrict connotations, to fix particular connotations, to produce new connotations. An example should make clear what Barthes has in mind. A Conservative Party political broadcast transmitted in 1990 ended with the word 'socialism' being transposed into red prison bars. What was being suggested is that the socialism of the Labour Party is synonymous with social, economic and political imprisonment. The broadcast was attempting to fix the connotations of the word socialism. Moreover, it hoped to locate socialism in a binary relationship in which it connoted unfreedom, while conservatism connoted freedom. For Barthes, this would be a classic example of the operations of ideology, the attempt to make universal and legitimate what is in fact partial and particular; an attempt to pass off that which is cultural as something which is natural.

So far we have briefly examined different ways of defining culture and ideology. What should be clear by now is that culture and ideology do cover much the same conceptual landscape, the main difference between them being that ideology brings a political dimension to the shared terrain. In addition, the introduction of the concept of ideology suggests that the culture/ideology landscape is inescapably marked by relations of power and politics. It suggests that the study of popular culture amounts to something more than a simple discussion of entertainment and leisure.[16]

## Popular culture

There are various ways to define popular culture. This book is of course in part about that very process, about the various ways in which different critical approaches have attempted to fix the meaning of popular culture. Therefore, all I intend to do for the remainder of this chapter is to sketch out six definitions of popular culture which in their different, general ways inform the study of popular culture. But first a few words about the term popular. Williams suggests four current meanings: 'well liked by many people'; 'inferior kinds of work'; 'work deliberately setting out to win favour with the people'; 'culture actually made by the people for themselves'.[17] Clearly, then, any definition of popular culture will bring into play a complex combination of the different meanings of the term culture with the different meanings of the term popular. The history of cultural theory's engagement with popular culture is, therefore, a history of the different ways in which the two terms have been connected by theoretical labour within particular historical and social contexts.

An obvious starting point in any attempt to define popular culture is to say that popular culture is simply culture that is widely favoured or well liked by many people. And, undoubtedly, such a quantitative index would meet the approval of many people. We could examine sales of books, sales of singles and albums. We could also examine attendance records at concerts, sporting events, festivals. We could scrutinize market research figures on audience preferences for different television programmes. Such counting would undoubtedly tell us a great deal. The difficulty might prove to be that, paradoxically, it tells us too much. Unless we can agree on a figure over which something becomes popular culture, and below which it is just culture, we might find that widely favoured or well liked by many people included so much as to be virtually useless as a conceptual definition of popular culture. Despite this problem, what is clear is that any definition of popular culture must include a quantitative dimension. The popular of popular culture would seem to demand it. What is also clear, however, is that on its own, a quantitative index is not enough to provide an adequate definition of popular culture. Such counting would almost certainly include 'the officially sanctioned "high culture" which in terms of book and record sales and audience ratings for television dramatizations of the classics, can justifiably claim to be "popular" in this sense'.[18]

A second way of defining popular culture is to suggest that it is the culture that is left over after we have decided what is high

7

culture. Popular culture, in this definition, is a residual category, there to accommodate cultural texts and practices which fail to meet the required standards to qualify as high culture. In other words, it is a definition of popular culture as substandard culture. What the culture/popular culture test might include is a range of value judgements on the particular cultural text or practice. For example, we might want to insist on formal complexity. We might also want to suggest that moral worth is a fitting method of judgement. Other cultural critics might want to argue that in the end it all comes down to the critical insight provided by the text or practice. To be culturally worthwhile it has to be difficult. Being difficult ensures its exclusive status as high culture. Its very difficulty literally excludes; it guarantees the exclusivity of its audience. The French sociologist Pierre Bourdieu argues that cultural distinctions are used in this way to support class distinctions. Taste is a deeply ideological category: it functions as a marker of 'class' (using the term in a double sense to mean both a social economic category and a particular level of quality). For Bourdieu, the consumption of culture is 'predisposed, consciously and deliberately or not, to fulfil a social function of legitimating social differences' (see Chapter 8).[19] Such distinctions are often supported by claims that popular culture is mass-produced commercial culture, whereas high culture is the result of an individual act of creation. The latter, therefore, deserves a moral and aesthetic response, the former requires only a fleeting sociological inspection to unlock what little it has to offer. Whatever the method deployed, those who wish to make the case for the division between high and popular culture generally insist that the division between the two is absolutely clear.

Moreover, not only is the division clear, it is fixed for all time. This latter point is usually insisted on, especially if the division is dependent on supposed essential textual qualities. There are many problems with this certainty. For example, William Shakespeare is now seen as the epitome of high culture, yet as late as the nineteenth century his work was very much a part of popular theatre.[20] The same point can also be made about Charles Dickens's work. Similarly, film noir can be seen to have crossed the borderline dividing popular and high culture: what started as popular cinema is now the preserve of academics and film clubs. One recent example of cultural traffic moving in the other direction is Luciano

Pavarotti's recording of Puccini's 'Nessun Dorma' (None Shall Sleep). Even the most rigorous defenders of high culture would not want to exclude Pavarotti or Puccini from its select enclave. But in 1990, Pavarotti managed to take 'Nessun Dorma' to number one in the British charts. Such commercial success on any quantitative analysis would make the composer, the performer and the song, popular culture. In fact, one student I know actually complained about the way in which the song had been supposedly devalued by its commercial success. He claimed that he now found it embarrassing to play the song for fear that someone should think his musical taste was simply the result of the song being 'The Official BBC Grandstand World Cup Theme'. Other students laughed and mocked. But his complaint highlights something very significant about the high culture/popular culture divide: the élitist investment that some put in its continuation.[21]

On 30 July 1991, Pavarotti gave a free concert in London's Hyde Park. A quarter of a million people were expected, but owing to heavy rain, the number who actually attended was around 100,000. Two things about the event are of interest to a student of popular culture. The first is the enormous popularity of the event. We could connect this with the fact that Pavarotti's last two albums (*Essential Pavarotti 1* and *Essential Pavarotti 2*) had both topped the British album charts. His obvious popularity would appear to call into question any clear division between high and popular culture. Second, the extent of his popularity would appear to threaten the class exclusivity of a high culture/popular culture divide. It is therefore interesting to note the way in which the event was reported in the media. All the British tabloids carried news of the event on their front pages. The *Daily Mirror*, for instance, had five pages devoted to the concert. What the tabloid coverage reveals is a clear attempt to define the event for popular culture. The *Sun* quoted a woman who said, 'I can't afford to go to posh opera houses with toffs and fork out £100 a seat'. The *Daily Mirror* ran an editorial in which it claimed that Pavarotti's performance 'wasn't for the rich' but 'for the thousands . . . who could never normally afford a night with an operatic star'. When the event was reported on television news programmes the following lunchtime, the tabloid coverage was included as part of the general meaning of the event. Both the BBC's *One o'Clock News* and ITV's *12.30 News* referred to the way in which the tabloids had covered the concert and, moreover, the extent to which they had covered the concert. The old certainties of the cultural landscape suddenly seemed in doubt. However, there was some attempt made to introduce the old certainties: 'some critics said that a park is no place for opera' (*One o'Clock News*); 'some opera enthusiasts might think it all a bit vulgar' (*12.30 News*).

Although such comments invoked the spectre of high-culture exclusivity, they seemed strangely at a loss to offer any purchase on the event. The apparently obvious cultural division between high and popular culture no longer seemed so obvious. It suddenly seemed that the cultural had been replaced by the economic, revealing a division between 'the rich' and 'the thousands'. It was the event's very popularity which forced the television news to confront, and ultimately to find wanting, old cultural certainties. This can be partly illustrated by returning to the contradictory meaning of the term popular.[22] On the one hand, something is said to be good because it is popular. An example of this usage would be: it was a popular performance. Yet, on the other hand, something is said to be bad for the very same reason. Consider these binary oppositions:

| | |
|---|---|
| Popular press | Quality press |
| Popular cinema | Art cinema |
| Popular entertainment | Art culture |

This shows clearly the way in which popular and popular culture carries within our society connotations of inferiority, a second best culture for those unable to understand, let alone appreciate, real culture – what Matthew Arnold refers to as 'the best that has been thought and said in the world' (see Chapter 2). Hall argues that what is important here is not the fact that popular forms move up and down the 'cultural escalator'; more significant are 'the forces and relations which sustain the distinction, the difference . . . [the] institutions and institutional processes . . . required to sustain each – and to continually mark the difference between them'.[23] This is principally the work of the education system and its promotion of a selective tradition (see Chapter 3).[24]

A third way of defining popular culture is as 'mass culture'. This draws heavily on the previous definition. The mass culture perspective will be discussed in some detail in Chapter 2, and all I want to do here is to suggest the basic outline of this definition.

10

The first point that those who refer to popular culture as mass culture want to establish is that popular culture is a hopelessly commercial culture. It is mass-produced for mass consumption. Its audience is a mass of non-discriminating consumers. The culture itself is formulaic, manipulative (to the political right or left, depending on who is doing the analysis). It is a culture which is consumed with brain-numbed and brain-numbing passivity. But as John Fiske points out, 'between 80 and 90 per cent of new products fail despite extensive advertising . . . many films fail to recover even their promotional costs at the box office'.[25] Simon Frith also points out that about 80 per cent of singles and albums lose money.[26] Such statistics should clearly call into question the notion of cultural consumption as an automatic and passive activity (see Chapters 6 and 8).

Those working within the mass culture perspective usually have in mind a previous 'golden age' when cultural matters were very different. This usually takes one of two forms: a lost organic community or a lost folk culture. But as Fiske points out, 'In capitalist societies there is no so-called authentic folk culture against which to measure the "inauthenticity" of mass culture, so bemoaning the loss of the authentic is a fruitless exercise in romantic nostalgia.'[27] This also holds true for the 'lost' organic community. The Frankfurt School, as we will see in Chapter 5, paradoxically locates the lost golden age, not in the past, but in the future.

For some cultural critics working within the mass culture paradigm, mass culture is not just an imposed and impoverished culture, it is in a clear identifiable sense an imported American culture: 'If popular culture in its modern form was *invented* in any one place, it was . . . in the great cities of the United States, and above all in New York' [my italics].[28] The claim that popular culture is mass American culture has a long history within the theoretical mapping of popular culture. It operates under the term 'Americanization'. Its central theme is that British culture has declined under the homogenizing influence of American culture. There are two things we can say with some confidence about the United States and popular culture. First, as Andrew Ross has pointed out, 'popular culture has been socially and institutionally central in America for longer and in a more significant way than in Europe.'[29] Second, the influence of American culture world-wide is undoubted. But the nature of that influence is at the very least contradictory. What is true is that in the 1950s (one of the key periods of Americanization), for many young people in Britain, American culture represented a force of liberation against the grey certainties of British cultural life. What is also clear is that the fear of Americanization is closely related to a distrust (regardless of national origin) of emerging forms of popular culture. As with the mass culture perspective generally, there are political left and political right versions of the argument. What is under threat is either the traditional values of high culture, or the traditional way of life of a 'tempted' working class.[30] There is what we might call a benign version of the mass culture perspective. The texts and practices of popular culture are seen as forms of public fantasy. Popular culture is understood as a collective dream world. As Richard Maltby claims, popular culture provides 'escapism that is not an escape from or to anywhere, but an escape of our utopian selves'.[31] In this sense, cultural practices such as Christmas and the seaside holiday, it could be argued, function in much the same way as dreams: they articulate in a disguised form collective (but suppressed and repressed) wishes and desires. This is a benign version of the mass culture critique because, as Maltby points out, 'If it is the crime of popular culture that it has taken our dreams and packaged them and sold them back to us, it is also the achievement of popular culture that it has brought us more and more varied dreams than we could otherwise ever have known'.[32]

Structuralism, although not usually placed within the mass culture perspective, and certainly not sharing its moralistic approach, nevertheless sees popular culture as a sort of ideological machine which more or less effortlessly reproduces the dominant ideology. Readers are seen as locked into specific 'reading positions'. There is little space for reader activity or textual contradiction. Part of post-structuralism's critique of structuralism is the opening up of a critical space in which such questions can be addressed. Chapter 4 will consider these issues in some detail.

A fourth definition contends that popular culture is the culture which originates from 'the people'. It takes issue with any approach which suggests that popular culture is something imposed on 'the people' from above. Popular culture is thus the authentic culture of 'the people'. It is popular culture as folk culture. It is a culture of the people for the people. As a definition of popular culture, it is 'often equated with a highly romanticised concept of working class culture construed as the major source of symbolic protest within contemporary capitalism'.[33] One problem with this approach is the question of who qualifies for inclusion in the category 'the people'. Another problem with it is that it evades the nature of the resources from which the culture is made. No matter how much we might insist on this definition, the fact remains that people do not spontaneously produce culture from raw materials they make themselves. Whatever popular culture is, what is certain is that its raw materials are those that are commercially provided. This approach tends to avoid the implications of this conclusion. Critical analysis of pop and rock music is particularly replete with this kind of analysis of popular culture. At a conference I attended in 1991, a contribution from the floor suggested that Levi would never be able to use a song from the Jam to sell its jeans. The fact that it had already used a song from the Clash would not shake his conviction. What underpinned this conviction was a clear sense of cultural difference – television commercials for Levi jeans are mass culture, the music of the Jam is popular culture defined as an oppositional culture of 'the people'. The only way the two could meet would be through the Jam 'selling out'. As this was not going to happen, Levi jeans would never use a song by the Jam to sell its product. But this had already happened to the Clash, a band with equally sound political credentials. The exchange stalled to a stop. The cultural use of the concept of hegemony would have, at the very least, fuelled further discussion.

A fifth definition of popular culture, then, is one that draws on the political analysis of the Italian Marxist Antonio Gramsci, particularly on his development of the concept of hegemony. Gramsci uses the term hegemony to refer to the way in which dominant groups in society through a process of 'intellectual and moral leadership' win the consent of the subordinate groups in society.[34] This will be discussed in some detail in Chapter 5. What I want to do here is to offer a general outline of how cultural theorists have taken Gramsci's political concept and used it to explain the nature and politics of popular culture – the relationship between hegemony and popular culture. Those using this approach, sometimes referred to as neo-Gramscian hegemony theory,[35] see popular culture as a site of struggle between the forces of 'resistance' of subordinate groups in society, and the forces of 'incorporation' of dominant groups in society. Popular culture in this usage is not the imposed culture of the mass culture theorists, nor is it an emerging-from-below spontaneously oppositional culture of 'the people'. Rather, it is a terrain of exchange between the two; a terrain, as already stated, marked by resistance and incorporation. The texts and practices of popular culture move within what Gramsci calls a 'compromise equilibrium'.[36] The process is historical (labelled popular culture one moment, and another kind of culture the next), but it is also synchronic (moving between resistance and incorporation at any given historical moment). For instance, the seaside holiday began as an aristocratic event and within a hundred years it had become an example of popular culture. Film noir started as despised popular cinema and within thirty years had become art cinema. In general terms, those looking at popular culture from a neo-Gramscian perspective tend to see it as a terrain of ideological struggle between dominant and subordinate classes, dominant and subordinate cultures. As Bennett explains,

> The field of popular culture is structured by the attempt of the ruling class to win hegemony and by forms of opposition to this endeavour. As such, it consists not simply of an imposed mass culture that is coincident with dominant ideology, nor simply of spontaneously oppositional cultures, but is rather an area of negotiation between the two within which – in different particular types of popular culture – dominant, subordinate and oppositional cultural and ideological values and elements are 'mixed' in different permutations.[37]

The compromise equilibrium of hegemony can also be employed to analyze different types of conflict within and across popular culture. Bennett highlights class conflict, but hegemony theory can also be used to explore and explain conflicts involving race, gender, region, generation, sexual preference, etc. – all are at different moments engaged in forms of cultural struggle against the homogenizing forces of incorporation of the official or dominant culture. The key concept in this use of the neo-Gramscian perspective is the concept of articulation (the word being employed in its double sense to mean both to express and to join together). Popular culture is said to be marked by what Chantal Mouffe calls 'a process of disarticulation–articulation'.[38] The Conservative Party political broadcast, discussed earlier, reveals this process in action. What was being attempted was the disarticulation of socialism as a political movement concerned with economic, social and political emancipation, in favour of its articulation as a political movement concerned to impose restraints on individual freedom. Also, as we will see in Chapter 6, feminism has always recognized the importance of cultural struggle within the contested landscape of popular culture. Feminist presses have published science fiction, detective fiction and romance fiction. Such cultural interventions represent an attempt to articulate popular genres for feminist politics. It is also possible, using hegemony theory, to locate the struggle between resistance and incorporation as taking place within and across individual popular texts and practices. Williams[39] suggests that we can identify different moments within a popular text or practice – what he calls 'dominant', 'emergent' and 'residual' – each pulling the text in a different direction. Thus a text is made up of a contradictory mix of different cultural forces. How these elements are articulated will depend in part on the social circumstances and historical conditions of production and reception. Hall uses Williams's insight to construct a theory of reading positions: 'subordinate', 'dominant', 'negotiated'. David Morley has modified the model to take into account discourse and subjectivity: seeing reading as always an interaction between the discourses of the text and the discourses of the reader.[40]

There is another aspect of popular culture which is suggested by the neo-Gramscian approach. This is the claim that theories of popular culture are really theories about the constitution of 'the people'. Hall, for instance, argues that popular culture is a contested site for political constructions of 'the people' and their relation to 'the power bloc'.[41] In neo-Gramscian terms,

> 'the people' refers neither to everyone nor to a single group within society but to a variety of social groups which, although differing from one another in other respects (their class position or the particular struggles in which they are most immediately engaged), are distinguished from the economically, politically and culturally powerful groups within society and are hence potentially capable of being united – of being organised into 'the people versus the power bloc' – if their separate struggles are connected.[42]

This is of course to make popular culture a profoundly political concept:

Popular culture is a site where the construction of everyday life may be examined. The point of doing this is not only academic – that is, as an attempt to understand a process or practice – it is also political, to examine the power relations that constitute this form of everyday life and thus reveal the configurations of interests its construction serves.[43]

In Chapter 8, I will consider John Fiske's 'semiotic' use of Gramsci's concept of hegemony (filtered, as it is, by Fiske through his reading of Michel de Certeau's work on popular culture, and Michel Foucault's theorization of the operations of power. Foucault's usefulness for the study of popular culture will be considered in Chapter 4). Fiske argues, as does Paul Willis from a slightly different perspective (also discussed in Chapter 8), that popular culture is what people make from the products of the culture industries – mass culture is the repertoire, and popular culture is what people actively make from it and actually do with it.

A sixth definition of popular culture is one informed by recent thinking around the debate on postmodernism. This will be the subject of Chapter 7. All I want to do now is to draw attention to some of the basic points in the debate about the relationship between postmodernism and popular culture. The main point to insist on here is the claim that postmodern culture is a culture which no longer recognizes the distinction between high and popular culture. As we shall see, for some this is a reason to celebrate an end to an élitism constructed on arbitrary distinctions of culture; for others it is a reason to despair at the final victory of commerce over culture. An example of the supposed interpenetration of commerce and culture (the postmodern blurring of the distinction between 'authentic' and 'commercial' culture) can be found in the relationship between television commercials and pop music. For example, there is a growing list of artists who have had hit records as a result of their songs appearing in television commercials:

| | |
|---|---|
| The Clash: | Levi Jeans |
| Ben E. King: | Levi Jeans |
| The Hollies: | Miller Lite |
| Free: | Wrigley's Spearmint Gum |
| Steve Miller Band: | Levi Jeans |
| Freakpower: | Wrangler Jeans |
| Babylon Zoo: | Levi Jeans |

One of the questions this relationship raises is: 'What is being sold, song or product?' I suppose the obvious answer is both. For those with little sympathy for either postmodernism or the celebratory theorizing of some postmodernists, the real question is: 'What is such a relationship doing to culture?' Those on the political left might worry about its effect on the oppositional possibilities of popular culture. Those on the political right might worry about what it is doing to the status of real culture. This has resulted in a sustained debate in cultural studies. The significance and place of popular culture is central to this debate; as is the role (the privileged position) of the student or intellectual of popular culture. These, and other questions, will be explored in Chapter 7. The chapter will also examine different attempts to fix the audience for postmodern culture to particular social and generational groupings. It will also consider claims made about what Lawrence Grossberg calls postmodernism's 'empowering sensibility'.[44] But most of all, the chapter will address, from the perspective of the student of popular culture, the question: 'What is postmodernism?'

Finally, what all these definitions have in common is the insistence that whatever else popular culture might be, it is definitely a culture that only emerged following industrialization and urbanization. As Williams argues in the Foreword to *Culture and Society*, 'The organising principle of this book is the discovery that the idea of culture, and the word itself in its general modern uses, came into English thinking in the period which we commonly describe as that of the Industrial Revolution.'[45] It is a definition of culture and popular culture which depends on there being in place a capitalist market economy. This of course makes Britain the first country to produce popular culture defined in this historically restricted way. There are other ways of defining popular culture, which do not depend on this particular history or these particular circumstances, but they are definitions that fall outside the range of the cultural theorists and cultural theory discussed in this book. The argument that underpins this particular periodization of popular culture is that the experience of industrialization and urbanization fundamentally changed the cultural relations across the landscape of popular culture. Before industrialization and urbanization, Britain had two cultures: a common culture which was shared, more or less, by all classes, and a separate élite culture produced and consumed by the dominant classes in society. As a result of industrialization and urbanization, three things happened, which together had the effect of redrawing the cultural map. First of all, industrialization changed the relations between employees and employers. This involved a shift from a relationship based on mutual obligation to one based solely on the demands of what Thomas Carlyle calls the 'cash nexus'.[46] Second, urbanization produced a residential separation of classes. For the first time in British history there were whole sections of towns and cities inhabited only by working men and women. Third, the panic engendered by the French Revolution – the fear that it might be imported into Britain – encouraged successive governments to enact a variety of repressive measures aimed at defeating radicalism. Political radicalism and trade unionism was not destroyed, but driven underground to organize beyond the influence of middle class interference and control. These three factors combined to produce a cultural space outside the paternalist considerations of the earlier common culture. The result was the production of a cultural space for the generation of a popular culture more or less outside the controlling influence of the dominant classes. How this space was filled was a subject of some controversy for the founding fathers of culturalism (see Chapter 3). Whatever we decide was its content, the anxieties engendered by the new cultural space were directly responsible for the emergence of the 'culture and civilization' approach to popular culture (see Chapter 2).

## Popular culture as *other*

What should be clear by now is that the term popular culture is not as definitionally obvious as we might have first thought. A great deal of the difficulty arises from the absent/present *other* which always haunts any definition we might use. It is never enough to speak of popular culture, we have always to acknowledge that with which it is being contrasted. And whichever of popular culture's others we employ, mass culture, high culture, working class culture, folk culture, etc., it will carry into the definition of popular culture a specific theoretical and political inflection. 'There is', as Bennett indicates, 'no single or "correct" way of resolving these problems; only a series of different solutions which have different implications and effects.'[47] The main purpose of this book is to chart the many problems encountered, and the many solutions suggested, in cultural theory's complex engagement with popular culture. As we shall discover, there is a lot of ground between Arnold's view of popular culture as anarchy and Dick Hebdige's claim that, 'In the West popular culture is no longer marginal, still less subterranean. Most of the time and for most people it simply is culture'.[48] Or, as Geoffrey Nowell-Smith notes, 'popular cultural forms have moved so far towards centre stage in British cultural life that the separate existence of a distinctive popular culture in an oppositional relation to high culture is now in question'.[49] This of course makes an understanding of the range of ways of theorizing popular culture all the more important.

This book, then, is about the theorizing that has brought us to our present state of thinking on popular culture. It is about how the changing terrain of popular culture has been explored and mapped by different cultural theorists and different theoretical approaches. It is upon their shoulders that we stand when we think critically about popular culture. The aim of this book is to introduce students to the different ways in which popular culture has been analyzed and the different popular cultures that have been articulated as a result of the act of cultural analysis. For it must be remembered that popular culture is not a historically fixed set of popular texts and practices, nor is it a historically fixed conceptual category. The object under theoretical scrutiny is both historically variable and always in part constructed by the very act of theoretical engagement. This is further complicated by the fact that different theoretical perspectives have tended to focus on particular areas of the popular cultural landscape. The most common division is between the study of texts (popular fiction, television, pop music, etc.) and lived cultures or cultural practices (seaside holidays, youth subcultures, the celebration of Christmas, etc.). The aim of this book, therefore, is to provide students with a map of the terrain to enable them to begin their own explorations, to begin their own mapping of the main theoretical and political debates which have characterized the study of popular culture.

## Further reading

Ben Agger, *Cultural Studies as Cultural Theory*, London: Falmer Press, 1992. As the title implies, this is a book about cultural studies written from a perspective sympathetic to the Frankfurt School. It offers some useful commentary on popular culture, especially Chapter 2: 'Popular culture as serious business'.

Robert C. Allen (ed.), *Channels of Discourse, Reassembled*, London: Routledge, 1992. Although this collection is specifically focused on television, it contains some excellent essays of general interest to the student of popular culture.

Tony Bennett, Colin Mercer and Janet Woolacott (eds), *Popular Culture and Social Relations*, Milton Keynes: Open University Press, 1986. An interesting collection of essays, covering both theory and analysis.

Gary Day (ed.), *Readings in Popular Culture*, London: Macmillan, 1990. A mixed collection of essays, some interesting and useful, others too unsure about how seriously to take popular culture.

John Fiske, *Understanding Popular Culture*, London: Unwin Hyman, 1989. A clear presentation of his particular approach to the study of popular culture.

John Fiske, *Reading the Popular*, London: Unwin Hyman, 1989. A collection of essays analyzing different examples of popular culture.

Andrew Milner, *Contemporary Cultural Studies* (second edition), London: UCL Press, 1994. A useful introduction to contemporary cultural theory.

Chandra Mukerji and Michael Schudson (eds), *Rethinking Popular Culture*, Berkeley: University of California Press, 1991. A collection of essays, with an informed and interesting introduction. The book is helpfully divided into sections on different approaches to popular culture: historical, anthropological, sociological, cultural.

James Naremore and Patrick Brantlinger, *Modernity and Mass Culture*, Bloomington and Indianapolis: Indiana University Press, 1991. A useful and interesting collection of essays on cultural theory and popular culture.

Dominic Strinati, *An Introduction to Theories of Popular Culture*, London: Routledge, 1995. A clear and comprehensive guide to theories of popular culture.

Andrew Tolson, *Mediations: Text and Discourse in Media Studies*, London: Edward Arnold, 1996. An excellent introduction to the study of popular media culture.

Graeme Turner, *British Cultural Studies* (second edition), London: Routledge, 1996. Still the best introduction to British cultural studies.

# 2

# THE 'CULTURE AND CIVILIZATION' TRADITION

The popular culture of the majority has always been a concern of powerful minorities. Those with political power have always thought it necessary to police the culture of those without political power, reading it symptomatically for signs of political unrest; reshaping it continually through patronage and direct intervention. In the nineteenth century, however, there was a fundamental change in this relationship. Those with power lost, for a crucial period, the means to control the culture of the subordinate classes. When they began to recover control, it was culture itself, and not culture as a symptom or sign of something else, that became, really for the first time, the actual focus of concern. As we noted at the end of Chapter 1, two factors are crucial to an understanding of these changes: industrialization and urbanization. Together they produce other changes which contribute to the making of a popular culture which marks a decisive break with the cultural relationships of the past.

If we take early nineteenth century Manchester as our example of the new industrial urban civilization, certain points become clear. First of all, the town evolved clear lines of class segregation. Second, residential separation was compounded by the new work relations of industrial capitalism. Third, on the basis of changes in living and working relations, there developed cultural changes. Put very simply, the Manchester working class was given space to develop an independent culture at some remove from the direct intervention of the dominant classes. Industrialization and urbanization had redrawn the cultural map. No longer was there a shared common culture, with an additional

21

culture of the powerful. Now, for the first time in history, there was a separate culture of the subordinate classes of the urban and industrial centres. It was a culture of two main sources: (i) a culture supplied for profit by the new cultural entrepreneurs, and (ii) a culture made by and for political agitation by radical artisans, the new urban working class, and middle class reformers described so well by E. P. Thompson in *The Making of the English Working Class* (see Chapter 3). Each of these developments in different ways threatened traditional notions of cultural cohesion and social stability. One weakened authority through the commercial dismantling of cultural cohesion, the other offered a direct challenge to all forms of political and cultural authority. These were not developments guaranteed to hearten those who feared for the continuation of a social order based on power and privilege. Such developments, it was argued, could only mean a weakening of social authority, a destabilizing of the social order. It marked the beginning of what Benjamin Disraeli would call the 'two nations', and it eventually gave birth to the first political and cultural movement of the new urban working class – Chartism. It is out of this context, and its continuing aftermath, that the *political* study of popular culture first emerges.


## Matthew Arnold


The study of popular culture in the modern age can be said to begin with the work of Matthew Arnold. In some ways this is surprising as he had very little to say directly about popular culture. Arnold's significance is that he inaugurates a tradition, a particular way of seeing popular culture, a particular way of placing popular culture within the general field of culture. The tradition has come to be known as the 'culture and civilization' tradition. My discussion of Arnold's contribution to the study of popular culture will focus mainly (but not exclusively) on *Culture and Anarchy*, the work that secured, and continues to sustain, his reputation as a cultural critic. Arnold established a cultural agenda which remained dominant in debate from the 1860s until the 1950s. His significance, therefore, lies not with any body of empirical work, but with the enormous influence of his general perspective – the Arnoldian perspective – on popular culture.

For Arnold, culture begins by meaning two things. First and foremost, it is a body of knowledge. In Arnold's famous phrase, 'the best that has been thought and said in the world.'[1] Second, culture is concerned 'to make reason and the will of God prevail'.[2] It is in the 'sweetness and light' of the second claim that 'the moral, social, and beneficial character of culture becomes manifest'.[3] That is, 'culture . . . is a study of perfection . . . perfection which consists in becoming something rather than in having something, in an inward condition of the mind and spirit, not in an outward set of circumstances'.[4] In other words, culture is the endeavour to know the best and to make this knowledge prevail for the good of all humankind. But how is culture to be attained? According to Arnold, we shall attain it 'by means of reading, observing, and thinking',[5] by 'the disinterested and active use of reading, reflection, and observation, in the endeavour to know the best that can be known'.[6] Culture, therefore, no longer consists of two things, but three. Culture is now the means to know the best that has been thought and said, as well as that body of knowledge and the application of that knowledge to the 'inward condition of the mind and spirit'.[7] There is, however, a fourth aspect to consider: Arnold insists that culture seeks 'to minister to the diseased spirit of our time'.[8] This would appear to be an example of culture's third aspect. However, we are quickly told that culture will play its part 'not so much by lending a hand to our friends and countrymen in their *actual operations* [my italics] for the removal of certain definite evils, but rather in getting our countrymen to seek culture'.[9] This is Arnold's fourth and final definition: culture is the seeking of culture, what Arnold calls 'cultivated inaction'.[10] For Arnold, then, culture is: (1) the ability to know what is best; (2) what is best; (3) the mental and spiritual application of what is best, and (4) the pursuit of what is best.

Popular culture is never actually defined. However, it becomes clear reading through Arnold's work, that the term 'anarchy' operates in part as a synonym for popular culture. Specifically, anarchy/popular culture is used to refer to Arnold's conception of the disruptive nature of working class lived culture: the political dangers that he believes to be inevitably concomitant with the entry of the male urban working class into formal politics in 1867. The upshot of this is that anarchy and culture are for Arnold deeply political concepts. The social function of culture is to police this disruptive presence: the 'raw and uncultivated . . . masses';[11] 'the raw and unkindled masses';[12] 'our masses . . . quite as raw and uncultivated as the French';[13] 'those vast, miserable unmanageable masses of sunken people'.[14] The problem is working class lived culture: 'The rough [i.e. a working-class political protester] . . . asserting his personal liberty a little, going where he likes, assembling where he likes, bawling as he likes, hustling as he likes'.[15] Again:

> the working class . . . raw and half developed . . . long lain half hidden amidst its poverty and squalor . . . now issuing from its hiding place to assert an Englishman's heaven born privilege of doing as he likes, and beginning to perplex *us* by marching where it likes, meeting where it likes, bawling what it likes, breaking what it likes [my italics].[16]

The context of all this is the suffrage agitation of 1866–67. Arnold's employment of the phrase 'beginning to perplex us' is a clear indication of the class nature of his discourse. His division of society into Barbarians (aristocracy), Philistines (middle class) and Populace (working class) would seem at first sight to defuse the class nature of this discourse. This seems to be supported by his claim that 'under all our class divisions, there is a common basis of human nature'.[17] However, if we examine what Arnold means by a common basis, we are forced to a different conclusion. If we imagine the human race existing on an evolutionary continuum with itself at one end and a common ancestor shared with the ape at the other, what Arnold seems to be suggesting is that the aristocracy and middle class are further along the evolutionary continuum than the working class. This is shown quite clearly in his example of the common basis of our human nature. He claims that

> every time that *we* snatch up a vehement opinion in ignorance and passion, every time that *we* long to crush an adversary by sheer violence, every time that *we* are envious, every time that *we* are brutal, every time that *we* adore mere power or success, every time that *we* add *our* voice to swell a blind clamour against some unpopular personage, every time that *we* trample savagely on the fallen [*we* have] found in *our* own bosom the eternal spirit of the Populace [my italics].[18]

According to Arnold, it takes only a little help from 'circumstances' to make this 'eternal spirit' triumph in both Barbarian and

Philistine. Culture has two functions in this scenario. First, it must carefully guide the aristocracy and the middle class from such circumstances. Second, it must bring to the working class, the class in which this so-called human nature is said to reside, 'a much wanted principle . . . of authority, to counteract the tendency to anarchy which seems to be threatening *us*'.[19] The principle of authority is to be found in a strong centralized State.

Why did Arnold think like this? The answer has a great deal to do with the historical changes witnessed by the nineteenth century. When he recommends culture 'as the great help out of our present difficulties', it is these changes he has in mind. The 'present difficulties' have a double context. On the one hand, they are the immediate 'problems' raised by the granting of the franchise to the male urban working class. On the other, they are a recognition of a historical process which had been in play from at least the seventeenth century. Arnold believed that the franchise had given power to men as yet uneducated for power. A working class which had lost 'the strong feudal habits of subordination and deference'[20] is a very dangerous working class. It is the function of education to restore a sense of subordination and deference to the class. In short, education would bring to the working class a 'culture' which would in turn remove the temptations of trade unionism, political agitation and cheap entertainment. In short, culture would remove popular culture. Against such 'anarchy', culture recommends the State: 'We want an authority . . . culture suggests the idea of the State.'[21] Two factors make the State necessary. First, the decline of the aristocracy as a centre of authority. Second, the rise of democracy. Together they create a terrain favourable to anarchy. The solution is to occupy this terrain with a mixture of culture and coercion. Arnold's cultured State is to function to control and curtail the social, economic and cultural aspirations of the working class until the middle class is sufficiently cultured to take on this function itself. The State will operate in two ways: (1) through coercion to ensure no more Hyde Park riots, and (2) through the instilling of the 'sweetness and light' of culture.

*Culture and Anarchy* informs its reader that 'education is the road to culture'.[22] It is therefore worth looking briefly at his vision of education. Arnold does not envisage working class, middle class and aristocratic children all walking down the same road to culture. For the aristocracy, education is to accustom it to decline, to banish it as a class to history. For the working class, education is to civilize it for subordination, deference and exploitation. Arnold saw working class schools (primary and elementary) as little more than outposts of civilization in a dark continent of working class barbarism: 'they civilize the neighbourhood where they are placed'.[23] In a letter to his mother written in 1862, he writes, 'the State has an interest in the primary school as a civilizing agent, even prior to its interest in it as an instructing agent'.[24] According to Arnold, working class children had to be civilized before they could be instructed. It was culture's task to accomplish this. For the middle class, education was something quite different. Its essential function is to prepare middle class children for the power that is to be theirs. Its aim is to convert 'a middle class, narrow, ungenial, and unattractive [into] a cultured, liberalised, ennobled, transformed middle class, [one to whom the working class] may with joy direct its aspirations'.[25]

Arnold called his various proposals, quoting the Duke of Wellington, 'a revolution by due course of law'.[26] What it amounts to is a revolution from above; a revolution to prevent popular revolution from below. It works on the principle that a reform given is always better than a reform taken, forced or won. Popular demands are met, but in such a way as to weaken claims for further demands. It is not that Arnold did not desire a better society, one with less squalor, less poverty, less ignorance, etc., but that a better society could never be envisaged as other than a better bourgeois society.

Most of what I have said is a roundabout way of saying that the first grand theorist of popular culture had in fact very little to say about popular culture, except, that is, to say that it was symptomatic of a profound political disorder. Culture is not the main concern of Arnold's work, rather the main concern is social order, social authority, won through cultural subordination and deference. Working class culture is significant to the extent that it signals evidence of social and cultural disorder and decline – a breakdown in social and cultural authority. The fact that it exists at all is evidence enough of decline and disorder. Working class 'anarchy' is to be suppressed by the harmonious influences of culture – 'the best that has been thought and said in the world'.

Many of Arnold's ideas are derived from the Romantic critique of industrialism.[27] One writer in particular seems especially

26

relevant, Samuel Taylor Coleridge. Coleridge distinguishes between 'civilization' ('a mixed good, if not far more a corrupting influence') and 'cultivation' ('the harmonious development of those qualities and faculties which characterise our humanity').[28] To simplify, Coleridge suggests that civilization refers to the nation as a whole; cultivation is the property of a small minority, whom he calls the 'clerisy'. It is the function of the cultivated clerisy to guide the progress of civilization:

> the objects and final intention of the whole order being these – preserve the stores, and to guard the treasures, of past civilisation, and thus to bind the present to the past; to perfect and add to the same, and thus to connect the present with the future; but especially to diffuse through the whole community, and to every native entitled to its laws and rights, that quantity and quality of knowledge which was indispensable both for understanding of those rights, and for the performance of the duties correspondent.[29]

Arnold builds on Coleridge's ideas. Instead of a clerisy, he writes of 'aliens' or 'the remnant'. But the purpose is essentially the same: the mobilisation of culture to police the unruly forces of mass society. According to Arnold, history shows that societies have always been destroyed by 'the moral failure of the unsound majority'.[30] Such a reading of history is hardly likely to inspire much confidence in democracy – let alone in popular culture. Arnold's vision is based on a curious paradox; the men and women of culture know the best that has been thought and said, but for whom are they preserving these treasures when the majority is unsound and has always been unsound? The inescapable answer seems to be: for themselves, a self-perpetuating cultural élite. All that is required from the rest of us is to recognize our cultural difference and acknowledge our cultural deference. Arnold is clear on this point:

> The mass of mankind will never have any ardent zeal for seeing things as they are; very inadequate ideas will always satisfy them. On these inadequate ideas reposes, and must repose, the general practice of the world. That is as much as saying that whoever sets himself to see things as they are will find himself one of a very small circle; but it is only by this small circle resolutely doing its own work that adequate ideas will ever get current at all.[31]

And again,

> The highly instructed few, and not the scantily instructed many,
> will ever be the organ to the human race of knowledge and truth.
> Knowledge and truth in the full sense of the words, are not
> attainable by the great mass of the human race at all.[32]

These are very revealing statements. If the mass of humankind is to
be always satisfied with inadequate ideas, never able to attain truth
and knowledge, for whom are the small circle working? And what
of the adequate ideas they will make current – current for whom?
For other small circles of élites? If they are never to engage in
practical politics, and never to have any real influence on the mass
of humankind, what is the purpose of all the grand humanistic
claims to be found scattered throughout Arnold's work? It would
appear that Arnold has been ensnared by his own élitism: and the
working class are destined to remain to wallow in 'their beer, their
gin, and their fun'.[33] However, Arnold does not so much reject
practical politics, as leave them in the safe hands of established
authority. Therefore, the only politics which are being rejected are
the politics of protest, the politics of opposition. This is a very stale
defence of the dominant order. Despite this, or perhaps because
of it, his influence has been enormous in that the Arnoldian
perspective virtually mapped out the way of thinking about popular culture and cultural politics which dominated the field until
the late 1950s.

## Leavisism

> For Matthew Arnold it was in some ways less difficult. I am think-
> ing of the so much more desperate plight of culture today.[34]

The influence of Arnold on F. R. Leavis is there for all to see.
Leavis takes Arnold's cultural politics, and applies them to the
supposed 'cultural crisis' of the 1930s. According to Leavis and the
Leavisites, the twentieth century is marked by an increasing
cultural decline. What had been identified by Arnold in the nineteenth century had continued and been compounded in the twentieth. It was a culture of 'standardisation and levelling down'.[35]
Against this 'the citizen . . . must be trained to discriminate and to
resist'.[36]

Leavis's work spans a forty-year period. However, his attitude to popular culture was formed in the early 1930s with the publication of three works: *Mass Civilisation and Minority Culture, Fiction and the Reading Public,* written by Q. D. Leavis, and *Culture and Environment,* written with Denys Thompson. Together these three books form the basis of the Leavisite response to popular culture.

Leavisism is based on the assumption that 'culture has always been in minority keeping':[37]

> Upon the minority depends our power of profiting by the finest human experience of the past; they keep alive the subtlest and most perishable parts of tradition. Upon them depend the implicit standards that order the finer living of an age, the sense that this is worth more than that, this rather than that is the direction in which to go, that the centre is here rather than there.[38]

What has changed is the status of this minority. No longer can it command cultural deference, no longer is its cultural authority unchallenged. Q. D. Leavis refers to a situation in which 'the minority, who had hitherto set the standard of taste without any serious challenge' have experienced a 'collapse of authority'.[39] Just as Arnold regretted the passing of 'the strong feudal habits of subordination and deference' (see p. 25 above), Q.D. Leavis is nostalgic for a time when the masses exhibited an 'unquestioning assent to authority'.[40] She quotes Edmund Gosse to confirm the seriousness of the situation:

> One danger which I have long foreseen from the spread of the democratic sentiment, is that of the traditions of literary taste, the canons of literature, being reversed with success by a popular vote. Up to the present time, in all parts of the world, the masses of uneducated or semieducated persons, who form the vast majority of readers, though they cannot and do not appreciate the classics of their race, have been content to acknowledge their traditional supremacy. Of late there have seemed to me to be certain signs, especially in America, of a revolt of the mob against our literary masters . . . . If literature is to be judged by a plebiscite and if the plebs recognises its power, it will certainly by degrees cease to support reputations which give it no pleasure and which it cannot comprehend. The revolution against taste, once begun, will land us in irreparable chaos.[41]

According to F. R. Leavis, what Gosse had only feared had now come to pass:

> I have said earlier that culture has always been in minority keeping. But the minority now is made conscious, not merely of an uncongenial, but of a hostile environment . . . . 'Civilisation' and 'culture' are coming to be antithetical terms. It is not merely that the power and the sense of authority are now divorced from culture, but that some of the most disinterested solicitude for civilisation is apt to be, consciously or unconsciously, inimical to culture.[42]

Mass civilization and its mass culture pose a subversive front, threatening 'to land us in irreparable chaos'. It is against this threat that Leavisism writes its manifestos, and proposes 'to introduce into schools a training in resistance [to mass culture]';[43] and outside schools, to promote a 'conscious and directed effort . . . [to] take the form of resistance by an armed and active minority'.[44] The threat of democracy in matters both cultural and political is a terrifying thought for Leavisism. Moreover, according to Q. D. Leavis, 'The people with power no longer represent intellectual authority and culture'.[45] Like Arnold, she sees the collapse of traditional authority coming at the same time as the rise of mass democracy. Together they squeeze the cultured minority and produce a terrain favourable for 'anarchy'.

F. R. Leavis claims that prior to the nineteenth century, and certainly in the seventeenth century, England had a vigorous common culture. After the changes brought about by the Industrial Revolution, the common culture fragmented into two cultures. On the one hand, a minority culture; on the other, a mass civilization. The minority culture embodied the values and standards of 'the best that has been thought and said', now reduced to a literary tradition. This was a culture of the educated minority. In opposition to this was mass civilization. This consisted of mass culture, commercial culture consumed by the 'uneducated' majority. In *Mass Civilisation and Minority Culture*, and *Culture and Environment*, F. R. Leavis isolates certain key aspects of mass culture for special discussion. Popular fiction, for example, is condemned for offering addictive forms of 'compensation' and 'distraction':

> This form of compensation . . . is the very reverse of recreation, in that it tends, not to strengthen and refresh the addict for living, but to increase his unfitness by habituating him to weak evasions, to the refusal to face reality at all.[46]

Q. D. Leavis refers to such reading as 'a drug addiction to fiction'[47] and for those readers of romantic fiction it can lead to 'a habit of fantasying [which] will lead to maladjustment in actual life'.[48] Self-abuse is one thing, but there is worse: their addiction 'helps to make a social atmosphere unfavourable to the aspirations of the minority. They actually get in the way of genuine feeling and responsible thinking.'[49] For those not addicted to popular fiction there is always the danger of cinema. Its increasing popularity makes it a very dangerous source of pleasure indeed: 'they [films] involve surrender, under conditions of hypnotic receptivity, to the cheapest emotional appeals, appeals the more insidious because they are associated with a compellingly vivid illusion of actual life.'[50] For Q. D. Leavis, Hollywood films are 'largely masturbatory'.[51] Although the popular press is described as 'the most powerful and pervasive de-educator of the public mind',[52] and radio is claimed to be putting an end to critical thought,[53] it is for advertising, with its 'unremitting, pervasive, masturbatory manipulations', that F. R. Leavis saves his most condemnatory tone.

Advertising is Leavisism's main symptom of cultural disease. To understand why we must understand Leavisism's attitude to language. In *Culture and Environment*, Leavis states: 'it should be brought home to learners that this debasement of language is not merely a matter of words; it is a debasement of emotional life, and the quality of living.'[54] Therefore advertising is not just blamed for debasing the language, but condemned for debasing the emotional life of the whole language community; reducing 'the standard of living'. He provides examples (mostly written by himself) for analysis. The questions he poses are very revealing of his general attitude. Here is a typical example, an advert for 'Two Quakers' tobacco:

### The Tobacco of Typical Twist

'Yes, it's the best I've ever smoked. But it's deuced expensive.'
'What's the tuppence extra? And anyway, you get it back an'
more. Burns clean and slow – that's the typical twist, – gives it the
odd look. Cute scientific dodge. You see, they experimented
. . . .' 'Oh! cut the cackle, and give us another fill. You talk like
an advertisement.'
Thereafter peace and a pipe of Two Quakers.

He then suggests the following question for school students in the fifth and sixth forms:

    i. Describe the type of person represented.

   ii. How are you expected to feel towards him?

  iii. What do you think his attitude would be towards us? How would he behave in situations where mob passions run high?[55]

Two things are remarkable about these questions. First of all, the connection that is made between the advertisement and so-called mob passions. This is an unusual question, even for students of cultural studies. Second, notice the exclusive 'we'; and note also how the pronoun attempts to construct membership of a small educated élite. Other questions operate in the same way. Here are a few examples:

> Describe the kind of reader this passage would please, and say why it would please him.[56]
>
> What kind of person can you imagine responding to such an appeal as this last? What acquaintance would you expect them to have of Shakespeare's work and what capacity for appreciating it?
>
> Pupils can be asked to recall their own observations of the kind of people they may have seen visiting 'shrines'.[57]
>
> In the light of the 'Gresham Law', what kind of influence do you expect the cinema to have on general taste and mentality?[58]
>
> What kind of standards are implied here? What would you judge to be the quality of the 'literature' he reads, and the reading he devotes to it?[59]
>
> Why do we wince at the mentality that uses this idiom?[60]
>
> [After describing the cinema as 'cheapening, debasing, distorting']. Develop the discussion of the educational value of cinema as suggested here.[61]

Rather than encouraging 'discrimination and resistance', it is difficult to see how such questions would invite anything other than a debilitating and self-confirming snobbery.

    F. R. Leavis looks back longingly to a cultural golden age, a mythic rural past, when there was a shared culture uncorrupted by commercial interests. This was a time before the cultural fall of the nineteenth century. The Elizabethan period of Shakespeare's theatre is often cited as such a time of cultural coherence before the cultural disintegration of the nineteenth and twentieth centuries. F. R. Leavis writes of Shakespeare belonging 'to a genuinely national culture, to a community in which it was possible for the theatre to appeal to the cultivated and the populace at the same time'.[62] Q. D. Leavis, in *Fiction and the Reading Public*, has charted this decline. Her own comment on the organic relations between populace and cultivated are very revealing: 'the masses were receiving their amusement from above. . . . They had to take the same amusements as their betters. . . . Happily, they had no choice.'[63] According to Q. D. Leavis,

> the spectator of Elizabethan drama, though he might not be able to follow the 'thought' minutely in the great tragedies, was getting his amusement from the mind and sensibility that produced those passages, from an artist and not from one of his own class. There was then no such complete separation as we have . . . between the life of the cultivated and the life of the generality.[64]

The golden age was not just marked by cultural coherence, but, happily for the Leavisites, a cultural coherence based on authoritarian and hierarchical principles. It was a common culture which gave intellectual stimulation at one end, and affective pleasure at the other. This was a mythic world in which everyone knew their place, knew their station in life. Despite these qualifications, F. R. Leavis is insistent 'that there was in the seventeenth century, a real culture of the people . . . a rich traditional culture . . . a positive culture which has disappeared.'[65] Most of this culture was, according to Leavisism, destroyed by the changes brought about by the Industrial Revolution. The last remnants of the organic community, however, could still be found in rural communities in nineteenth century England. He cites the work of George Bourne, *Change in the Village* and *The Wheelwright's Shop*, as evidence of this.[66] In the opening pages of *Culture and Environment*, F. R. Leavis offers a reminder of what had been lost:

> What we have lost is the organic community with the living culture it embodied. Folk songs, folk dances, Cotswold cottages and handicraft products are signs and expressions of something more: an art of life, a way of living, ordered and patterned, involving social arts, codes of intercourse and a responsive adjustment, growing out of immemorial experience, to the natural environment and the rhythm of the year.[67]

The quality of work has also deteriorated with the loss of the organic community. He sees the need for leisure as a sign of this loss. Whereas in the past a worker lived in his or her work, he or she now works in order to live outside his or her work. But the quality of work, as a result of industrialization, has deteriorated to such an extent that workers are actually 'incapacitated by their work'.[68] Therefore, instead of recreation (recreating what was lost in work), leisure provides them with only 'decreation' (a compounding of the loss experienced through work). Given such a situation, it is little wonder that people turn to mass culture for compensation and passive distraction; the drug habit develops and they become junkies addicted to 'substitute living'.[69]

A world of rural rhythms has been lost to the monotony and mediocrity of, 'almost universally, suburbanism'.[70] Whereas in the organic community everyday culture was a constant support to the health of the individual, in mass civilization one must make a conscious and directed effort to avoid the unhealthy influence of everyday culture. F. R. Leavis fails to mention, as Williams remarks, 'the penury, the petty tyranny, the disease and mortality, the ignorance and frustrated intelligence which were also among its ingredients'.[71] What we are presented with is not a historical account, but a literary myth to draw attention to the nature of our supposed loss: 'the memory of the old order must be the chief incitement towards a new'.[72] But, although the organic community is lost, it is still possible to get access to its values and standards. Literature is a treasury embodying all that is to be valued in human experience. Unfortunately, literature as the jewel in the crown of culture, has, like culture, lost its authority. F. R. Leavis plans to remedy this by dispatching cultural missionaries, a small select band of literary intellectuals, to establish outposts of culture within universities to maintain the literary/cultural tradition and encourage its 'continuous collaborative renewal',[73] and in schools to arm students to wage war against the general barbarism of mass culture and mass civilization. The re-establishment of literature's authority would not of course herald the return of the organic community, but it would keep under control the expansion of the influence of mass culture and thus present and maintain the continuity of England's cultural tradition. In short, it would help maintain and produce an 'educated public' who would continue the Arnoldian tradition of keeping in circulation 'the best that has been thought and said'.

It is very easy to be critical of the Leavisite approach to popular culture. But, as Bennett points out,

> Even as late as the mid fifties . . . 'Leavisism' [provided] the only developed intellectual terrain on which it was possible to engage

with the study of popular culture. Historically, of course, the work produced by the 'Leavisites' was of seminal importance, constituting the first attempt to apply to popular forms techniques of literary analysis previously reserved for 'serious' works. . . . Perhaps more importantly, the general impact of 'Leavisism' – at least as scathing in its criticisms of established 'high' and 'middle brow' culture as of popular forms – tended to unsettle the prevailing canons of aesthetic judgment and evaluation with, in the long term, quite radical and often unforeseen consequences.[74]

In Chapter 3, we will begin to consider some of these radical and often unforeseen consequences as they appeared in the work of Richard Hoggart and Raymond Williams.

## Mass culture in America: the post-war debate

In the first fifteen or so years following the end of the Second World War, American intellectuals engaged in a debate about so-called mass culture. Andrew Ross sees 'mass' as 'one of the key terms that governs the official distinction between American/ UnAmerican'.[75] He argues that, 'The history behind this official distinction is in many ways the history of the formation of the modern national culture.'[76] Following the Second World War, America experienced the temporary success of a cultural and political consensus – supposedly based on liberalism, pluralism and classlessness. Until its collapse in the agitation for black civil rights, the formation of the counterculture, the opposition to America's war in Vietnam, the women's liberation movement, the campaign for gay rights, it was a consensus dependent to a large extent on the cultural authority of American intellectuals. As Ross points out, 'For perhaps the first time in American history, intellectuals, as a social grouping, had the opportunity to recognize themselves as national agents of cultural, moral, and political leadership'.[77] This newly found significance was in part due to 'the intense, and quite public, debate about "mass culture" that occupied intellectuals for almost fifteen years, until the late fifties'.[78] Ross spends most of his time relating the debate to the Cold War ideology of 'containment': the need to maintain a healthy body politic both within (from the dangers of mass culture) and without (from the dangers of Soviet communism). He identifies three positions in the debate: (1) an aesthetic–liberal position which bemoans the fact that given the choice the majority of the population choose so-called second- and third-rate cultural texts and practices in preference to the texts and practices of high culture; (2) the corporate–liberal or progressive–evolutionist position which claims that popular culture serves a benign function of socializing people into the pleasures of consumption in the new capitalist–consumerist society; and (3) the radical or socialist position which views mass culture as a form of, or means to, social control. As the 1950s wore on, the debate became increasingly dominated by the first two positions. This reflected in part the growing (McCarthyite) pressure to renounce anything resembling a socialist analysis.

Given limited space, I will focus only on the debate about the health of the body politic within. In order to understand the debate one publication is essential reading, the anthology *Mass Culture: The popular arts in America*, published in 1957. Reading the many contributions, one quickly gets a sense of the parameters of the debate – what is at stake in the debate, and who the principal participants are. Let us begin with the editors, Bernard Rosenberg and David Manning White. Rosenberg argues that the material wealth and well-being of American society is being undermined by the dehumanizing effects of mass culture. His greatest anxiety is that, 'At worst, mass culture threatens not merely to cretinize our taste, but to brutalize our senses while paving the way to totalitarianism'.[79] He claims that mass culture is not American by nature or by example; nor is it the inevitable culture of democracy. Mass culture, according to Rosenberg, is nowhere more widespread than in the Soviet Union. Its author is not capitalism, but technology. Therefore America cannot be held responsible for its emergence or its persistence. White makes a similar point but for a different purpose. 'The critics of mass culture', according to White, 'take an exceedingly dim view of contemporary American society.'[80] White's defence of American (mass) culture is to compare it with aspects of the popular culture of the past. He maintains that critics romanticize the past in order to castigate the present. He condemns those 'who discuss American culture as if they were holding a dead vermin in their hands',[81] and yet forget the sadistic and brutal reality of animal baiting that was the everyday culture in which Shakespeare's plays first appeared. His point is that every period in history has produced 'men who preyed upon the ignorance and insecurities of the largest part of the populace . . . and therefore we need not be so shocked that such men exist today'.[82] The second part of his defence consists of cataloguing the extent to which high culture flourishes in America: Shakespeare on TV, record figures for book borrowing from libraries, a successful tour by the Sadler's Wells ballet, the fact that more people attend classical music events than attend baseball games and growth in symphony orchestras.

A key figure in the debate is Dwight Macdonald. In a very influential essay, 'A theory of mass culture', he attacks mass culture on a number of fronts. First of all, mass culture undermines the vitality of high culture. It is a parasitic culture, feeding on high culture, while offering nothing in return:

> Folk art grew from below. It was a spontaneous, autochthonous expression of the people, shaped by themselves, pretty much without the benefit of High Culture, to suit their own needs. Mass Culture is imposed from above. It is fabricated by technicians hired by businessmen; its audience are passive consumers, their participation limited to the choice between buying and not buying. The Lords of *kitsch*, in short, exploit the cultural needs of the masses in order to make a profit and/or to maintain their class rule – in Communist countries, only the second purpose obtains. . . . Folk art was the people's own institution, their private little garden walled off from the great formal park of their masters' High Culture. But Mass Culture breaks down the wall, integrating the masses into a debased form of High Culture and thus becoming an instrument of political domination.[83]

Like other contributors to the debate, Macdonald is quick to deny the claim that America is the land of mass culture: 'the fact is that the U.S.S.R. is even more a land of Mass Culture than is the U.S.A.'[84] This fact, he claims, is often missed by critics who focus only on the 'form' of mass culture in the Soviet Union. But it is mass culture (not folk culture: the expression of the people, nor high culture: the expression of the individual artist); and it differs from American mass culture in that 'its quality is even lower', and in that 'it exploits rather than satisfies the cultural needs of the masses . . . for political rather than commercial reasons'.[85] Despite its superiority to Soviet mass culture, American mass culture is still a problem ('acute in the United States'): 'The eruption of the masses onto the political stage [produced] . . . disastrous cultural results'.[86] The problem is the absence of 'a clearly defined cultural élite'.[87] If one existed, the masses could have mass culture and the élite could have high culture. However, without a cultural élite, America is under threat from a Gresham's Law of culture: the bad will drive out the good; the result will be not just an homogeneous culture but an 'homogenized culture . . . that threatens to engulf everything in its spreading ooze',[88] dispersing the cream from the top and turning the American people into infantile masses.[89] His conclusions are pessimistic to say the least: 'far from Mass Culture getting better, we will be lucky if it doesn't get worse.'[90]

The analysis changes again as we move from the disillusioned ex-Trotskyism of Macdonald to the optimistic liberalism of Gilbert Seldes. Seldes shares some of Macdonald's distaste for mass culture. He, however, blames the producers of mass culture for underestimating the cultural tastes of the American public. Ernest van den Haag suggests that in some ways this is inevitable; it is in the nature of mass production:

> The mass-produced article need not aim low, but it must aim at an average of tastes. In satisfying all (or at least many) individual tastes in some respects, it violates each in other respects. For there are – so far – no average persons having average tastes. Averages are but statistical composites. A mass-produced article, while reflecting nearly everybody's taste to some extent, is unlikely to embody anybody's taste fully. This is one source of the sense of violation which is rationalized vaguely in theories about deliberate debasement of taste.[91]

He also suggests another reason: the temptations offered by mass culture to high culture. Two factors must be particularly tempting: (1) the financial rewards of mass culture, and (2) the potentially enormous audience. He uses Dante as an illustration. Although he may have suffered religious and political pressures, Dante was not tempted to shape his work to appeal to an average of tastes. Had he been 'tempted to write for *Sports Illustrated*' or been asked 'to condense his work for *Readers' Digest*' or been given a contract 'to adapt it for the movies', would he have been able to maintain his aesthetic and moral standards? Dante was fortunate; his talent was never really tempted to stray from the true path of creativity: 'there were no alternatives to being as good a writer as his talent permitted'.[92] It is not so much that mass taste has deteriorated, van den Haag argues, but that it has become more important to the cultural producers in Western societies. Like White, he notes the plurality of cultural texts and practices consumed in America. However, he also notes the way in which high culture and folk culture are absorbed into mass culture, and are consequently consumed as mass culture: 'it is not new nor disastrous that few people read classics. It is new that so many people misread them.'[93] He cannot help in the end declaring that mass culture is a drug which 'lessens people's capacity to experience life itself'.[94] Mass culture is ultimately a sign of impoverishment. It marks the de-individualization of life; an endless search after what Sigmund Freud calls 'substitute gratifications' (Freud is referring to all art, and not just popular culture); and what Leavis refers to as 'substitute living'. The trouble with substitute gratifications, according to the mass culture critique, is that they shut out 'real gratifications'. This leads van den Haag to suggest that the consumption of mass culture is a form of repression; the empty texts and practices of mass culture are consumed to fill an emptiness within, which grows the more, the more the empty texts and practices of mass culture are consumed. The working of this cycle of repression of 'fundamental impulses' makes it increasingly impossible to experience 'real gratification'.[95] The result is a cultural nightmare in which the 'addict' or the 'masturbator' of mass culture moves endlessly on a continuum of non-fulfilment, between boredom and distraction:

> Though the bored person hungers for things to happen to him, the disheartening fact is that when they do he empties them of the very meaning he unconsciously yearns for by using them as distractions. In popular culture even the second coming would become just another 'barren' thrill to be watched on television till Milton Berle comes on.[96]

Van den Haag differs from the 'cultural nostalgics', who use romanticized versions of the past to condemn the present, in his uncertainty about the historical relationship: 'popular culture impoverishes life without leading to contentment. But whether "the mass of men" felt better or worse without mass production techniques of which popular culture is an ineluctable part, we shall never know.'[97] Edward Shils believes he does know. Moreover, he knows that when van den Haag says that industry has impoverished life he is talking nonsense:

> The present pleasures of the working and lower middle class are
> not worthy of profound aesthetic, moral or intellectual esteem
> but they are surely not inferior to the villainous things which gave
> pleasure to their European ancestors from the Middle Ages to
> the nineteenth century.[98]

Shils rejects completely

> the utterly erroneous idea that the twentieth century is a period
> of severe intellectual deterioration and that this alleged deterio-
> ration is a product of a mass culture. . . . Indeed, it would be far
> more correct to assert that mass culture is now less damaging to
> the lower classes than the dismal and harsh existence of earlier
> centuries had ever been.[99]

As far as Shils can see the problem is not mass culture, but the
response of intellectuals to mass culture. In similar fashion, D. W.
Brogan, while in agreement with much of Macdonald's argument,
remains more optimistic. He believes that Macdonald in being 'so
grimly critical of the present America, is too kind to the past in
America and to the past and present in Europe'.[100] His pessimism
about the present is only sustained by his overly optimistic view of
the past. In short, Macdonald 'exaggerates . . . the bad eminence
of the United States'.[101] The situation in Europe is much the same
as the situation in the United States. Whereas both Europe and the
United States have faced the difficulties of transition from rural to
urban societies, the States has faced the additional burden of having to create a unified national culture from fragments of European and other cultures.

In 'The middle against both ends', Leslie Fiedler, unlike most
other contributors to the debate, claims that mass culture

> is a peculiarly American phenomenon. . . . I do not mean . . . that
> it is found only in the United States, but that wherever it is found,
> it comes first from us, and is still to be discovered in fully de-
> veloped form only among us. Our experience along these lines is,
> in this sense, a preview for the rest of the world of what must follow
> the inevitable dissolution of the older aristocratic cultures.[102]

For Fiedler, mass culture is popular culture which 'refuses to know
its place':[103]

> contemporary vulgar culture is brutal and disturbing: the quasi-
> spontaneous expression of the uprooted and culturally dis-
> possessed inhabitants of anonymous cities, contriving mythologies

which reduce to manageable form the threat of science, the horror of unlimited war, the general spread of corruption in a world where the social bases of old loyalties and heroisms have long been destroyed.[104]

Fiedler poses the question: 'What is wrong with American mass culture?' He knows that for some critics, at home and abroad, the fact that it is American is enough reason to condemn it. But, for Fiedler, the inevitability of the American experience makes the argument meaningless; that is, unless those who support the argument are also against industrialization, mass education and democracy. He sees America 'in the midst of a strange two-front class war'. In the centre is 'the genteel middling mind', at the top is 'the ironical-aristocratic sensibility', and at the bottom is 'the brutal-populist mentality'.[105] The attack on popular culture is a symptom of timidity and an expression of conformity in matters of culture: 'the fear of the vulgar is the obverse of the fear of excellence, and both are aspects of the fear of difference; symptoms of a drive for conformity on the level of the timid, sentimental, mindless-bodiless genteel'.[106] The genteel middling mind wants cultural equality on its own terms. This is not the Leavisite demand for cultural deference, but an insistence on an end to cultural difference. Therefore, Fiedler sees American mass culture as hierarchical and pluralist, rather than homogenized and levelling. Moreover, he celebrates it as such.

Shils suggests a similar model – American culture is divided into three cultural 'classes', each embodying different versions of the cultural: ' "superior" or "refined" culture' at the top, ' "mediocre" culture' in the middle, and ' "brutal" culture' at the bottom.[107] Mass society has changed the cultural map, reducing the significance of 'superior or refined culture', and increasing that of both 'mediocre' end 'brutal'.[108] However, Shils does not see this as a totally negative development: 'It is an indication of a crude aesthetic awakening in classes which previously accepted what was handed down to them or who had practically no aesthetic expression and reception.'[109] Like Fiedler, he does not shy away from the claim that America is the home of mass culture. He calls America 'that most massive of all mass societies'.[110] But he remains optimistic: 'As a matter of fact, the vitality, the individuality, which may rehabilitate our intellectual public will probably be the fruits of the liberation of powers and possibilities inherent in mass societies.'[111]

As Ross suggests, in Fiedler's essay, and in the work of other writers in the 1950s and early 1960s,

> the concept of 'class' makes a conditional return after its years in the intellectual wilderness. This time, however, class analysis returns not to draw attention to conflicts and contradictions, as had been the case in the thirties, but rather to serve a hegemonic moment in which a consensus was being established about the non-antagonistic coexistence of different political conceptions of the world. Cultural classes could exist as long as they kept themselves to themselves.[112]

Cultural choice and consumption become both the sign of class belonging and the mark of class difference. However, instead of class antagonism, there is only plurality of consumer choice within a general consensus of the dangers within and the dangers without. In short, the debate about mass culture had become the terrain on which to construct the Cold War ideology of containment. After all, as Melvin Tumin points out, 'America and Americans have available to them the resources, both of mind and matter, to build and support the finest culture the world has ever known.'[113] The fact that this has not yet occurred does not dismay Tumin; for him it simply prompts the question: How do we make it happen? For the answer, he looks to American intellectuals, who 'never before have . . . been so well placed in situations where they can function as intellectuals',[114] and through the debate on mass culture, to take the lead in helping to build the finest *popular* culture the world has ever known.

## The culture of other people

It is easy to be critical of the 'culture and civilization' tradition's approach to popular culture. Given the recent developments in the field of cultural theory, it is almost enough to present a narrative of its approach to condemn it to 'populist' disapproval. However, it must be remembered that from a historical point of view, the tradition's work is absolutely foundational to the project of the study of popular culture within British cultural studies. Furthermore, the impact of the tradition is difficult to overestimate: for more than a century it was undoubtedly the dominant paradigm in cultural analysis. Indeed, it could be argued that it still forms a kind of repressed 'common sense' in certain areas of British and American academic and non-academic life.[115]

Although the 'culture and civilization' tradition, especially in its Leavisite form, created an educational space for the study of popular culture, there is a sense in which this approach to popular culture 'actively impeded its development as an area of study'.[116] The principal problem is its working assumption that popular culture always represents little more than an example of cultural decline and potential political disorder. Given this assumption, theoretical research and empirical investigation continued to confirm what it always expected to find:

> It was an assumption of the theory that there was something wrong with popular culture and, of course, once that assumption had been made, all the rest followed: one found what one was looking for – signs of decay and deterioration – precisely because the theory required that these be found. In short, the only role offered to the products of popular culture was that of fall guy.[117]

As we have noted, popular culture is condemned for many things. However, as Bennett points out, the 'culture and civilization' tradition is not noted for its detailed analyses of the texts and practices of popular culture. Instead, it looked down from the splendid heights of high culture to the commercial wastelands of popular culture, seeking only confirmation of cultural decline, cultural difference and the need for cultural deference, regulation and control. It

> was very much a discourse of the 'cultured' about the culture of those without 'culture'. . . . In short, popular culture was approached from a distance and gingerly, held at arm's length by outsiders who clearly lacked any sense of fondness for or participation in the forms they were studying. It was always the culture of 'other people' that was at issue.[118]

The anxieties of the 'culture and civilization' tradition are anxieties about social and cultural extension; how to deal with challenges to cultural and social exclusivity. As the nineteenth century receded, and those traditionally outside 'culture' and 'society' demanded inclusion, strategies were adopted to incorporate and to exclude. Acceptance brought into being 'high society' and 'high culture' to be distinguished from society and culture or, better still, mass society and mass culture. The situation was complexly compounded in the twentieth century. In short, it is a tradition which demanded two responses from the 'masses'[119] – cultural and social difference and cultural and social deference. As we shall see (Chapters 7 and 8), the debates around postmodernism and, say, political correctness and multiculturalism, may be little more than the latest struggle for inclusion in and exclusion from a cultural canon, which ultimately is less about texts and much more about people and their lived cultures.

## Further reading

Chris Baldick, *The Social Mission of English 1848–1932*, Oxford: Clarendon Press, 1983. Contains interesting and informed chapters on Arnold and Leavisism.

R. P. Bilan, *The Literary Criticism of F. R. Leavis*, Cambridge: Cambridge University Press, 1979. Although mostly on Leavis as a literary critic, it contains some useful material on his attitude to high and popular culture.

Leon Bramson, *The Political Context of Sociology*, Princeton, NJ: Princeton University Press, 1961. Contains an illuminating chapter on the mass culture debate in America.

Herbert J. Gans, *Popular Culture and High Culture: An analysis and evaluation of taste*, New York: Basic Books, 1974. The book is a late contribution to the mass culture debate in the USA. It presents a compelling argument in defence of cultural pluralism.

Lesley Johnson, *The Cultural Critics*, London: Routledge & Kegan Paul, 1979. Contains useful chapters on Arnold and F. R. Leavis.

Francis Mulhern, *The Moment of 'Scrutiny'*, London: New Left Books, 1979. Perhaps the classic account of Leavisism.

Andrew Ross, *No Respect: Intellectuals and popular culture*, London: Routledge, 1989. An interesting book, with a useful chapter on the mass culture debate in America.

Lionel Trilling, *Matthew Arnold*, London: Unwin University Books, 1949. Still the best introduction to Arnold.

Bernard Waites, Tony Bennett and Graham Martin (eds), *Popular Culture: Past and present*, London: Croom Helm, 1982. A collection of essays on different examples of popular culture. Chapters 1–4 and 6 address popular culture and the historical context which gave rise to the anxieties of the 'culture and civilization' tradition.

Raymond Williams, *Culture and Society*, Harmondsworth: Penguin, 1963. Perhaps still the best general book on the 'culture and civilization' tradition: includes chapters on Arnold and F. R. Leavis.

# 3

# CULTURALISM

In this chapter I will consider the work produced by Richard Hoggart, Raymond Williams, E. P. Thompson, and Stuart Hall and Paddy Whannel in the late 1950s and early 1960s. This body of work, despite certain differences between its authors, constitutes the founding texts of culturalism. As Hall was later to observe, 'Within cultural studies in Britain, "culturalism" has been the most vigorous, indigenous strand.'[1] The chapter will end with a brief discussion of the institutionalization of culturalism at the Centre for Contemporary Cultural Studies.

Both Hoggart and Williams develop positions in response to Leavisism. As we noted in Chapter 2, the Leavisites opened up in Britain an educational space for the study of popular culture. Both Hoggart and Williams occupy this space in ways that challenge many of the basic assumptions of Leavisism, while also sharing some of these assumptions. It is this contradictory mixture – looking back to the 'culture and civilization' tradition, while at the same time moving forward to culturalism and the foundations of the cultural studies approach to popular culture – which has led *The Uses of Literacy*, *Culture and Society* and *The Long Revolution* to be called both texts of the 'break' and examples of 'left-Leavisism'.[2]

Thompson, on the other hand, would describe his work, then and always, as Marxist. The term culturalism was coined to describe his work, and the work of Hoggart and Williams, by one of the former directors of the Centre for Contemporary Cultural Studies, Richard Johnson.[3] Johnson uses the term to indicate the presence of a certain theoretical coherence connecting the work of the three theorists. Each, in his different way, breaks with key aspects of the tradition he inherits. Hoggart and Williams break

45

with Leavisism; Thompson breaks with mechanistic and economistic forms of Marxism. What unites them is an approach that insists that by analyzing the culture of a society – the textual forms and documented practices of a culture – it is possible to reconstitute the patterned behaviour and constellations of ideas shared by the men and women who produce and consume the cultural texts and practices of that society. It is a perspective which stresses 'human agency', the active production of culture, rather than its passive consumption. Although not usually included in accounts of the formation of culturalism out of left-Leavisism, Hall and Whannel's *The Popular Arts* is included here because of its classic left-Leavisite focus on popular culture. Taken together as a body of work, the contributions of Hoggart, Williams, Thompson, and Hall and Whannel, clearly mark the emergence of what is now known as the cultural studies approach to popular culture. The institutional home of these developments has been the Centre for Contemporary Cultural Studies, at the University of Birmingham.

## Richard Hoggart: *The Uses of Literacy*

*The Uses of Literacy* is divided into two parts: 'An "older" order', describing the working class culture of Hoggart's childhood in the 1930s; and 'Yielding place to new', describing a traditional working class culture under threat from the new forms of mass entertainment of the 1950s. Dividing the book in this way in itself speaks volumes about the perspective taken and the conclusions expected. On the one hand, we have the traditional 'lived culture' of the 1930s. On the other, we have the cultural decline of the 1950s. Hoggart is in fact aware that during the course of writing the book, 'nostalgia was colouring the material in advance: I have done what I could to remove its effects'.[4] He is also aware that the division he makes between the 'older' and the 'new', underplays the amount of continuity between the two. It should also be noted that his evidence for the 'older' depends not on 'invoking some rather mistily conceived pastoral tradition the better to assault the present, [but] to a large extent on memories of my childhood about twenty years ago'.[5] This is clearly a rebuke to Leavisism. His evidence for the cultural decline represented by the popular culture of the 1950s is material gathered as a university lecturer and researcher. In short, the 'older' is based on personal experience; the 'new' on academic research. This is a significant and informing distinction.

It is also worth noting something about Hoggart's project which is often misunderstood. What he attacks is not a 'moral' decline in the working class as such, but what he perceives as a decline in the 'moral seriousness' of the culture provided for the working class. He repeats on a number of occasions his confidence in the working class's ability to resist many of the manipulations of mass culture: 'This is not simply a power of passive resistance, but something which, though not articulate, is positive. The working classes have a strong natural ability to survive change by adapting or assimilating what they want in the new and ignoring the rest'.[6] His confidence stems from his belief that their response to mass culture is always partial: 'with a large part of themselves they are just "not there", are living elsewhere, living intuitively, habitually, verbally, drawing on myth, aphorism, and ritual. This saves them from some of the worst effects.'[7]

According to Hoggart,

> working class people have traditionally, or at least for several generations, regarded art as escape, as something enjoyed but not assumed to have much connexion with the matter of daily life. Art is marginal, 'fun' . . . 'real' life goes on elsewhere. . . . Art is for you to use.[8]

He describes the aesthetic of the working class as an 'overriding interest in the close detail' of the everyday; a profound interest in the already known; a taste for culture that 'shows' rather than 'explores'. It therefore seeks not 'an escape from ordinary life' but its intensification, in the assumption 'that ordinary life is intrinsically interesting'.[9] The new mass entertainment of the 1950s is said to undermine this aesthetic:

> Most mass entertainments are in the end what D. H. Lawrence described as 'anti life'. They are full of a corrupt brightness, of improper appeals and moral evasions . . . they offer nothing which can really grip the brain or heart. They assist a gradual drying up of the more positive, the fuller, the more cooperative kinds of enjoyment, in which one gains much by giving much.[10]

It is not just that the pleasures of mass entertainment are 'irresponsible' and 'vicarious';[11] they are also destroying the very fabric of an older, more healthy, working class culture. He is adamant that

> we are moving towards the creation of a mass culture; that the remnants of what was at least in parts an urban culture 'of the people' are being destroyed; and that the new mass culture is in some important ways less healthy than the often crude culture it is replacing.[12]

He claims that the working class culture of the 1930s expressed what he calls 'The rich full life', marked by a strong sense of community. This is a culture which is by and large made by the people. Here is a fairly well-known example of what he means – his description of a typical day at the seaside:

> the 'charas' go rolling out across the moors for the sea, past the road houses which turn up their noses at coach parties, to one the driver knows where there is coffee and biscuits or perhaps a full egg and bacon breakfast. Then on to a substantial lunch on arrival, and after that a fanning out in groups. But rarely far from one another, because they know their part of the town and their bit of beach, where they feel at home. . . . They have a nice walk past the shops; perhaps a drink; a sit in a deck chair eating an ice cream or sucking mint humbugs; a great deal of loud laughter – at Mrs Johnson insisting on a paddle with her dress tucked in her bloomers, at Mrs Henderson pretending she has 'got off' with the deck chair attendant, or in the queue at the ladies lavatory. Then there is the buying of presents for the family, a big meat tea, and the journey home with a stop for drinks on the way. If the men are there, and certainly if it is a men's outing, there will probably be several stops and a crate or two of beer in the back for drinking on the move. Somewhere in the middle of the moors the men's parties all tumble out, with much horseplay and noisy jokes about bladder capacity. The driver knows exactly what is expected of him as he steers his warm, fuggy, and singing community back to the town; for his part he gets a very large tip, collected during the run through the last few miles of the town street.[13]

This is a popular culture that is communal and self-made. Hoggart can be criticized for his romanticism, but we should also recognize this (in the passage's Utopian energy) as an example of his continually striving to distinguish between a culture 'of the people' and a 'world where things are done for the people'.[14]

The first half of *The Uses of Literacy* consists mostly of examples of communal and self-made entertainment. The analysis is often in considerable advance of Leavisism. For example, he defends working class appreciation of popular song against the dismissive hostility of Cecil Sharp's (Leavisesque) longing for the 'purity' of folk music[15] in terms which were soon to become central to the project of cultural studies. Songs only succeed, he argues, 'no matter how much Tin Pan Alley plugs them',[16] if they can be made to meet the emotional requirements of their popular audience. As he says of the popular appropriation of 'After the Ball is Over', 'they have taken it on their own terms, and so it is not for them as poor a thing as it might have been'.[17]

The idea of an audience appropriating for its own purposes – on its own terms – the products offered to it by the culture industries is never fully explored. But the idea is there in Hoggart; again indicating the under-exploited sophistication of *parts* of *The Uses of Literacy* too often dismissed as a rather unacademic, and nostalgic, semi-autobiography. On the contrary, the real weakness of the book is its inability to carry forward the insights from its treatment of the popular culture of the 1930s to its treatment of the popular culture of the 1950s. If it had done, it would have, for example, quickly found totally inadequate the contrasting descriptive titles, 'The full rich life' and 'Invitations to a candy floss world'. It is worth noting at this point that it is not necessary to say that Hoggart's picture of the 1930s is romanticized in order to prove that his picture of the 1950s is exaggeratedly pessimistic and overdrawn; he does not have to be proved wrong about the 1930s, as some critics seem to think, in order to be proved wrong about the 1950s. It is possible that he is right about the 1930s, while being wrong about the 1950s. Like many intellectuals whose origins are working class, he is perhaps prone to bracket off his own working class experience against the real and imagined condescension of his new middle class colleagues: 'I know *this* working class is deplorable, but *mine* was different'. Although I would not wish to overstress this motivation, it does get some support in Williams's review of *The Uses of Literacy*, when he comments on 'lucky Hoggart's' account of the scholarship boy: 'which I think has been well received by some readers (and why not? it is much what they wanted to hear, and now an actual scholarship boy is saying it)'.[18] Again, in a discussion of the 'strange allies' dominant groups often attract, Williams makes a similar, but more general, point:

In our own generation we have a new class of the same kind: the young men and women who have benefited by the extension of public education and who, in surprising numbers, identify with the world into which they have been admitted, and spend much of their time, to the applause of their new peers, expounding and documenting the hopeless vulgarity of the people they have left: the one thing that is necessary now, to weaken belief in the practicability of further educational extension.[19]

When, in the second part of his study, Hoggart turns to consider 'some features of contemporary life',[20] the self-making aspect of working class culture is mostly kept from view. The popular aesthetic, so important for an understanding of the working class pleasure on show in the 1930s, is now forgotten in the rush to condemn the popular culture of the 1950s. The success of 'the radio "soap operas", with working class women . . . is due to the consumateness of their attention . . . to their remarkably sustained presentation of the perfectly ordinary and unremarkable'.[21] This is repeated in newspaper cartoons featuring such figures as 'the "little man" worrying for days on end about his daughter's chances in the school cookery competition . . . a daily exercise in spinning out the unimportant and insignificant'.[22] What has happened to the intrinsic significance of the everyday? Instead of talk of a popular aesthetic, we are invited on a tour of the manipulative power of mass culture. The popular culture of the 1950s, as described by Hoggart, no longer offers the possibility of a full rich life; everything is now far too thin and insipid. The power of 'commercial culture' has grown, relentless in its attack on the old (traditional working class culture) in the name of the new (the 'shiny barbarism'[23] of mass culture). This is a world in which 'To be "old fashioned" is to be condemned.'[24] It is a condition to which the young are particularly vulnerable. These 'barbarians in wonderland'[25] demand more, and are given more, than their parents and their grandparents had or expected. But such supposedly mindless hedonism, fed by thin and insipid fare, leads only to a debilitating excess.

> 'Having a good time' may be made to seem so important as to override almost all other claims; yet when it has been allowed to do so, having a good time becomes largely a matter of routine. The strongest argument against modern mass entertainments is not that they debase taste – debasement can be alive and active – but that they over excite it, eventually dull it, and finally kill

it. . . . They kill it at the nerve, and yet so bemuse and persuade their audience that the audience is almost entirely unable to look up and say, 'But in fact this cake is made of sawdust'.[26]

Although that stage had not yet been reached, all the signs, according to Hoggart, indicate that this is the way in which the world is travelling. But even in this 'candy floss wonderland' there are still signs of resistance. For example, although mass culture may produce some awful popular songs,

> people do not have to sing or listen to these songs, and many do not: and those who do, often make the songs better than they really are . . . people often read them in their own way. So that even there they are less affected than the extent of their purchases would seem to indicate.[27]

Again, this reminds us that Hoggart's target is (mostly) the producers of popular culture and not its consumers. He offers many examples of 'proof' of cultural decline, but popular fiction is arguably his key example of deterioration. He compares a piece of contemporary writing (in fact it is an imitation written by himself) with an extract from *East Lynne* and an extract from *Adam Bede*. He concludes that in comparison the contemporary extract is thin and insipid: a 'trickle of tinned milk and water which staves off the pangs of a positive hunger and denies the satisfactions of a solidly filling meal'.[28] Leaving aside the fact that the contemporary extract is an imitation (as are all his examples), Hoggart argues that its inferiority is due to the fact that it lacks the 'moral tone'[29] of the other two extracts. This may be true, but what is also significant is the way in which the other two extracts are *full* of 'moral tone' in a quite definite sense: they attempt to tell the reader what to think; they are, as he admits, 'oratory'.[30] The contemporary extract is similarly *thin* in a quite definite sense: it does not tell the reader what to think. Therefore, although there may be various grounds on which we might wish to rank the three extracts, with *Adam Bede* at the top and the contemporary extract at the bottom, 'moral tone' (meaning fiction should tell people what to think) seems to lead us nowhere but back to the rather bogus certainties of Leavisism. Moreover, we can easily reverse the judgement: the contemporary extract is to be valued for its elliptic and interrogative qualities; it invites us to think by not thinking for us; this is not to be dismissed as an absence of thought (or 'moral tone' for that matter), but as an absence full of potential presence, which the reader is invited to *actively* produce.

One supposedly striking portent of the journey into the candy floss wonderland is the habitual visitor to the new milk bars, 'the juke box boy'[31] – his term for the Teddy boy. Milk bars are themselves symptomatic: they 'indicate at once, in the nastiness of their modernistic knick-knacks, their glaring showiness, an aesthetic breakdown so complete'.[32] Patrons are mostly 'boys between fifteen and twenty, with drape suits, picture ties, and an American slouch'.[33] Their main reason for being there is to 'put copper after copper into the mechanical record player'.[34] Records are played loud: the music 'is allowed to blare out so that the noise would be sufficient to fill a good sized ballroom. . . . The young men waggle one shoulder or stare, as desperately as Humphrey Bogart, across the tubular chairs.'[35]

> Compared even with the pub around the corner, this is all a peculiarly thin and pallid form of dissipation, a sort of spiritual dry-rot amid the odour of boiled milk. Many of the customers – their clothes, their hair styles, their facial expressions all indicate – are living to a large extent in a myth world compounded of a few simple elements which they take to be those of American life.[36]

To Hoggart,

> They are a depressing group . . . perhaps most of them are rather less intelligent than the average [working class youth], and are therefore even more exposed than others to the debilitating mass trends of the day . . . they have no responsibilities, and little sense of responsibilities, to themselves or to others.[37]

Although 'they are not typical', they are an ominous sign of things to come:

> these are the figures some important contemporary forces are tending to create, the directionless and tamed helots of a machine-minding class. . . . The hedonistic but passive barbarian who rides in a fifty-horse-power bus for threepence, to see a five-million-dollar film for one-and-eightpence, is not simply a social oddity; he is a portent.[38]

The juke box boy symptomatically bears the prediction of a society in which 'the larger part of the population is reduced to a condition of obediently receptive passivity, their eyes glued to television sets, pin ups, and cinema screens'.[39]

However, Hoggart does not totally despair at the march of mass culture. He knows, for instance, that the working class 'are not living lives which are imaginatively as poor as a mere reading of their literature would suggest'.[40] The old communal and self-made popular culture still remains in working class ways of speaking, in 'the Working-Men's Clubs, the styles of singing, the brass bands, the older types of magazines, the close group games like darts and dominoes'.[41] Moreover, he trusts their 'considerable moral resources'[42] to allow them, and to encourage them, to continue to adapt for their own purposes the products and practices of the culture industries. In short, they 'are a good deal less affected than they might well be. The question, of course, is how long this stock of moral capital will last, and whether it is being renewed.'[43] For all his guarded optimism, he warns that it is a 'form of democratic self-indulgence to over stress this resilience' in the face of the 'increasingly dangerous pressures' of mass culture,[44] with all its undermining of genuine community with an increasingly 'hollow . . . invitation to share in a kind of palliness'.[45] His ultimate fear is that 'competitive commerce'[46] may have totalitarian designs:

> Inhibited now from ensuring the 'degradation' of the masses economically . . . competitive commerce . . . becomes a new and stronger form of subjection; this subjection promises to be stronger than the old because the chains of cultural subordination are both easier to wear and harder to strike away than those of economic subordination.[47]

Hoggart's approach to popular culture has much in common with the approach of Leavisism (this is most noticeable in the analysis of popular culture in the second part of the book); both operate with a notion of cultural decline; both see education in discrimination as a means to resist the manipulative appeal of mass culture. However, what makes his approach different from that of Leavisism is his detailed preoccupation with, and, above all, his clear commitment to, working class culture. His distance from Leavisism is most evident in the content of his own 'good past/bad present' binary opposition: instead of the organic community of the seventeenth century, his 'good past' is the working class culture of the 1930s. What Hoggart celebrates from the 1930s is, ironically, the very culture which the Leavisites were armed to resist. This alone makes his approach an implicit critique of, and an advance on, Leavisism. But, as Hall points out, although Hoggart 'refused many of Leavis's embedded cultural judgements', he, nevertheless, in his use of Leavisite literary methodology, 'continued "a tradition" while seeking, in practice, to transform it'.[48]

## Raymond Williams: *The Long Revolution*

Williams's influence on cultural studies has been enormous. The range of his work alone is formidable. He has made significant contributions to our understanding of cultural theory, cultural history, television, the press, radio and advertising. Alan O'Connor's bibliography[49] of Williams's published work runs to thirty-nine pages. His contribution is all the more remarkable when one considers his origins in the Welsh working class (his father was a railway signalman), and that as an academic he was Professor of Drama at Cambridge University. In this section, I will comment only on his contribution to the founding of culturalism and its contribution to the study of popular culture.

In *The Long Revolution*, Williams outlines the 'three general categories in the definition of culture'.[50] First, there is 'the "ideal", in which culture is a state or process of human perfection, in terms of certain absolute or universal values'.[51] The role of cultural analysis, using this definition, 'is essentially the discovery and description, in lives and works, of those values which can be seen to compose a timeless order, or to have permanent reference to the universal human condition'.[52] This is the definition inherited from Arnold and used by Leavisism: what he calls, in *Culture and Society*, culture as an ultimate 'court of human appeal, to be set over the processes of practical social judgement and yet to offer itself as a mitigating and rallying alternative'.[53] Second, there is the 'documentary' record: the recorded texts and practices of culture. In this definition, 'culture is the body of intellectual and imaginative work, in which, in a detailed way, human thought and experience are variously recorded'.[54] The purpose of cultural analysis, using this definition, is one of critical assessment. This can take a form of analysis similar to that adopted with regard to the 'ideal'; an act of critical sifting until the discovery of what Arnold calls 'the best that has been thought and said' (see Chapter 2). It can also involve a less exalted practice: the cultural as the critical object of interpretative description and evaluation (literary studies is the obvious example of this practice). Finally, it can also involve a more historical, less literary evaluative function: an act of critical reading to measure its significance as a 'historical document' (historical studies is the obvious example of this practice). Third, 'there is the "social" definition of culture, in which culture is a description of a particular way of life'.[55]

It is this latter definition which proved crucial for the founding of culturalism. The 'social' definition of culture introduces three new ways of thinking about culture. First of all, the 'anthropological' claim that culture is a description of a particular way of life; second, the claim that culture 'expresses certain meanings and values';[56] third, the claim that the work of cultural analysis should be the 'clarification of the meanings and values implicit and explicit in a particular way of life, a particular culture'.[57] Williams is aware that the kind of analysis the 'social' definition of culture demands will often 'involve analysis of elements in the way of life that to followers of the other definitions are not "culture" at all'.[58] Moreover, while such analysis might still operate modes of evaluation of the 'ideal' and the 'documentary' type, it will also range

> to an emphasis which, from studying particular meanings and values, seeks not so much to compare these, as a way of establishing a scale, but by studying their modes of change to discover certain general 'laws' or 'trends', by which social and cultural development as a whole can be better understood.[59]

Taken together, the three points embodied in the 'social' definition of culture – culture as a particular way of life, culture as expression of a particular way of life and cultural analysis as a method of reconstituting a particular way of life establish both the general perspective and the basic procedures of culturalism.

Williams, however, is reluctant to lose any of the three definitions: 'there is a significant reference in each . . . and, if this is so, it is the relations between them that should claim our attention'.[60] He describes as 'inadequate' and 'unacceptable' any definition which fails to include the other definitions. 'However difficult it may be in practice, we have to try to see the process as a whole, and to relate our particular studies, if not explicitly at least by ultimate reference, to the actual and complex organization.'[61]

> I would then define the theory of culture as the study of relationships between elements in a whole way of life. The analysis of

culture is the attempt to discover the nature of the organization which is the complex of these relationships. Analysis of particular works or institutions is, in this context, analysis of their essential kind of organization, the relationships which works or institutions embody as parts of the organization as a whole.[62]

In addressing the 'complex organization' of culture as a particular way of life, the purpose of cultural analysis is always to understand what a culture is expressing; 'the actual experience through which a culture was lived'; the 'important common element'; 'a particular community of experience'.[63] In short, to reconstitute what Williams calls 'the structure of feeling'.[64] By structure of feeling, he means the shared values of a particular group, class or society. The term is used to describe a discursive structure which is a cross between a collective cultural unconscious and an ideology. He uses, for example, the term to explain the way in which many nineteenth century novels employ 'magic solutions' to close the gap in that society between 'the ethic and the experience'. He gives examples of how men and women are released from loveless marriages as a result of the convenient death or the insanity of their partners; legacies turn up unexpectedly to overcome reverses in fortune; villains are lost in the Empire; poor men return from the Empire bearing great riches; and those whose aspirations could not be met by prevailing social arrangements are put on a boat to make their dreams come true elsewhere. All these (and more) are presented as examples of a shared structure of feeling; the unconscious and conscious working out in fictional texts of the contradictions of nineteenth century society. The purpose of cultural analysis is to read the structure of feeling through the documentary record, 'from poems to buildings and dress-fashions'.[65] As he makes clear,

> What we are looking for, always, is the actual life that the whole organization is there to express. The significance of documentary culture is that, more clearly than anything else, it expresses that life to us in direct terms, when the living witnesses are silent.[66]

The situation is complicated by the fact that culture always exists on three levels:

> We need to distinguish three levels of culture, even in its most general definition. There is the lived culture of a particular time

and place, only fully accessible to those living in that time and place. There is the recorded culture, of every kind, from art to the most everyday facts: the culture of a period. There is also, as the factor connecting lived culture and period cultures, the culture of the selective tradition.[67]

The relationship between the three levels is historically active. Each historical period reorders the documentary record of past periods. Traditions rise and fall. Lived culture is culture as lived and experienced by people in their day-to-day existence in a particular place and moment in time, and the only people who have full access to this culture are those who actually live the structure of feeling. Once the historical moment is gone the structure of feeling begins to fragment. Cultural analysis has access only through the documentary record of the culture. But the documentary record itself fragments under the processes of 'the selective tradition'. Between a lived culture and its reconstitution in cultural analysis, clearly, a great deal of detail is lost. For example, as Williams points out, nobody can claim to have read all the novels of the nineteenth century. Instead, what we have is the specialist who can claim perhaps to have read many hundreds; the interested academic who has read somewhat fewer; the 'educated reader' who has read fewer again. This quite clear process of selectivity does not prevent the three groups of readers from sharing a sense of the nature of *the* nineteenth century novel. Williams is of course aware that no nineteenth century reader would in fact have read *all* the novels of the nineteenth century. His point, however, is that the nineteenth century reader 'had something which . . . no later individual can wholly recover: that sense of the life within which the novels were written, and which we now approach through our selection'.[68] For Williams, it is crucial to understand the selectivity of cultural traditions. It always (inevitably) produces a cultural record, a cultural tradition, marked by 'a rejection of considerable areas of what was once a living culture'.[69] Furthermore, as he explains in *Culture and Society*, 'there will always be a tendency for this process of selection to be related to and even governed by the interests of the class that is dominant'.[70]

> Within a given society, selection will be governed by many kinds of special interests, including class interests. Just as the actual social situation will largely govern *contemporary* selection, so the development of the society, the process of historical change, will

**57**

largely determine the selective tradition. The traditional culture of a society will always tend to correspond to its contemporary system of interests and values, for it is not an absolute body of work but a continual selection and interpretation.[71]

This has quite profound ramifications for the student of popular culture. Given that selection is invariably made on the basis of 'contemporary interests', and given the incidence of many 'reversals and rediscoveries', it follows that 'the relevance of past work, in any future situation, is unforeseeable'.[72] If this is the case, it also follows that absolute judgements about what is good and what is bad, about what is high and what is popular, in contemporary culture, should be made with a great deal less certainty; open as they are to historical realignment in a whirlpool of historical contingency. Williams advocates a form of cultural analysis which is conscious that 'the cultural tradition is not only a selection but also an interpretation'.[73] Although cultural analysis cannot reverse this, it can, by returning a text or practice to its historical moment, show other 'historical alternatives' to contemporary interpretation and 'the particular contemporary values on which it rests'.[74] In this way, we are able to make clear distinctions between 'the whole historical organization within which it was expressed' and 'the contemporary organization within which it is used'.[75] By working in this way, 'real cultural processes will emerge'.[76]

Williams's analysis breaks with Leavisism in a number of ways. First, there is no special place for Art − it is seen as a cultural practice like any other: 'art is there, as an activity, with the production, the trading, the politics, the raising of families.'[77] Art is a human activity alongside other human activities. Williams presses for a democratic account of culture: culture as a particular way of life. In *Culture and Society*, he distinguishes between bourgeois culture as 'the basic individualist idea and the institutions, manners, habits of thought, and intentions which proceed from that' and working class culture as 'the basic collective idea, and the institutions, manners, habits of thought, and intentions which proceed from this'.[78] He then gives this account of the achievements of working-class culture:

> The working class, because of its position, has not, since the Industrial Revolution, produced a culture in the narrower sense. The culture which it has produced, and which it is important to

recognise, is the collective democratic institution, whether in the trade unions, the cooperative movement, or a political party. Working class culture, in the stage through which it has been passing, is primarily social (in that it has created institutions) rather than individual (in particular intellectual or imaginative work). When it is considered in context, it can be seen as a very remarkable creative achievement.[79]

It is when Williams insists on culture as a definition of the 'lived experience' of 'ordinary' men and women, made in their daily interaction with the texts and practices of everyday life, that he finally breaks decisively with Leavisism. Here is the basis for a democratic definition of popular culture. He takes seriously Leavis's call for a common culture. But the difference between Leavisism and Williams on this point is that Williams does want a common culture, whilst Leavisism wants only an hierarchical culture of difference and deference. Williams's review of *The Uses of Literacy* indicates some of the difference between the two positions:

> The analysis of Sunday newspapers and crime stories and romances is . . . familiar, but, when you have come yourself from their apparent public, when you recognise in yourself the ties that still bind, you cannot be satisfied with the older formula: enlightened minority, degraded mass. You know how bad most 'popular culture' is, but you know also that the irruption of the 'swinish multitude', which Burke had prophesied would trample down light and learning, is the coming to relative power and relative justice of your own people, whom you could not if you tried desert.[80]

Although he still claims to recognize 'how bad most "popular culture" is', this is no longer a judgement made from within an enchanted circle of certainty, policed by 'the older formula: enlightened minority, degraded mass'. Hoggart's problem, according to Williams, is that he 'has taken over too many of the formulas', from 'Matthew Arnold' to 'contemporary conservative ideas of the decay of politics in the working class'; the result is an argument in need of 'radical revision'.[81] *The Long Revolution*, described by Hall as 'a seminal event in English postwar intellectual life',[82] did much to provide the radical revision necessary to lay the basis for a non-Leavisite study of popular culture.

## E. P. Thompson: *The Making of the English Working Class*

In the Preface to *The Making of the English Working Class*, E. P. Thompson states:

> This book has a clumsy title, but it is one which meets its purpose. *Making*, because it is a study in an active process, which owes as much to agency as conditioning. The working class did not rise like the sun at an appointed time. It was present at its own making.[83]

The English working class, like any class, is for Thompson 'a *historical* phenomenon'; it is not a 'structure' or a 'category', but the coming together of 'a number of disparate and seemingly unconnected events, both in the raw material of experience and in consciousness'; it is 'something which in fact happens (and can be shown to happen) in human relationships'.[84] Moreover, class is not a 'thing', it is always a historical relationship of unity and difference: uniting one class as against another class or classes. As he explains: 'class happens when some men, as a result of common experiences (inherited or shared), feel and articulate the identity of their interests as between themselves, and as against other men whose interests are different from (and usually opposed to) theirs'.[85] The common experience of class 'is largely determined by the productive relations into which men are born – or enter involuntarily'.[86] However, the consciousness of class, the translation of experience into culture, is not determined in this way: 'Class is defined by men as they live their own history, and, in the end, this is its only definition'.[87]

Class is for Thompson, then, 'a social and cultural formation, arising from processes which can be studied as they work themselves out over a considerable historical period'.[88] The book details the political and cultural formation of the English working class by approaching its subject from three different but related perspectives. First, it reconstructs the political and cultural traditions of English radicalism in the late eighteenth century: religious dissent, popular discontent, the influence of the French Revolution. Second, it focuses on the social and cultural experience of the Industrial Revolution as it was lived by different working groups: weavers, field labourers, cotton spinners, artisans, etc. Finally, it analyzes the growth of working class consciousness evidenced in the corresponding growth in a range of political, social and cultural, 'strongly based and self conscious working-class institutions'.[89] As he insists: 'The working class made itself as much as it was made.'[90] He basically draws two conclusions from his research. First, 'when every caution has been made, the outstanding fact of the period between 1790 and 1830 is the formation of "the working class"'.[91] Second, he claims that 'this was, perhaps, the most distinguished popular culture England has known'.[92]

*The Making of the English Working Class* is in so many ways a monumental contribution to social history (in size alone: the Penguin edition runs to over 900 pages). What makes it significant for the student of popular culture is the nature of its historical account. Thompson's history is not one of abstract economic and political processes; nor is it an account of the doings of the great and the worthy. The book is about 'ordinary' men and women; their experiences, their values, their ideas, their actions, their desires; in short, popular culture as a site of resistance to those in whose interests the Industrial Revolution was made. Hall calls it 'the most seminal work of social history of the post-war period', pointing to the way it challenges 'the narrow, élitist conception of "culture" enshrined in the Leavisite tradition, as well as the rather evolutionary approach which sometimes marked Williams's *The Long Revolution*'.[93] In an interview a decade or so after the publication of the book, Thompson commented on his historical method as follows: 'If you want a generalization I would have to say that the historian has got to be listening all the time.'[94] He is by no means the only historian who listens; the conservative historian G. M. Young also listens, if in a rather more selective fashion: 'history is the conversation of people who counted'.[95] What makes Thompson's listening radically different is the people to whom he listens. As he explains in a famous passage from the Preface to *The Making of the English Working Class*:

> I am seeking to rescue the poor stockinger, the Luddite cropper, the 'obsolete' hand loom weaver, the 'utopian' artisan, and even the deluded follower of Joanna Southcott, from the enormous condescension of posterity. Their crafts and traditions may have been dying. Their hostility to the new industrialism may have been backward looking. Their communitarian ideals may have been fantasies. Their insurrectionary conspiracies

**61**

may have been foolhardy. But they lived through these times of acute social disturbance, and we did not. Their aspirations were valid in terms of their own experience; and, if they were casualties of history, they remain, condemned in their own lives, as casualties.[96]

*The Making of the English Working Class* is the classic example of 'history from below'. Thompson's aim is to place the 'experience' of the English working class as central to any understanding of the formation of an industrial capitalist society in the decades leading up to the 1830s. It is a history from below in the double sense suggested by Gregor McLellan:[97] a history from below in that it seeks to reintroduce working class experience into the historical process; and a history from below in that it insists that the working class were the conscious agents of their own making. Thompson is working within Marx's famous claim about the way in which men and women make history: 'Men make their own history, but they do not make it just as they please; they do not make it under circumstances chosen by themselves, but under circumstances directly encountered, given and transmitted from the past.'[98] What Thompson does is to emphasize the first part of Marx's claim (human agency) against what he considers to have been an over-emphasis by Marxist historians on the second part (structural determinants). Paradoxically, or perhaps not so, he has himself been criticized for over-stressing the role of human agency – human experiences, human values at the expense of structural factors.[99]

Before concluding this brief account of Thompson's contribution to the study of popular culture, it should be noted that he himself does not accept the term culturalism as a description of his work. This and other related points were the subject of a heated 'History Workshop' debate between Johnson, Hall and Thompson himself.[100] One of the difficulties when reading the contributions to the debate is the way that culturalism is made to carry two quite different meanings. On the one hand, it is employed as a description of a particular methodology (this is how I am using it here). On the other, it is used as a term of critique (usually from a more 'traditional' Marxist position or from the perspective of Marxist structuralism). This is a complex issue, but as a coda to this discussion of Hoggart, Williams and Thompson, here is a very simplified clarification: positively, culturalism is a methodology which stresses culture (human agency, human values, human experience) as of crucial importance for a full sociological and historical understanding of a given social formation; negatively, culturalism is used to suggest the employment of such assumptions without full recognition and acknowledgement that culture is the effect of structures beyond itself, and that these have the effect of ultimately determining, constraining and, finally, producing culture (human agency, human values and human experience). Thompson disagrees strongly with the second proposition, and refutes totally any suggestion that culturalism, regardless of the definition, can be applied to his own work.[101]

## Stuart Hall and Paddy Whannel: *The Popular Arts*

The 'main thesis' of the *The Popular Arts* is that 'in terms of actual quality . . . the struggle between what is good and worthwhile and what is shoddy and debased is not a struggle against the modern forms of communication, but a conflict *within* these media'.[102] Hall and Whannel's concern is with the difficulty of making these distinctions. They set themselves the task to develop 'a critical method for handling . . . problems of value and evaluation' in the study of popular culture.[103] In this task they pay specific thanks to the work of Hoggart and Williams; and passing thanks to the key figures of Leavisism. The book was written against a background of concern about the influence of popular culture in the classroom. In 1960 the National Union of Teachers (NUT) Annual Conference passed a resolution which read in part:

> Conference believes that a determined effort must be made to counteract the debasement of standards which result from the misuse of press, radio, cinema and television. . . . It calls especially upon those who use and control the media of mass communication, and upon parents, to support the efforts of teachers in an attempt to prevent the conflict which too often arises between the values inculcated in the classroom and those encountered by young people in the world outside.[104]

The resolution led to the NUT Special Conference, 'Popular culture and personal responsibility'. One speaker at the conference, the composer Malcolm Arnold, said: 'Nobody is in any way a better person morally or in any other way for liking Beethoven more than Adam Faith. . . . Of course the person who likes both is in a very happy position since he is able to enjoy much more in his life than a lot of other people.'[105] Although Hall and Whannel recognize 'the honest intention' in Arnold's claim, they question what they call 'the random use of Adam Faith as an example' because, as they claim, 'as a singer of popular songs he is by any serious standards far down the list'. Moreover, as they explain, 'By serious standards we mean those that might be legitimately applied to popular music – the standards set, for example, by Frank Sinatra or Ray Charles'.[106] What Hall and Whannel are doing here is rejecting the arguments of both Leavisism, and the (mostly American) mass culture critique, which claims that all high culture is good and that all popular culture is bad, for an argument which says on the one hand that most high culture is good, and on the other, contrary to Leavisism and the mass culture critique, that some popular culture is also good – it is ultimately a question of popular discrimination.

Part of the aim of *The Popular Arts*, then, is to replace the 'misleading generalizations' of earlier attacks on popular culture by helping to facilitate popular discrimination within the range of popular culture itself. Instead of worrying about the 'effects' of popular culture, 'we should be seeking to train a more demanding audience'.[107] A more demanding audience, according to Hall and Whannel, is one that prefers jazz to pop, Miles Davis to Liberace, Frank Sinatra to Adam Faith, Polish films to mainstream Hollywood, *L' Année Dernière à Marienbad* to *South Pacific*; and knows intuitively and instinctively that high culture ('Shakespeare, Dickens and Lawrence') is usually always best. They take from Clement Greenberg (who took it from Theodor Adorno) the idea that mass culture is always 'pre-digested' (our responses are predetermined rather than the result of a genuine interaction with the text or practice), and use the idea as a means to discriminate, not just between good and bad popular culture, but to suggest that it can also be applied to examples of high culture: 'The important point about such a definition is that it cuts across the commonplace distinctions. It applies to films but not all, to some TV but not all. It covers segments of the traditional as well as the popular culture.'[108]

Their approach leads them to reject two common teaching strategies often encountered when popular culture is introduced into the classroom. First, the defensive strategy which introduces popular culture in order to condemn it as second rate culture.

Second, the 'opportunist' strategy which embraces the popular tastes of students in the hope of eventually leading them to better things.[109] 'In neither case', they contend, 'is there a genuine response, nor any basis for real judgements.'[110] Neither would lead to what they insist is necessary: 'a training in discrimination'.[111] This is not the classic discrimination of Leavisism, defending the 'good' high culture against the encroachments of the 'bad' popular culture, but discrimination within popular culture: the necessity to discriminate within and not just against popular culture; sifting the good popular culture from the bad popular culture. However, although they do not believe in introducing the texts and practices of popular culture into education 'as steppingstones in a hierarchy of taste' leading ultimately to real culture, they do still insist (as do Hoggart and Williams) that there is a fundamental categorical difference – a difference of value – between high and popular culture. Nevertheless, the difference is not necessarily a question of superiority/inferiority; it is more about different kinds of satisfaction: 'it is not useful to say that the music of Cole Porter is inferior to that of Beethoven. The music of Porter and Beethoven is not of equal value, but Porter was not making an unsuccessful attempt to create music comparable to Beethoven's.'[112]

Not unequal, but of different value, is a very difficult distinction to unload. What it seems to suggest is that we must judge cultural texts and practices on their own terms: 'recognize different aims . . . assess varying achievements with defined limits'.[113] Such a strategy will open up discrimination to a whole range of cultural activity and prevent the defensive ghettoization of high against the rest. Although they acknowledge the 'immense debt' they owe to the 'pioneers' of Leavisism, and accept more or less the Leavisite view (modified by a reading of William Morris) of the organic culture of the past, they, nevertheless, in a classic left-Leavisite move, reject the conservatism and pessimism of Leavisism, and insist, against calls for 'resistance by an armed and conscious minority' to the culture of the present (Q. D. Leavis), that 'if we wish to re-create a genuine popular culture we must seek out the points of growth within the society that now exists'.[114] By adopting 'a critical and evaluative attitude'[115] and an awareness that it is 'foolish to make large claims for this popular culture',[116] it is possible 'to break with the false distinction . . . between the "serious" and the "popular" and between "entertainment" and "values"'.[117]

This leads Hall and Whannel to what we might call the second part of their thesis: the necessity to recognize within popular culture a distinct category they call 'popular art'. Popular art is not art which has attempted and failed to be 'real' art, but art which operates within the confines of the popular. Using the best of music hall, especially Marie Lloyd, as an example (but also thinking of Charles Dickens, the early Charlie Chaplin, *The Goon Show*, and jazz musicians), they offer this definition:

> while retaining much in common with folk art, it became an *individual* art, existing within a literate commercial culture. Certain 'folk' elements were carried through, even though the artist replaced the anonymous folk artist, and the 'style' was that of the performer rather than a communal style. The relationships here are more complex – the art is no longer simply created by the people from below – yet the interaction, by way of the conventions of presentation and feeling, re-establishes the rapport. Although this art is no longer directly the product of the 'way of life' of an 'organic community', and is not 'made by the people', it is still, in a manner not applicable to the high arts, a popular art, for the people.[118]

According to this argument, good popular culture (popular art) is able to re-establish the relationship ('rapport') between performer and audience that was lost with the advent of industrialization and urbanization. As they explain:

> Popular art . . . is essentially a conventional art which re-states, in an intense form, values and attitudes already known; which measures and reaffirms, but brings to this something of the surprise of art as well as the shock of recognition. Such art has in common with folk art the genuine contact between audience and performer: but it differs from folk art in that it is an individualized art, the art of the known performer. The audience as community has come to depend on the performer's skills, and on the force of a personal style, to articulate its common values and interpret its experiences.[119]

One problem with their distinction between art and popular art is that it depends for its clarity on art as 'surprise', but this is art as defined in modernist terms. Before the modernist revolution in art, everything here claimed for popular art could equally have been claimed for art in general. They make a further distinction to include mass art. There is popular art (good and bad), and there is art (good and not so good), and there is mass art. Mass art is a 'corrupt' version of popular art; here they adopt uncritically the standard criticisms made of mass culture: it is formulaic, escapist, aesthetically worthless, emotionally unrewarding. . . .

Rather than confront the mass culture critique, they instead seek to privilege and thus to remove certain of the texts and practices of popular culture from the condemnation of the critics of mass culture. In order to do this they introduce a new category – the popular arts. Popular art is mass culture which has risen above its origins. Unlike 'average films or pop music [which] are processed mass art', popular art is, for example, the 'best cinema', the 'most advanced jazz'.[120] They claim that, 'Once the distinction between popular and mass art has been made, we find we have bypassed the cruder generalizations about "mass culture", and are faced with the full range of material offered by the media'.[121]

The main focus of *The Popular Arts* is on the textual qualities of popular culture. However, when Hall and Whannel turn to questions of youth culture they find it necessary to discuss the interaction between text and audience. Moreover, they recognize that to do full justice to the relationship, they have to include other aspects of teenage life: 'work, politics, the relation to the family, social and moral beliefs and so on'.[122] This of course begs the question why this is not also necessary when other aspects of popular culture are discussed. In the discussion of pop music culture, they concede that the claim that 'the picture of young people as innocents exploited' by the pop music industry 'is over-simplified'.[123] Against this, they argue that there is very often conflict between the use made of a text or practice by an audience, and the use intended by the producers. Significantly, they concede, 'This conflict is particularly marked in the field of teenage entertainments . . . [although] it is to some extent common to the whole area of mass entertainment in a commercial setting'.[124] Pop music culture – songs, magazines, concerts, festivals, comics, interviews with pop stars, films, etc. – helps to establish a sense of identity among youth:

> The culture provided by the commercial entertainment market
> . . . plays a crucial role. It mirrors attitudes and sentiments which
> are already there, and at the same time provides an expressive
> field and a set of symbols through which these attitudes can be
> projected. . . . Teenage culture is a contradictory mixture of the
> authentic and manufactured: it is an area of self-expression for

the young and a lush grazing pasture for the commercial providers.[125]

Moreover, pop songs

reflect adolescent difficulties in dealing with a tangle of emotional and sexual problems. They invoke the need to experience life directly and intensely. They express the drive for security in an uncertain and changeable emotional world. The fact that they are produced for a commercial market means that the songs and settings lack a certain authenticity. Yet they dramatize authentic feelings. They express vividly the adolescent emotional dilemma.[126]

Pop music exhibits 'emotional realism'; young men and women 'identify with these collective representations and . . . use them as guiding fictions. Such symbolic fictions are the folklore by means of which the teenager, in part, shapes and composes his mental picture of the world'.[127] Hall and Whannel also identify the way in which teenagers use particular ways of talking, particular places to go, particular ways of dancing and particular ways of dressing, to establish distance from the world of adults: they describe dress style as 'a minor popular art . . . used to express certain contemporary attitudes . . . for example, a strong current of social nonconformity and rebelliousness'.[128] This line of investigation would come to full fruition in the work of the Centre for Contemporary Cultural Studies, carried out during the 1970s, under the directorship of Hall himself. But here Hall and Whannel draw back from the full possibilities of their enquiries; anxious that an 'anthropological . . . slack relativism', with its focus on the functionality of pop music culture, would prevent them from posing questions of value and quality, about likes ('are those likes enough?') and needs ('are the needs healthy ones?') and taste ('perhaps tastes can be extended').

As we have noted already, they compare pop music unfavourably with jazz. They claim that jazz is 'infinitely richer . . . both aesthetically and emotionally'.[129] They also claim that the comparison is 'much more rewarding' than the more usual comparison between pop music and classical music, as both jazz and pop are popular musics. Now all this may be true, but what is the ultimate purpose of the comparison? In the case of classical against pop music, it is always to show the banality of pop music and to say something about those who consume it. Is Hall and Whannel's comparison fundamentally any different?

> The point behind such comparisons ought not to be *simply* to wean teenagers away from the juke-box heroes, but to alert them to the severe limitations and ephemeral quality of music which is so formula-dominated and so directly attuned to the standards set by the commercial market. It is a genuine widening of sensibility and emotional range which we should be working for – an extension of tastes which might lead to an extension of pleasure. The worst thing which we would say of pop music is not that it is vulgar, or morally wicked, but, more simply, that much of it is not very good.[130]

Despite the theoretical suggestiveness of much of their analysis, and despite their protests to the contrary, their position on pop music culture is a position still struggling to free itself from the theoretical constraints of Leavisism: teenagers should be persuaded that their taste is deplorable and that by listening to jazz instead of pop music they might break out of imposed and self-imposed limitations, widen their sensibilities, broaden their emotional range, and perhaps even increase their pleasure. In the end, Hall and Whannel's position seems to drift very close to the teaching strategy they condemn as 'opportunist' – in that they seem to suggest that because most school students do not have access, for a variety of reasons, to the best that has been thought and said, they can instead be given critical access to the best that has been thought and said within the popular arts of the new mass media: jazz and good films will make up for the absence of Beethoven and Shakespeare:

> This process – the practical exclusion of groups and classes in society from the selective tradition of the best that has been and is being produced in the culture – is especially damaging in a democratic society, and applies to both the traditional and new forms of high art. However, the very existence of this problem makes it even more important that some of the media which are capable of communicating work of a serious and significant kind should remain open and available, and that the quality of popular work transmitted there should be of the highest order possible, on its own terms.[131]

Where they do break significantly with Leavisism is in that they advocate a training in critical awareness, not as a means of defence *against* popular culture, but as a means to discriminate between what is good and what is bad *within* popular culture. It is a move which was to lead to a decisive break with Leavisism when the ideas of Hall and Whannel, and those of Hoggart, Williams and Thompson, were brought together under the banner of culturalism at the Birmingham University Centre for Contemporary Cultural Studies.

## The Centre for Contemporary Cultural Studies

In the introduction to *The Long Revolution,* Williams regrets the fact that 'there is no academic subject within which the questions I am interested in can be followed through; I hope one day there might be'.[132] Three years after the publication of these comments, Hoggart established the Centre for Contemporary Cultural Studies at the University of Birmingham. In the inaugural lecture, 'Schools of English and contemporary society', establishing the Centre, Hoggart states: 'It is hard to listen to a programme of pop songs . . . without feeling a complex mixture of attraction and repulsion'.[133] Once the work of the Centre began its transition, as Michael Green describes it, 'from Hoggart to Gramsci',[134] especially under the directorship of Hall, we find emerging a very different attitude towards pop music culture, and popular culture in general. Many of the researchers who followed Hoggart into the Centre (including myself), did not find listening to pop music in the least repulsive; on the contrary, they found it profoundly attractive. They focused on a different Hoggart, one critical of taking what is said at face value, and who proposed a procedure which would eventually resonate through the reading practices of cultural studies:

> we have to try and see beyond the habits to what the habits stand for, to see through the statements to what the statements really mean (which may be the opposite of the statements themselves), to detect the differing pressures of emotion behind idiomatic phrases and ritualistic observances. . . . [And to see the way] mass publications [for example] connect with commonly accepted attitudes, how they are altering those attitudes, and how they are meeting resistance.[135]

Culturalists study cultural texts and practices in order to reconstitute or reconstruct the experiences, values, etc. – the 'structure of feeling' of particular groups or classes or whole societies, in order to better understand the lives of those who lived the culture. In different ways – Hoggart's example, Williams's social definition of culture, Thompson's act of historical rescue, Hall and Whannel's 'democratic' extension of Leavisism – each contribution discussed here argues that popular culture (defined as the lived culture of ordinary men and women) is worth studying. It is on the basis of these and other assumptions of culturalism, channelled through the traditions of English, sociology and history, that British cultural studies began. However, research at the Centre quickly brought culturalism into complex and often contradictory and conflictual relations with imports of French structuralism (see Chapter 4), in turn bringing the two approaches into critical dialogue with developments in 'Western Marxism', especially the work of Louis Althusser and Antonio Gramsci (see Chapter 5). It is from this complex and critical mixture that the 'disunified' field of British cultural studies was born.

## Further reading

Iain Chambers, *Popular Culture: The metropolitan experience*, London: Routledge, 1986. An interesting and informed survey – mostly from the perspective of culturalism – of the rise of urban popular culture since the 1880s.

John Clarke, Chas Critcher and Richard Johnson (eds), *Working Class Culture: Studies in history and theory*, London: Hutchinson, 1979. Some good essays from a culturalist perspective. See especially Richard Johnson's 'Three problematics: elements of a theory of working class culture'.

Terry Eagleton (ed.), *Raymond Williams: Critical perspectives*, Cambridge: Polity Press, 1989. Essays in critical appreciation of the work of Raymond Williams.

Stuart Hall and Tony Jefferson (eds), *Resistance Through Rituals*, London: Hutchinson, 1976. The Centre for Contemporary Cultural Studies' foundational account of youth subcultures. Chapter 1 provides a classic statement of the Centre's version of culturalism.

Stuart Hall, Dorothy Hobson, Andrew Lowe and Paul Willis (eds), *Culture, Media, Language*, London: Hutchinson, 1980. A selection of essays covering almost the first ten years of the Centre's published work. See especially Chapter 1, Stuart Hall's important account of the theoretical development of work at the Centre: 'Cultural studies and the Centre: some problematics and problems'.

Harvey J. Kaye and Keith McClelland (eds), *E. P. Thompson: Critical perspectives*, Oxford: Polity Press, 1990. A collection of critical essays on different aspects of Thompson's contribution to the study of history; some useful references to *The Making of the English Working Class*.

Alan O'Connor (ed.), *Raymond Williams: Writing, culture, politics*, Oxford: Basil Blackwell, 1989. Provides a critical survey of Williams's work. Excellent bibliography.

# 4
# STRUCTURALISM AND POST-STRUCTURALISM

Structuralism is a theoretical method and not a political position. Moreover, unlike the other approaches discussed already, structuralism is, as Terry Eagleton points out, 'quite indifferent to the cultural value of its object: anything from *War and Peace* to *The War Cry* will do. The method is analytical, not evaluative'.[1] It is a way of approaching texts and practices which is derived from the theoretical work of the Swiss linguist Ferdinand de Saussure. Its principal exponents are French: Claude Lévi-Strauss in anthropology, Roland Barthes in literary and cultural studies, Michel Foucault in philosophy and history, Jacques Lacan in psychoanalysis and Louis Althusser in Marxist theory. Their work is often very different, and at times very difficult. What unites them is the influence of Saussure, and the use of a particular vocabulary drawn from his work. It is as well, then, to start our exploration with a consideration of his work in linguistics. This is best approached by examining a number of key concepts.

## Ferdinand de Saussure

Saussure divides language into two component parts. When I write the word dog it produces the inscription dog, but also the concept or mental image of a dog: a four-legged canine creature. He calls the first the signifier, and the second the signified. Together (like two sides of a coin or a sheet of paper) they make up the sign. He then goes on to argue that the relationship between signifier and signified is completely arbitrary. The word dog, for example, has no dog-like qualities, there is no reason why the signifier dog should produce the signified dog: four-legged canine creature. The relationship between the two is simply the result of convention – of cultural agreement. The signifier dog could just as easily produce the signified cat: four-legged feline creature. On the basis of this claim, he suggests that meaning is not the result of an essential correspondence between signifiers and signifieds, it is rather the result of difference and relationship. The signifier 'dog' is taken to mean the signified dog because the signifier is not cog, log or jog, for instance. Another example might make the point clearer. Traffic lights operate within a system of four signs: red = stop, green = go, amber = prepare for red, amber and red = prepare for green. The relationship between the signifier green and the signified go is arbitrary; there is nothing in the colour green that naturally attaches it to the verb go. Traffic lights would work equally well if red signified go and green signified stop. The system works not by expressing a *natural* meaning but by marking a difference, a distinction within a system of difference and relationships.

According to Saussure, meaning is also the result of a process of combination and selection. The sentence, 'I saw a dog today', is meaningful through the accumulation of its different parts: I/saw/a dog/today. Its meaning is only complete once the final word is spoken or inscribed. Saussure calls this process the syntagmatic axis of language. One can add other parts to extend its meaningfulness: 'I saw a dog today in the rain'. Meaning is thus accumulated along the syntagmatic axis of language. Meaning can be changed by substituting certain parts of the sentence for new parts. For example, I could write instead, 'I saw a dog yesterday in the rain'. Such substitutions are said to be operating along a plane of associations, or along the paradigmatic axis of language.

Let us consider a more politically charged example. 'Terrorists carried out an attack on an army base today'. Substitutions from the paradigmatic axis could alter the meaning of this sentence considerably. If we substitute 'freedom fighters' or 'anti-imperialist volunteers' for the word 'terrorists' we would have a sentence meaningful in quite a different way. This would be achieved without any reference to a corresponding reality outside of the sentence itself. The meaning of the sentence is produced through a process of selection and combination. Structuralists argue that language does not reflect an already existing reality. The function of language is to organize and construct our access to reality – different languages in effect produce a different mapping of the real. When, for example, a European gazes at a snowscape, he or she sees snow. An Eskimo, with over fifty words to describe snow, looking at the same snowscape would presumably see so much more. Therefore an Eskimo and a European standing together surveying the snowscape would in fact be seeing two quite different conceptual scenes. Similarly, Australian Aborigines have many words to describe the desert. What these examples demonstrate to a structuralist is that the way we conceptualize the world is ultimately dependent on the language we speak. And by analogy, it will depend on the culture we inhabit. The meanings made possible by language are thus the result of the interplay of a network of relationships between combination and selection, similarity and difference. Meaning cannot be accounted for by reference to an extra linguistic reality. As Saussure insists, 'in language there are only differences *without positive terms* . . . language has neither ideas nor sounds that existed before the linguistic system, but only conceptual and phonic differences that have issued from the system'.[2] We might want to query this assumption by noting that the snowscape is named differently by Eskimos because of the material bearing it has on their day-to-day existence. It could also be objected that substituting 'terrorists' for 'freedom fighters' produces meanings not accounted for purely by linguistics (see Chapter 5).

Saussure distinguishes between two theoretical approaches to linguistics: the diachronic approach which studies the historical development of a given language, and the synchronic approach which studies a given language at one particular moment in time. He argues that in order to found a science of linguistics it is necessary to adopt a synchronic approach. Structuralists have, generally speaking, taken the synchronic approach to the study of texts or practices. They argue that in order to understand a text or practice thoroughly it is necessary to focus exclusively on its structural properties. This of course allows critics hostile to structuralism to criticize it as ahistorical in its approach to culture.

Saussure makes one other distinction which has proved essential to the development of structuralism. That is the division of language into *langue* and *parole*. *Langue* refers to the system of language; the rules and conventions that organize it. This is language as a social institution: and as Roland Barthes points out, 'it is essentially a collective contract which one must accept in its entirety if one wishes to communicate'.[3] *Parole* refers to the individual utterance, the individual use of language. To clarify this point, he compares language to the game of chess. Here we can distinguish between the rules of the game and an actual game of chess. Without the body of rules there could be no actual game, but it is only in an actual game that these rules are made manifest. Therefore, there is *langue* and *parole*, structure and performance. It is the homogeneity of the structure which makes the heterogeneity of the performance possible.

Structuralism takes two basic ideas from Saussure's work. First, a concern with the underlying relations of cultural texts and practices – the 'grammar' which makes meaning possible. Second, the view that meaning is always the result of the interplay of relationships of selection and combination made possible by the underlying structure. In other words, cultural texts and practices are studied as analogous to language. Imagine, for example, that aliens from outer space had landed in London in May 1996, and as an earthly display of welcome they were invited to attend the FA Cup Final between Manchester United and Liverpool. What would they witness? Two groups of men in different coloured costumes, one red, the other green and white, moving at different speeds, in different directions, across a green surface, marked with white lines. They would notice that a white spherical projectile appeared to have some influence on the various patterns of cooperation and competition. They would also notice a man dressed in black, with a whistle which he blew to stop and start the combinations of play. They would also note that he appeared to be supported by two other men in black, one on either side of the main activity, each using a flag to support the main man in black's limited authority. Finally, they would note the presence of two men, one at each end of the playing area, standing in front of partly netted structures. They would see that periodically these men engaged in acrobatic routines which involved contact with the white projectile. The visiting aliens could observe the occasion and describe what they saw to each other, but unless someone explained to them the rules of association football, its *structure*, the FA Cup Final, in which Manchester United became the first team in history to win the league and cup double twice, would make very little sense to them at all. It is the underlying rules of cultural texts and practices that interest structuralists. It is structure that makes meaning possible. The task of structuralism, therefore, is to make explicit the rules and conventions (the structure) which govern the production of meaning (an act of *parole*).

## Claude Lévi-Strauss, Will Wright and the American Western

Claude Lévi-Strauss uses Saussure to help him discover the 'unconscious foundations'[4] of the culture of so-called 'primitive' societies. He analyzes cooking, manners, modes of dress, aesthetic activity and other forms of cultural and social practices as analogous to a system of language; each in its different way being a mode of communication, a form of expression. As Terence Hawkes points out, 'His quarry, in short, is the *langue* of the whole culture; its system and its general laws: he stalks it through the particular varieties of its *parole*.'[5] In pursuit of his quarry Lévi-Strauss investigates a number of 'systems'. It is, however, his analysis of myth which is of central interest to the student of popular culture. He claims that beneath the vast heterogeneity of myths there can be discovered a homogeneous structure. In short, he argues that individual myths are examples of *parole*, articulations of an underlying structure or *langue*. By understanding this structure we should be able truly to understand the meaning – 'operational value'[6] – of particular myths. Myths work like language: composed of individual 'mythemes', analogous to individual units of language, 'morphemes' and 'phonemes'. Like morphemes and phonemes, mythemes only take on meaning when combined in particular patterns. Seen in this way, the anthropologist's task is to discover the underlying 'grammar': the rules and regulations which make it possible for myths to be meaningful. He also argues that myths are structured in terms of 'binary oppositions'. Meaning is produced by dividing the world into mutually exclusive categories: culture/nature, man/woman, black/white, good/bad, us/them, for example. Drawing on Saussure, he sees meaning as a result of the interplay between a process of similarity and difference. For example, in order to say what is bad we must have some notion of what is good. In the same way, what it means to be a man is defined against what it means to be a woman.

Lévi-Strauss claims that all myths have a similar structure. Moreover, he also claims – although this is by no means his primary focus – that all myths have a similar sociocultural function within society. That is, the purpose of myth is to make the world explicable, magically to resolve its problems and contradictions. As he contends, 'mythical thought always progresses from the awareness of oppositions toward their resolution. . . . The purpose of myth is to provide a logical model capable of overcoming a contradiction.'[7] Myths are stories we tell ourselves as a culture in order to banish contradictions and make the world understandable and therefore habitable; they attempt to put us at peace with ourselves and our existence.

In *Sixguns and Society*, Will Wright uses Lévi-Strauss's structuralist methodology to analyze the Hollywood Western. He argues that much of the narrative power of the Western is derived from its structure of binary oppositions. However, Wright differs from Lévi-Strauss in that his concern 'is not to reveal a mental structure but to show how the myths of a society, through their structure, communicate a conceptual order to the members of that society'.[8] In short, whereas Lévi-Strauss's primary concern is the structure of the human mind, Wright's focus is on the way the Western 'presents a symbolically simple but remarkably deep conceptualization of American social beliefs'.[9] He contends that the Western has evolved through three stages: 'classic' (including a variation he calls 'vengeance'), 'transition theme' and 'professional'. Despite the genre's different types, he identifies a basic set of structuring oppositions:

| Inside society | Outside society |
| --- | --- |
| Good | Bad |
| Strong | Weak |
| Civilization | Wilderness[10] |

But, as he insists (taking him beyond Lévi-Strauss), in order to understand the social meaning of a myth fully, it is necessary to analyze not only its binary structure but its narrative structure 'the progression of events and the resolution of conflicts'.[11] The 'classic' Western is divided into sixteen narrative 'functions':[12]

1. The hero enters a social group.
2. The hero is unknown to the society.

3. The hero is revealed to have an exceptional ability.
4. The members of the society recognize a difference between themselves and the hero; the hero is given a special status.
5. The society does not completely accept the hero.
6. There is a conflict of interests between the villains and the society.
7. The villains are stronger than the society; the society is weak.
8. There is a strong friendship or respect between the hero and a villain.
9. The villains threaten the society.
10. The hero avoids involvement in the conflict.
11. The villains endanger a friend of the hero.
12. The hero fights the villains.
13. The hero defeats the villains.
14. The society is safe.
15. The society accepts the hero.
16. The hero loses or gives up his special status.[13]

*Shane* is the classic example of the classic Western: the story of a stranger who rides out of the wilderness and helps a group of farmers defeat a powerful rancher, and then rides away again, back into the wilderness. In the classic Western, the hero and society are (temporarily) aligned in opposition to the villains who remain outside society. In the 'transition theme' Western, which Wright claims provides a bridge between the classic Western, the form which dominated the 1930s, the 1940s and most of the 1950s, and the professional Western, the form which dominated the 1960s and 1970s, the binary oppositions are reversed, and we see the hero outside society struggling against a strong, but corrupt and corrupting, civilization:

| Hero | Society |
|---|---|
| Outside society | Inside society |
| Good | Bad |
| Weak | Strong |
| Wilderness | Civilization[14] |

Many of the narrative functions are also inverted. Instead of being outside the society, the hero begins as a valued member of the society. But the society is revealed to be the real 'villain' in opposition to the hero and those outside society and civilization.

In his support for, and eventual alignment with, those outside society and civilization, he himself crosses from inside to outside and from civilization to wilderness. But in the end the society is too strong for those outside it, who are ultimately powerless against its force. The best they can do is escape to the wilderness.

Although, according to Wright, the last 'transition theme' Western was *Johnny Guitar* in 1954, it appears clear, using his own binary oppositions and narrative functions, that *Dances with Wolves*, made in 1990, is a perfect example of the form. A cavalry officer, decorated for bravery, rejects the East ('civilization') and requests a posting to the West ('wilderness') – as the film publicity puts it, 'in 1864 one man went in search of the frontier and found himself'. He also found *society* among the Sioux. The film tells the story of how 'he is drawn into the loving and honourable folds of a Sioux tribe . . . and ultimately, the crucial decision he must make as white settlers continue their violent and ruthless journey into the lands of the Native Americans'.[15] His decision is to fight on the side of the Sioux against the 'civilization' he has rejected. Finally, considered a traitor by the cavalry, he decides to leave the Sioux, so as not to give the cavalry an excuse to butcher them. The final scene, however, shows his departure as, unbeknown to him or the Sioux, the cavalry close in for what is to be undoubtedly the massacre of the tribe.

If we accept *Dances with Wolves* as a 'transition theme' Western, it raises some interesting questions about the film as myth. Wright claims that each type of Western 'corresponds' to a different moment in the recent economic development of the United States:

> the classic Western plot corresponds to the individualistic conception of society underlying a market economy. . . . [T]he vengeance plot is a variation that begins to reflect changes in the market economy. . . . [T]he professional plot reveals a new conception of society corresponding to the values and attitudes inherent in a planned, corporate economy.[16]

Each type in turn articulates its own mythic version of how to achieve the *American Dream*:

> The classical plot shows that the way to achieve such human rewards as friendship, respect, and dignity is to separate yourself from others and use your strength as an autonomous individual to succor them. . . . The vengeance variation . . . weakens the

compatibility of the individual and society by showing that the path to respect and love is to separate yourself from others, struggling individually against your many and strong enemies but striving to remember and return to the softer values of marriage and humility. The transition theme, anticipating new social values, argues that love and companionship are available at the cost of becoming a social outcast to the individual who stands firmly and righteously against the intolerance and ignorance of society. Finally, the professional plot . . . argues that companionship and respect are to be achieved only by becoming a skilled technician, who joins an élite group of professionals, accepts any job that is offered, and has loyalty only to the integrity of the team, not to any competing social or community values.[17]

Given the critical and financial success of *Dances with Wolves* (winner of seven Oscars; fifth most successful film in both the United Kingdom and the United States, grossing £10.9 million and $122.5 million in the first year of release in the United Kingdom and United States respectively),[18] it may well (if we accept Wright's rather reductive correspondence theory) represent a 'transition theme' Western that marks the beginning of a reverse transition, back to a time of less mercenary social and community values – back in fact to a time of society and community.

## Roland Barthes: *Mythologies*

Roland Barthes's early work on popular culture is concerned with the process of signification, the means by which meanings are produced and put into circulation. *Mythologies* is a collection of essays on French popular culture. In it he discusses, among many things, wrestling, soap powders and detergents, toys, steak and chips, tourism and popular attitudes towards science. He uses Saussure's linguistic model to analyze French popular culture. His aim is to make explicit what too often remains implicit in the texts and practices of popular culture. His guiding principle is always interrogate 'the falsely obvious'.[19] His purpose is political; his target is what he calls the 'bourgeois norm'.[20] As he states in the Preface to the 1957 edition, 'I resented seeing Nature and History confused at every turn, and I wanted to track down, in the decorative display of *what-goes-without-saying*, the ideological abuse which, in my view, is hidden there'.[21] *Mythologies* represents the most significant attempt to bring the methodology of semiology to bear on popular culture. Semiology itself was first posited by Saussure:

> Language is a system of signs that express ideas, and is therefore comparable to a system of writing, the alphabet of deaf mutes, symbolic rites, polite formulas, military signals, etc. . . . *A science that studies the life of signs within society is conceivable*. . . I shall call it semiology.[22]

*Mythologies* is also quite simply one of the founding texts of cultural studies.[23] The collection concludes with a theoretical essay, 'Myth today'. In the essay Barthes outlines a semiological model for reading popular culture. He takes Saussure's schema of signifier/signified = sign and adds to it a second level of signification.

As we noted earlier, the signifier dog produces the signified dog: a four-legged canine creature. Barthes argues that this indicates only primary signification. The sign dog produced in this formulation can become the signifier dog in a second level of signification. This produces at the secondary level the signified dog: an unpleasant human being. As illustrated in Figure 4.1, the sign of primary signification becomes the signifier of secondary signification. In *Elements of Semiology*, Barthes substitutes the more familiar terms denotation (primary signification) and connotation (secondary signification): 'the first system [denotation] becomes the plane of expression or signifier of the second system [connotation]. . . . The signifiers of connotation . . . are made up of signs (signifiers and signifieds united) of the denoted system.'[24]

He claims that it is at the level of secondary signification or connotation that myth is produced for consumption. He calls myth a type of speech. What he means by this is that myth can consist of any discursive practice analogous to language. Myth is therefore

| Primary signification | 1. Signifier       2. Signified | |
| --- | --- | --- |
| Denotation | 3. Sign | |
| Secondary signification | I.  SIGNIFIER | II.  SIGNIFIED |
| Connotation | III.  SIGN | |

*Figure 4.1*  Primary and secondary signification.

what he calls 'a second order semiological system'. But as we have noted, Barthes's purpose is political. By myth he also means ideology understood as a body of ideas and practices which defend the prevailing structure of power by actively promoting the values and interests of the dominant groups in society. To understand this aspect of his argument we need to understand the polysemic nature of signs; that is, that they have the potential to signify multiple meanings. An example might make the point clearer. I discussed in Chapter 1 how the Conservative Party presented a party political broadcast which concluded with the word socialism being transposed into red prison bars. This was a clear attempt to fix the secondary signification or connotations of the word socialism to mean restrictive, imprisoning, against freedom. Barthes would see this as an example of the fixing of new connotations in the production of myth – the production of ideology. He argues that all forms of signification can be shown to operate in this way. His most famous example of the workings of secondary signification is taken from the cover of the French magazine *Paris Match* (1955). He begins his analysis by establishing that the primary level of signification consists of a signifier: patches of colour and figuration. This produces the signified: 'a black soldier saluting the French flag'. Together they form the primary sign. The primary sign then becomes the signifier 'black soldier saluting the French flag', producing the signified 'French imperiality'. Here is his account of his encounter with the cover of the magazine:

1 am at the barber's, and a copy of *Paris Match* is offered to me. On the cover, a young Negro in a French uniform is saluting, with his eyes uplifted, probably fixed on the fold of the tricolour. All this is the meaning of the picture. But, whether naively or not, I see very well what it signifies to me: that France is a great Empire, that all her sons, without colour discrimination, faithfully serve under her flag, and that there is no better answer to the detractors of an alleged colonialism than the zeal shown by this Negro in serving his so-called oppressors. I am therefore faced with a greater semiological system: there is a signifier, itself already formed with a previous system (*a black soldier is giving the French salute*); there is a signified (it is a purposeful mixture of Frenchness and militariness); finally there is a presence of the signified through the signifier.[25]

At the first level: black soldier saluting the French flag. At the second level: a positive image of French imperialism. The cover illustration represents *Paris Match*'s attempt to produce a positive image of French imperialism. Following the defeat in Vietnam (1946–54), and the then current war in Algeria (1954–62), such an image would seem by many to be of some political urgency. And as Barthes suggests, 'myth has . . . a double function: it points out and it notifies, it makes us understand something and it imposes it on us.'[26] What makes this a possibility are the shared cultural codes on which both Barthes and the readership of *Paris Match* are able to draw. Connotations are therefore not simply produced by the makers of the image, but activated from an already existing cultural repertoire. In other words, the image both draws from the cultural repertoire and at the same time adds to it. Moreover, the cultural repertoire does not form a homogeneous block. Myth is continually confronted by counter-myth. For example, an image containing references to pop music culture might be seen by a young audience as an index of freedom and heterogeneity, but to an older audience it might signal manipulation and homogeneity. Which codes are mobilized will largely depend on the triple context of the location of the text, the historical moment and the cultural formation of the reader.

In 'The photographic message'[27] Barthes introduces a number of further considerations. Context of publication is important, as I have already said. If the photograph of the black soldier saluting the flag had appeared on the cover of the *Socialist Review*, its connotative meaning(s) would have been very different. Readers would have looked for irony. Rather than being read as a positive image of French imperialism, it would have been seen as a sign of imperial exploitation and manipulation. In addition to this, a socialist reading the original *Paris Match* would not have seen the image as a positive image of French imperialism, but as a desperate attempt to project such an image given the general historical context of France's defeat in Vietnam and its pending defeat in Algeria. But despite all this the intention behind the image is clear:

> Myth has an imperative, buttonholing character . . . [it arrests] in both the physical and the legal sense of the term: French imperialism condemns the saluting Negro to be nothing more than an instrumental signifier, the Negro suddenly hails me in the name of French imperiality; but at the same moment the Negro's salute thickens, becomes vitrified, freezes into an eternal reference meant to *establish* French imperiality.[28]

This is not the only way French imperialism might be given positive connotations. Barthes suggests other mythical signifiers the press might use: 'I can very well give to French imperiality many other signifiers beside a Negro's salute: a French general pins a decoration on a one-armed Senegalese, a nun hands a cup of tea to a bed ridden Arab, a white schoolmaster teaches attentive piccaninnies'.[29]

Barthes envisages three possible reading positions from which the image can be read. The first would simply see the black soldier saluting the flag as an 'example' of French imperiality, a 'symbol' for it. This is the position of those who produce such myths. The second would see the image as an 'alibi' for French imperiality. This is the position of the socialist reader discussed above. The final reading position is that of the 'reader of myths'. He or she reads the image not as an example or a symbol, nor as an alibi: the black soldier saluting the flag 'is the very presence of French imperiality'. There is of course a fourth reading position, that of Barthes himself – the mythologist. This reading produces what he calls a 'structural description'. It is a reading position which seeks to determine the image's means of ideological production, its transformation of history into nature. What is meant by this is the way the black soldier saluting the flag can be seen as *naturally* conjuring up the concept of French imperiality. There is not anything to discuss, it is obvious that one implies the presence of the other. The relationship between the black soldier saluting the flag and French imperiality has been 'naturalized'. As Barthes explains,

> what allows the reader to consume myth innocently is that he does not see it as a semiological system but as an inductive one. Where there is only equivalence, he sees a kind of causal process: the signifier and the signified have, in his eyes, a natural relationship. This confusion can be expressed otherwise: any semiological system is a system of values; now the myth-consumer takes the signification for a system of facts: myth is read as a factual system, whereas it is but a semiological system.[30]

Again, according to Barthes, 'Semiology has taught us that myth has the task of giving an historical intention a natural justification, and making contingency appear eternal. Now this process is exactly that of bourgeois ideology.'[31] His argument is that 'myth is constituted by the loss of the historical quality of things: in it, things lose the memory that they once were made.'[32] It is what he calls 'depoliticized speech'.

> In the case of the soldier Negro . . . what is got rid of is certainly
> not French imperiality (on the contrary, since what must be
> actualized is its presence); it is the contingent, historical, in one
> word: *fabricated*, quality of colonialism. Myth does not deny
> things, on the contrary, its function is to talk about them; simply,
> it purifies them, it makes them innocent, it gives them a natural
> and eternal justification, it gives them a clarity which is not that
> of an explanation but that of a statement of fact. If I *state the fact*
> of French imperiality without explaining it, I am very near to
> finding that it is natural and goes *without saying.* . . . In passing
> from history to nature, myth acts economically: it abolishes the
> complexity of human acts . . . it organizes a world which is with-
> out contradictions because it is without depth, a world wide open
> and wallowing in the evident, it establishes a blissful clarity:
> things appear to mean something by themselves.[33]

Images rarely appear without the accompaniment of a linguistic text of one kind or another. A newspaper photograph, for
example, will be surrounded by a title, a caption, a story and the
general layout of the page. It will also, as we have already noted, be
situated within the context of a particular newspaper or magazine.
The context provided by the *Daily Telegraph* is very different from
that provided by the *Socialist Worker.* Readership and reader expec-
tation form part of this context.

> Formerly, the image illustrated the text (made it clearer); today,
> the text loads the image, burdening it with culture, a moral, an
> imagination. Formerly, there was reduction from text to image;
> today, there is amplification from one to the other. The connota-
> tion is now experienced only as the natural resonance of the
> fundamental denotation constituted by the photographic anal-
> ogy and we are thus confronted with a typical process of natural-
> ization of the cultural.[34]

In other words, image does not illustrate text, it is the text which
amplifies the connotative potential of the image. He refers to this
process as 'relay'. The relationship can of course work in other
ways. For example, rather than 'amplifying a set of connotations
already given in the photograph . . . the text produces (invents) an
entirely new signified which is retroactively projected into the image, so much so as to appear denoted there.'[35] An example might
be a photograph taken in 1996 of a rock star looking reflective,
and originally used to promote a love song: 'My Baby Done Me

Very Wrong'. In 1997 the photograph is reused to accompany newspaper accounts of the death by a drug overdose of one of the rock star's closest friends. The photograph is retitled: 'Drugs killed my friend'. The caption would feed into the image producing (inventing) connotations of loss, despair and a certain thoughtfulness about the role of drugs in rock music culture. Barthes refers to this process as 'anchorage'. What the example of the different meanings of the photograph of the rock star reveals is the polysemic nature of all signs. That is, their potential for multiple signification. Without the addition of a linguistic text, the meaning of the image is very difficult to pin down. The linguistic message works in two ways. It helps the reader to identify the denotative meaning of the image: this is a rock star looking reflective. Second, it limits the potential proliferation of the connotations of the image: the rock star is reflective because of the drug overdose by one of his or her closest friends. Therefore, the rock star is contemplating the role of drugs in rock music culture. Moreover, it tries to make the reader believe that the connotative meaning is actually present at the level of denotation.

What makes the move from denotation to connotation possible is the store of social knowledge (a cultural repertoire) upon which the reader is able to draw when he or she reads the image. Without access to this shared code (conscious or unconscious) the operations of connotation would not be possible. And of course such knowledge is always both historical and cultural. That is to say, it might differ from one culture to another, and from one historical moment to another. Cultural difference might also be marked by differences of class, race, gender, generation or sexual preference. As Barthes points out,

> reading closely depends on my culture, on my knowledge of the world, and it is probable that a good press photograph (and they are all good, being selected) makes ready play with the supposed knowledge of its readers, those prints being chosen which comprise the greatest possible quantity of information of this kind in such a way as to render the reading fully satisfying.[36]

Again, as he explains, 'the variation in readings is not, however, anarchic; it depends on the different kinds of knowledge – practical, national, cultural, aesthetic – invested in the image [by the reader]'.[37] Here we see once again the analogy with language.

Every class contains children *of widely differing abilities and interests.*

## ONE GIRL WANTS TO GO TO UNIVERSITY.
## THE OTHER WANTS TO LEAVE AT 16.
## HOW DO YOU KEEP THEM BOTH INTERESTED?

Jackie on the right is motivated to learn at school by her long-term goals. However,
contrary to appearances, Susan on the left may see little point in paying attention at all.

MUSIC, clothes and boys are the sort of things 14 year olds like Susan are usually most interested in. Electromagnetism, genetics and Charles Dickens, unfortunately, are not. Unless, of course, the teacher makes them interesting.

If you think that sounds difficult, you're right. The trick is to make whatever you're teaching relevant to the interests of less motivated pupils and, most important of all, make it enjoyable.

Remembering at the same time you have to keep your lessons stimulating and challenging for the keener ones.

This is where a strong imagination and a sense of humour come in handy. (And of course these days, there are all sorts of interesting teaching aids to help you as well, many of which you will learn about in your training).

You'll also need a lot of energy, as any teacher will tell you, but it is rewarding when you see all your efforts pay off. For example, when pupils like Jackie go on to do well in higher education (especially if they choose to pursue their subject).

And equally when pupils like Susan go on to do well at work. Or better still, decide not to leave at 16 after all.

But is it rewarding when it comes to the end of the month? Well, you may be surprised to learn that teachers' starting salaries now compare well with those of graduates in general.

From December, teachers in inner London with a good honours degree will start on around £14,000 (including inner London supplement and allowance).

And if you make it to the top of your profession as a Head teacher of a large secondary school in

inner London, you could earn up to £48,000.

Interested? For more information, fill in the coupon or call 0345 300121, quoting the department code xxxxxx.

[coupon form]

Teaching brings out the best in people.

*Figure 4.2*  Department of Education and Science advertisement.
(Crown Copyright. Reproduced by kind permission of the Department of Education.)

The individual image is an example of *parole*, and the code of connotations is an example of *langue*. The best way to draw together the different elements of this model of reading is to demonstrate it. In 1991 the Department of Education and Science (DES) produced an advertisement which they placed in the popular film magazine *Empire* (Figure 4.2). The image shows two 14-year-old schoolgirls: Jackie intends to go to university, Susan intends to leave school at 16. The poster's aim is to attract men and women to the teaching profession. It operates a double bluff. That is, we see the two girls, read the caption and decide which girl wants to go to university, which girl wants to leave at 16. The double bluff is that the girl who wants to leave is the one convention – those without our cultural competence – would consider studious. It is a double bluff because we are not intended to be taken in by the operation. We can congratulate ourselves on our perspicacity. We, unlike others, have not been taken in – we have the necessary cultural competence. Therefore we are excellent teacher material. The advertisement plays with the knowledge necessary to be a teacher and allows us to recognize that knowledge in ourselves: it provides us with a position from which to say: 'Yes, I should be a teacher.'

## Post-structuralism

Post-structuralists reject the idea of an underlying structure upon which meaning can rest secure and satisfied. Meaning is always in process. What we call meaning is a momentary stop in a continuing flow of interpretations of interpretations. For example, when Freud analyzed his patients' dreams, he was in effect interpreting his patients' interpretations of their dreams. The unconscious does not guarantee the meaning of a dream; rather, it is a metaphorical device (structure) which makes interpretation possible. For the post-structuralist Barthes, denotation is no longer a neutral level, it is no more than the last connotation. Denotation itself is a part of the production of myth. Denotation is just as ideological as connotation.

Saussure, as we have noted, posited language as consisting of the relationship between the signifier, signified and the sign. The theorists of post-structuralism suggest that the situation is more complex than this. Signifiers do not produce signifieds, they produce more signifiers. Meaning as a result is a very unstable thing. We have noted already how for structuralists the meaning of a word depends on it not being another word. We also noted how meaning is produced by the selection and combination processes of the paradigmatic and syntagmatic axes. Meaning is therefore always in a sense both present and absent. In 'The death of the author', Barthes insists that a text cannot be seen as the pure medium of an authorial intention. Rather, a text is 'a multi-dimensional space in which a variety of writings, none of them original, blend and clash. The text is a tissue of quotations drawn from the innumerable centres of culture.'[38] Only a reader can bring a temporary unity to a text. Unlike the work which can be seen lying in apparent completion on library shelves and in book shops, the text 'is experienced only in an activity of production'.[39] A text is a work seen as inseparable from the active process of the intertextuality of its many readings.

## Jacques Derrida

Post-structuralism is virtually synonymous with the work of Jacques Derrida. Derrida has invented a new word to describe the divided nature of the sign: *différence*,[40] meaning both to defer and to differ. The sign, as we have noted, is made meaningful for Saussure by being different. Derrida adds to this the notion that meaning is also always deferred, never fully present, always both absent and present (see discussion of defining popular culture in Chapter 1). For example, if we track the meaning of a word through a dictionary we encounter a relentless deferment of meaning. If we look up the signifier 'letter' in the *Collins Pocket Dictionary of the English Language*, we discover it has five possible signifieds: a written or printed message, a character of the alphabet, the strict meaning of an agreement, precisely (as in 'to the letter') and to write or mark letters on a sign. If we then look up one of these, the signified '[a written or printed] message', we find that it too is a signifier producing four more signifieds: a communication from one person or group to another, an implicit meaning, as in a work of art, a religious or political belief that someone attempts to communicate to others, and to understand (as in 'to get the message'). Tracking through the dictionary in this way confirms a relentless intertextual deferment of meaning, 'the indefinite referral of signifier to signifier . . . which gives the signified meaning no respite . . . so that it always signifies again'.[41] It is only when located in a discourse and read in a context that there is a temporary halt to the endless play of signifier to signifier. For example, if we read or hear the words 'nothing was delivered', they would mean something quite different depending on whether they were the opening words of a novel, a line from a poem, an excuse, a jotting in a shopkeeper's notebook, a line from a song, an example from a phrase book, part of a monologue in a play, part of a speech in a film, an illustration in an explanation of *différence*. But even context cannot fully control meaning: the phrase 'nothing was delivered' will carry with it the 'trace' of meanings from other contexts. If I know the line is from a song, this will resonate across the words as I read them in a shopkeeper's notebook.

The DES advertisement I discussed earlier contains what Derrida would call a 'violent hierarchy'[42] in its couplet: 'good' girl, who is interested in electromagnetism, genetics and Charles Dickens; and 'bad' girl, who prefers music, clothes and boys. Derrida refers to the 'strange economy of the supplement'[43] to point to the unstable interplay between such binary oppositions. In his analyses of Jean-Jacques Rousseau's 'confessional' and linguistic writings, Derrida deconstructs the binary opposition between speech and writing. Rousseau considers speech as the natural way to express thought; writing, he regards as a 'dangerous supplement'. However, when presence is no longer guaranteed by speech, writing becomes a necessary means to protect presence. But for Rousseau writing can *only* be a 'supplement to speech': 'it is not natural. It diverts the immediate presence of thought. . . . [It is] a sort of artificial and artful ruse to make speech present when it is actually absent. It is a violence done to the natural destiny of the language'.[44] To supplement means both to add and to substitute. Writing is therefore both an addition to speech and a substitute for speech. But speech itself is a supplement. It does not exist outside culture. Speech cannot therefore play *Edenic nature* to writing's *fallen culture*, both always already belong to 'the order of the supplement'.[45] For, as Derrida insists, 'the indefinite process of supplementarity has always already *infiltrated* presence, always already inscribed there the space of repetition and the splitting of the self [from pure self-presence].'[46] Nature may have preceded culture, but our sense of nature as pure presence is a product of culture. Writing is not the fall of language, it is inscribed in its origins. Rousseau, in a sense, already knows this: according to Derrida, he '*declares* what he *wishes to say*', but he also '*describes* that which he *does not wish to say*'.[47] It is in the unravelling of this contradiction that the binary oppositions speech/writing, nature/culture are deconstructed – the privileged term in the opposition is shown to be dependent on the other for its meaning.

We noted in Chapter 1 how high culture has often depended on popular culture to give it definitional solidity. Derrida's critique of Rousseau alerts us to the way in which one side in such couplets is always privileged over the other; one side always claims a position of status (of pure presence) over the other. Derrida also demonstrates that they are not pure opposites – each is *motivated* by the other, ultimately dependent on the absent other for its own presence and meaning. There is no naturally 'good' girl who stays on at school, which can be opposed to a naturally 'bad' girl who wants to leave at 16. Simply to reverse the binary opposition would be to keep in place the assumptions already constructed by the opposition. We must do more than 'simply . . . neutralize the binary oppositions. . . . One of the two terms controls the other . . . holds the superior position. To deconstruct the opposition [we must] . . . overthrow the hierarchy.'[48] Instead of accepting the double bluff, a 'deconstructive' reading would wish to dismantle the couplet to demonstrate that it can only be held in place by a certain 'violence' – a certain set of dubious assumptions about gender and sexuality. A Derridean reading could also be made of *Dances with Wolves*: instead of the film being seen to invert the binary oppositions and narrative functions of Wright's model, we might perhaps consider the way the film challenges the hierarchy implicit in the model. As Derrida points out,

> [A deconstructive] reading must always aim at a certain relationship, unperceived by the writer, between what he commands and what he does not command of the patterns of language that he uses. This relationship is . . . a signifying structure that critical [i.e. deconstructive] reading should *produce*. . . . [That is, a] production [which] attempts to make the not seen accessible to sight.[49]

## Jacques Lacan

Jacques Lacan rereads Freud using the theoretical methodology developed by structuralism. His account of the development of the subject has had an enormous influence on cultural studies, especially the study of film. Lacan takes Freud's developmental structure and rearticulates it through a critical reading of structuralism to produce a post-structuralist psychoanalysis. According to Lacan, we are born into a condition of 'lack', and subsequently spend the rest of our lives trying to overcome this condition. 'Lack' is experienced in different ways and as different things, but it is always a non-representable expression of the fundamental condition of 'lack'. As we move forward, we are driven by a desire to overcome the condition, and as we look back, we continue to believe that the union with the mother was a moment of plenitude before the fall into 'lack'. The result is an endless quest in search of an imagined moment of plenitude. Lacan figures this as a search for what he terms *l'objet petit a*: an endless quest for a non-existent object, signifying an imaginary moment in time. We console ourselves with a series of substitutes for a substitute.

According to Lacan, we make a journey through three determining stages of development. The first stage is the 'mirror phase', the second is the '*fort–da*' game, and the third is the 'Oedipus complex'. In the mythical moment of plenitude there is no clear distinction between subject and object. Our union with the mother is perfect and complete. This is followed by a period experienced as one of 'fragmentation': beyond the constant satisfactions of the womb, now dependent on the intermittent satisfactions of the breast. A sense of self to challenge the experience of fragmentation, and promise control over our own needs, emerges during what Lacan calls the 'mirror phase'. Looking in the mirror (real or imagined), we begin to construct a sense of self. The mirror phase is the moment (supposedly between the ages of 6 and 18 months) when we first recognize ourselves in a mirror. On the basis of this recognition or, more properly, *misrecognition* (not the self, but an image of the self), we begin to see ourselves as separate individuals; that is, we see ourselves as more complete, more unified than our physical development actually warrants. The 'mirror phase' heralds the moment of entry into an order of subjectivity Lacan calls the imaginary:

> The imaginary for Lacan is precisely this realm of *images* in which we make identifications, but in the very act of doing so are led to misperceive and misrecognize ourselves. As a child grows up, it will continue to make such imaginary identifications with objects,

and this is how the ego will be built up. For Lacan, the ego is just this narcissistic process whereby we bolster up a fictive sense of unitary selfhood by finding something in the world with which we can identify.[50]

With each new image we will attempt to return to a time before 'lack', to find ourselves in what is not ourselves; and each time we will fail.

The second stage of development is the '*fort–da*' game, originally named by Freud after watching his grandson throw a cotton reel away ('gone') and then pull it back again ('here') by means of an attached thread. Freud saw this as the child's way of coming to terms with its mother's absence – the reel symbolically representing the mother, over which the child is exerting mastery. Lacan rereads this as a representation of the child's introduction *into* language. Through language we enter what Lacan calls the symbolic. This is the order of culture. It is here that we acquire our human subjectivity. Language allows us to communicate with others, but it also intensifies our experience of 'lack'. Our demands can now be articulated through language, but they cannot make good our experience of 'lack' – they only intensify it. Our entry into language, and the symbolic, opens up a gap between our need for the original moment of plenitude and the promise and failure of language; it is in this gap that desire emerges. It is in and through language that the subject becomes a subject: subject in, subject of, and ultimately subject to, language. I can only be 'I' in and through language. But again there is a price to pay: Lacan distinguishes between the subject of the enunciation and the subject of the enounced.

When 'I' speak I am always different from the 'I' of whom I speak; always sliding into difference and defeat: 'when the subject appears somewhere as meaning, he is manifested elsewhere as "fading", as disappearance'.[51] Subjectivity is thus produced from the very processes of language, made and remade within its patterns and articulations, and not an essential pre-given as 'rational' accounts presuppose. The symbolic order is something which pre-exists us: it is already there waiting for us to take our places. It produces our very subjectivity and yet it is forever outside our sense of being, belonging to others in the same way as it belongs to us. I am 'I' when I speak to you and 'you' when you speak to me. It follows from this that our sense of being a unique individual is somewhat fragile. There can be no such thing as an essential self. It is nothing more than a fiction we live by. Not only does the language we speak produce our subjectivity, we are subjects of its structural processes. But more than this, Lacan insists that our unconscious is also constructed out of our contact with language. In this way, he argues, our sense of self and our sense of otherness are both composed from the language we speak and the cultural repertoire we encounter in our everyday existence. It is language which enables us to think ourselves as subjects: without language we would have no sense of self, and yet within language our sense of self is always slipping away – fragile and threatening to fragment.

The third stage of development is the 'Oedipus complex': the encounter with sexual difference. In a classic structuralist move, Lacan rewrites the 'Oedipus complex' in terms of language. The unconscious is itself structured like a language. What takes him beyond structuralism is his account of desire. The Oedipal movement from the imaginary to the symbolic leaves the child moving from one signifier to another. Desire itself is the process or pursuit of the fixed signified (the 'other', the 'real', the moment of plenitude, the mother's body), always forever becoming another signifier – the 'incessant sliding of the signified under the signifier'.[52] Desire is the impossibility of closing the gap between self and other – to make good that which we 'lack'. The 'lesson' of the 'Oedipus complex' is that

> The child must now resign itself to the fact that it can never have any *direct* access to reality, in particular to the prohibited body of the mother. It has been banished from this 'full', imaginary possession into the 'empty' world of language . . . the 'metaphorical' world of the mirror has yielded ground to the 'metonymic' world of language. . . . This potentially endless movement from one signifier to another is what Lacan means by desire. All desire springs from a lack, which it strives continually to fill. . . . To enter language is to be severed from what Lacan calls the 'real', that inaccessible realm which is always beyond the reach of signification, always outside the symbolic order. In particular, we are severed from the mother's body: after the Oedipus crisis, we will never again be able to attain this precious object, even though we will spend all our lives hunting for it. We have to make do instead with substitute objects . . . with which we try vainly to plug the gap at the very centre of our being. We move among substitutes for substitutes, metaphors for metaphors, never able

> to recover the pure (if fictive) self-identity and self-completion which we knew in the imaginary. . . . In Lacanian theory, it is an original lost object – the mother's body which drives forward the narrative of our lives, impelling us to pursue substitutes for this lost paradise in the endless metonymic movement of desire.[53]

The ideology of romance could be cited as an example of this endless search. What I mean by this is the way that romance as a discursive practice (see discussion of Foucault below) holds that 'love' is the ultimate solution to all our problems. Love makes us whole, it makes us full, it completes our being. Love in effect promises to return us to the blissful state of the moment of plenitude, warm against the body of the mother. We can see this played out in the masculine romance of *Paris, Texas*. The film can be read as a road movie of the unconscious, a figuration of Travis Henderson's impossible struggle to return to the moment of plenitude. We see three attempts at return: first he goes to Mexico in search of his mother's origins; then he goes to Paris (Texas) in search of the moment of his conception; finally, in an act of 'displacement', he returns Hunter to Jane (a son to his mother), in symbolic recognition that his own quest is doomed to failure.

## Discourse and power: Michel Foucault and Edward Said

Michel Foucault's 'genealogical' analysis is concerned with the relationship between power and knowledge and how this relationship operates within what he calls discursive formations, the conceptual frameworks that allow some modes of thought and deny others. Whereas structuralists focus on how the system of language, and systems analogous to language, 'determines' the nature of linguistic and cultural expression, post-structuralists such as Foucault are more concerned with how language is used and how language-use is always articulated with other social and cultural practices (his point also applies to other systems analogous to language). Language-use, and cultural practice generally, is seen as 'dialogical', in dialogue and potential conflict with other uses of language, other cultural texts and practices. In this sense discourse is inseparable from power. Discourse is the means by which institutions wield their power through a process of definition and exclusion. What he means by this is the way particular discourses or discursive formations define what it is possible to say on any given topic. A discursive formation consists of a body of unwritten rules which attempt to regulate what can be written, thought and acted upon in a particular field.

In *Discipline and Punish*, and *The History of Sexuality*, Foucault rejects notions of universal and timeless truth. He takes from Friedrich Nietzsche the view that knowledge works as a weapon of power. Foucault's aim is to discover 'how men govern (themselves and others) by the production of truth (. . . the establishment of domains in which the practice of true and false can be made at once ordered and pertinent)'.[54] He continually demonstrates how power operates through discourse and how discourses are always rooted in power: 'power produces knowledge . . . power and knowledge directly imply one another . . . there is no power relation without the correlative constitution of a field of knowledge, nor any knowledge that does not presuppose and constitute at the same time power relations'.[55] What concerns Foucault is the double question: 'how is power exercised and what are its effects?' This is posed against two more traditional questions: 'what is power and where does it come from?' For Foucault, power is not the property of, say, a ruling class; power is a strategic terrain, the site of an unequal *relationship* between the powerful and the powerless: 'where there is power, there is resistance'.[56] Moreover, power should not be thought of as a negative force, something which denies, represses, negates; power is productive,

> We must cease once and for all to describe the effects of power in negative terms: it 'excludes', it 'represses', it 'censors', it 'abstracts', it 'masks', it 'conceals'. In fact, power produces; it produces reality; it produces domains of objects and rituals of truth.[57]

Therefore when he considers the history of sexuality, he rejects what he calls 'the repressive hypothesis', which suggests an approach to sexuality in terms of censorship and prohibition. Instead he formulates a different set of questions:

> Why has sexuality been so widely discussed and what has been said about it? What were the effects of power generated by what was said? What are the links between these discourses, these effects of power, and the pleasures that were invested by them? What knowledge (*savoir*) was formed as a result of this linkage?[58]

Foucault tracks the discourse of sexuality through a series of discursive domains: medicine, demography, psychiatry, pedagogy, social work, criminology, government. Rather than silence, he encounters 'a political, economic and technical incitement to talk about sex'.[59] He argues that the different discourses on sexuality are not *about* sexuality, they actually *constitute* sexuality. This is not to say that sexuality does not exist as a non-discursive formation, but that our 'knowledge' of sexuality and the 'power–knowledge' relations of sexuality are discursive.

Edward Said shows how a Western discourse on the Orient – 'Orientalism' – has constructed a 'knowledge' of the East and a body of 'power–knowledge' relations articulated in the interests of the 'power' of the West. Said demonstrates Foucault's claim that the 'truth' of a discourse depends less on what is said and more on who is saying it and when and where it is said. According to Said, 'The Orient was a European invention.'[60] 'Orientalism' is the term he uses to describe the relationship between Europe and the Orient, in particular, the way 'the Orient has helped to define Europe (or the West) as its contrasting image, idea, personality, experience'.[61] He 'also tries to show that European culture gained in strength and identity by setting itself off against the Orient as a sort of surrogate and even underground self'.[62]

> Orientalism can be discussed and analyzed as the corporate institution for dealing with the Orient – dealing with it by making statements about it, authorizing views of it, describing it, by teaching it, settling it, ruling over it: in short, Orientalism as a Western style for dominating, restructuring, and having authority over the Orient.[63]

How does all this relate to the study of popular culture? It is not too difficult to see how the Tarzan stories, for example, and other imperial myths might be better understood using a Foucauldian approach. There are basically two imperial plot structures. First, stories that tell of white colonizers succumbing to the primeval power of the jungle and, as the racist myth puts it, 'going native'. Kurtz of both *Heart of Darkness* and *Apocalypse Now* is such a figure. Then there are stories of whites, who because of the supposed power of their racial heredity, impose themselves on the jungle and its inhabitants. 'Tarzan' (novels, films and *myth*) is the classic representation of this imperial fiction. From a Foucauldian perspective both narratives tell us a great deal more about the desires and anxieties of the culture of imperialism than they can ever tell us about the people and places of colonial conquest. What the approach does is to shift the focus of attention away from what and where the narratives are about to the 'function' that they serve to the producers and consumers of such myths. It prevents us from slipping into a form of naive realism; away from a focus on what the stories tell us about Africa or the Africans, to what such representations tell us about Europeans and Americans. In effect, it shifts our concern from 'how' the story is told to 'why'; and from those whom the story is about to those who tell and consume the story. For example, 'Tarzan' tells us nothing about the colonized, but a great deal about the colonizers.

Hollywood's Vietnam War is in many ways a classic example of a particular form of Orientalism. Rather than the silence of defeat, there has been a veritable 'incitement' to talk about Vietnam. America's most unpopular war has become its most popular when measured in discursive and commercial terms. Although America no longer has 'authority over' Vietnam, it continues to hold authority over Western accounts of America's war in Vietnam. Hollywood as a 'corporate institution' deals with Vietnam 'by making statements about it, authorizing views of it, describing it, by teaching it'. Hollywood has 'invented' Vietnam as a 'contrasting image' and a 'surrogate and . . . underground self' of America. In this way Hollywood – together with other discursive practices, songs, novels, TV serials, etc. – has succeeded in producing a very powerful discourse on Vietnam: telling America and the world – through a series of 'rituals of truth' – that what happened there, happened because Vietnam *is* like that. These different discourses are not *about* Vietnam, they increasingly *constitute* for many Americans the *experience* of Vietnam. This is not to argue that the war did not exist as a historical reality, but that for many Americans, 'knowledge' of the war, and the 'power– knowledge' relations which are constituted on the basis of this knowledge, are discursive. Even when Hollywood appears to be critical of American involvement in Vietnam, it is always critical within a discursive practice which ultimately works to contain such criticism, to redirect it into the procedures and protocols of Orientalism.

## Further reading

Simon During, *Foucault and Literature: Towards a genealogy of writing*, London: Routledge, 1992. Although the focus is on literature, this is nevertheless a very useful introduction to Foucault.

Terry Eagleton, *Literary Theory: An introduction*, Oxford: Basil Blackwell, 1983. Contains an excellent chapter on post-structuralism; especially good on Lacan.

Antony Easthope, *British Post-Structuralism*, London: Routledge, 1988. An ambitious attempt to map the field. Useful chapters on film theory, cultural studies, deconstruction and historical studies.

Terence Hawkes, *Structuralism and Semiotics*, London: Methuen, 1977. A useful introduction to the subject.

Christopher Norris, *Derrida*, London: Fontana, 1987. A clear and interesting introduction to Derrida.

Madan Sarup, *An Introductory Guide to Post-Structuralism and Postmodernism* (second edition), Hemel Hempstead: Harvester Wheatsheaf, 1993. An excellent introduction to post-structuralism.

Alan Sheridan, *Michel Foucault: The will to truth*, London: Tavistock, 1980. Still the most readable introduction to Foucault.

Kaja Silverman, *The Subject of Semiotics*, Oxford: Oxford University Press, 1983. An interesting and accessible account of structuralism, semiotics, psychoanalysis, feminism and post-structuralism. Especially useful on Barthes and Lacan.

John Sturrock (ed.), *Structuralism and Since: From Lévi-Strauss to Derrida*, Oxford: Oxford University Press, 1979. Contains good introductory essays on Lévi-Strauss, Barthes, Foucault, Lacan and Derrida.

Tony Twaites, Lloyd Davis and Mules Warwick, *Tools for Cultural Studies: An introduction*, Melbourne: Macmillan, 1994. Presents an informed account of the place of semiotics in the field of cultural studies.

Chris Weedon, *Feminist Practice and Poststructuralist Theory*, Oxford: Basil Blackwell, 1987. An interesting introduction to post-structuralism from a feminist perspective. Helpful chapters on Lacan and Foucault.

# 5
# MARXISM

## Classical Marxism

Marxism is a difficult and contentious body of work. But it is also *more* than this: it is a body of revolutionary theory with the purpose of changing the world. As Marx famously said: 'The philosophers have only *interpreted* the world, in various ways; the point is to change it'.[1] This makes Marxist analysis political in a quite specific way. But this is not to suggest that other methods and approaches are apolitical; on the contrary, Marxism insists that all are ultimately political. As the American Marxist cultural critic Fredric Jameson puts it, 'the political perspective [is] the absolute horizon of all reading and all interpretation'.[2]

The Marxist approach to culture insists that cultural texts and practices must be analyzed in relation to their historical conditions of production (and in some versions, the changing conditions of their consumption and reception). What makes the Marxist methodology different from other 'historical' approaches to culture is the Marxist conception of history. The fullest statement of the Marxist approach to history is contained in the Preface and Introduction to *A Contribution to the Critique of Political Economy*. Here Marx outlines the now famous 'base/superstructure' account of social and historical development. In Chapter 1, I discussed this formulation briefly, in relation to different concepts of ideology. I will now explain the formulation in more detail and demonstrate how it might be used to understand the 'determinations' which influence the production and consumption of popular culture.

Marx argues that each significant period in history is constructed around a particular 'mode of production'; that is, the way in which a society is organized (i.e. slave, feudal, capitalist) to produce the necessaries of life: food, shelter, etc. Each mode of production produces different ways of obtaining the necessaries of life, but it also produces different relationships between 'workers' end 'non-workers', and different social institutions (including cultural ones). At the heart of this analysis is the claim that how a society produces its means of existence (its particular mode of production) ultimately determines the political, social and cultural shape of that society and its possible future development. This claim is based on a revolutionary understanding of the relationship between base and superstructure.

It is on this relationship – between 'base' and 'superstructure' – that the Marxist account of culture rests. The 'base' consists of a combination of the 'forces of production' and the 'relations of production'. The forces of production refer to the raw materials, the tools, the technology, the workers and their skills, etc. The relations of production refer to the class relations of those engaged in production. That is, each mode of production, besides being different, say, in terms of its basis in agrarian or industrial production, is also different in that it produces particular relations of production: the slave mode produces master/slave relations; the feudal mode produces lord/peasant relations; the capitalist mode produces bourgeois/proletariat relations. It is in this sense that one's class position is determined by one's relationship to the mode of production. The 'superstructure' consists of the institutions (political, legal, educational, cultural, etc.), and 'definite forms of social consciousness' generated by these (political, religious, ethical, philosophical, aesthetic, cultural, etc.), which arise on the basis of the mode of production. The relationship between base and superstructure is twofold. On the one hand, the superstructure both expresses and legitimizes the base. On the other, the base is said to 'condition' or 'determine' the content and form of the superstructure. This relationship can be understood in a range of different ways. It can be seen as a mechanical relationship ('economic determinism') of cause and effect: what happens in the superstructure is a passive reflection of what is happening in the base. This often results in a vulgar Marxist 'reflection theory' of culture, in which the politics of a text or practice are read off from or reduced to the economic conditions of its production. The relationship can also be seen as the setting of limits, the providing of a specific framework in which some developments are probable and others unlikely.

After Marx's death, Frederick Engels, friend and collaborator, found himself having to explain, through a series of letters, many of the subtleties of Marxism to younger Marxists who, in their revolutionary enthusiasm, threatened to reduce it to a form of economic determinism. Here is part of his famous letter to Joseph Bloch:

> According to the materialist conception of history, the *ultimately* determining element in history is the production and reproduction of real life. Neither Marx nor I have ever asserted more than this. Therefore if somebody twists this into saying that the economic factor is the *only* determining one, he is transforming that proposition into a meaningless, abstract, absurd phrase. The economic situation is the basis, but the various components of the superstructure . . . also exercise their influence upon the course of the historical struggles and in many cases determine their *form*. . . . We make our own history, but, first of all, under very definite assumptions and conditions. Among these the economic ones are ultimately decisive. But the political ones, etc., and indeed even the traditions which haunt human minds also play a part, although not the decisive one.[3]

What Engels claims is that the economic base produces the superstructural terrain (this terrain and not that), but that the form of activity that takes place there is determined not just by the fact that the terrain was produced and is reproduced by the economic base (although this clearly sets limits and influences outcomes), but by the interaction of the institutions and the participants as they occupy the terrain. Therefore, culture can never be the primary force in history; but it can be an active agent in historical change or the servant of social stability.[4]

In *The German Ideology*, Marx and Engels claim that, 'The ideas of the ruling class are in every epoch the ruling ideas, i.e., the class which is the ruling *material* force in society, is at the same time its ruling *intellectual* force.'[5] What they mean by this is that the dominant class, on the basis of its ownership of and control over the means of material production, is virtually guaranteed to have control over the means of intellectual production. However, this does not mean that the ideas of the ruling class are simply imposed on subordinate classes. A ruling class is 'compelled . . . to represent its interest as the common interest of all the members of society . . . to give its ideas the form of universality, and represent them as the only rational, universally valid ones'.[6] Given the uncertainty of this project, ideological struggle is almost inevitable. During periods of social transformation it becomes chronic: as Marx points out, it is in the 'ideological forms' of the superstructure that men and women 'become conscious of . . . conflict and fight it out'.[7]

In Marxist terms, popular culture is one of the ideological forms of the superstructure. So, what are the implications of the materialist conception of history for the analysis of popular culture? First of all, to understand and explain a text or practice it must first be situated in its historical moment of production; analyzed in terms of the historical conditions which produced it. There are dangers here: historical conditions are ultimately economic, therefore cultural analysis can quickly collapse into economic analysis (the cultural becomes a passive reflection of the economic). It is crucial, as Engels and Marx warn and as Thompson demonstrates (see Chapter 3), to keep in play a subtle dialectic between agency and structure. For example, a full analysis of nineteenth century stage melodrama would have to weave together into focus both the economic changes which produced its audience and the theatrical tradition which produced its form. The same also holds true for a full analysis of music hall. In neither instance would performance be reduced to changes in the economic structure of society. But what would be insisted on is that a full analysis of melodrama or music hall would not be possible without reference to the changes in theatre attendance brought about by changes in the economic structure of society, which in turn produced the performance of a play like *My Poll and My Partner Joe*, and the emergence of a performer like Marie Lloyd. Thus a Marxist analysis would argue that ultimately, however indirectly, there is nevertheless a real and fundamental relationship between the emergence of melodrama and music hall and changes that took place in the capitalist mode of production.

## The Frankfurt School

The Frankfurt School is the name given to a group of German intellectuals associated with the Institute for Social Research at the University of Frankfurt. The Institute was established in 1923. Following the coming to power of Hitler in 1933, it moved to New York, attaching itself to the University of Columbia. In 1949 it moved back to Germany. 'Critical theory' is the name given to the Institute's critical mix of Marxism and psychoanalysis. The Institute's work on popular culture is mostly associated with the writings of Theodor Adorno, Walter Benjamin, Max Horkheimer, Leo Lowenthal and Herbert Marcuse.

In 1947 Max Horkheimer and Theodor Adorno coined the term 'culture industry' to designate the products and processes of mass culture. The products of the culture industry, they claim, are marked by two features: cultural homogeneity, 'film, radio and magazines make up a system which is uniform as a whole and in every part . . . all mass culture is identical';[8] and predictability:

> As soon as the film begins, it is quite clear how it will end, and who will be rewarded, punished, or forgotten. In light music [popular music], once the trained ear has heard the first notes of the hit song, it can guess what is coming and feel flattered when it does come.[9]

Whereas Arnold and Leavisism had worried that popular culture represented a threat to cultural and social authority, the Frankfurt School argue that it actually produces the opposite effect; it maintains social authority. Where Arnold and Leavisism saw 'anarchy', the Frankfurt School sees only 'conformity'. Here is Adorno reading an American situation comedy about a young schoolteacher who is both underpaid [some things don't change], and continually fined by her school principal. As a result, she is without money and therefore without food. The humour of the storyline consists in her various attempts to secure a meal at the expense of friends and acquaintances. In his reading of this situation comedy, Adorno is guided by the assumption that while it is always difficult, if not impossible, to establish the unmistakable 'message' of a work of 'authentic' culture, the 'hidden message' of a piece of mass culture is not at all difficult to discern. According to Adorno, 'the script implies':

> If you are humorous, good natured, quick witted, and charming as she is, do not worry about being paid a starvation wage. . . . In other words, the script is a shrewd method of promoting adjustment to humiliating conditions by presenting them as objectively comical and by giving a picture of a person who experiences even her own inadequate position as an object of fun apparently free of any resentment.[10]

This is one way of reading this TV comedy. But it is by no means the only way. Brecht, Benjamin's close friend (considered to be 'crude' by Adorno), might have offered another way of reading, one that implies a less passive audience. Discussing his own play, *Mother Courage*, Brecht suggests, 'Even if Courage learns nothing else at least the audience can, in my view, learn something by observing her.'[11] The same point can be made against Adorno with reference to the schoolteacher's behaviour.

Leo Lowenthal contends that the culture industry, by producing a culture marked by 'standardization, stereotype, conservatism, mendacity, manipulated consumer goods',[12] has worked to depoliticize the working class – limited its horizon to political and economic goals that could be realized within the oppressive and exploitative framework of capitalist society. He maintains that, 'Whenever revolutionary tendencies show a timid head, they are mitigated and cut short by a false fulfilment of wish-dreams, like wealth, adventure, passionate love, power and sensationalism in general'.[13] In short, the culture industry discourages the 'masses' from thinking beyond the confines of the present. As Marcuse claims in *One Dimensional Man*:

> the irresistible output of the entertainment and information industry carry with them prescribed attitudes and habits, certain intellectual and emotional reactions which bind the consumers more or less pleasantly to the producers and, through the latter, to the whole. The products indoctrinate and manipulate; they promote a false consciousness which is immune against its falsehood . . . it becomes a way of life. It is a good way of life much better than before – and as a good way of life, it militates against qualitative change. Thus emerges a pattern of *one-dimensional thought and behaviour* in which ideas, aspirations, and objectives that, by their content, transcend the established universe of discourse and action are either repelled or reduced to terms of this universe.[14]

In other words, by supplying the means to certain needs, capitalism is able to p·event the formation of more fundamental desires. The culture industry thus stunts the political imagination. As with Arnold and Leavisism, art or high culture is different. It embodies ideals denied by capitalism. As such it offers an implicit critique of capitalist society; an alternative, Utopian vision. 'Authentic' culture, according to Horkheimer, has taken over the Utopian function of religion: to keep alive the human desire for a better world beyond the confines of the present; it carries the key to unlock the prison-house of mass culture.[15] This is not to say that it functions didactically. On the contrary, it persuades through its 'form' rather than commands through its 'content'. But increasingly the radical potential of 'authentic' culture or 'autonomous' culture, called by Marcuse 'affirmative culture' (the culture or cultural space which emerged with the separation of culture and civilization discussed in Chapter 2), is threatened by the processes of the culture industry. Premodern culture worked within and on society, effecting and articulating change; the position of affirmative culture is quite different:

> By affirmative culture is meant that culture of the bourgeois epoch which led in the course of its own development to the segregation from civilization of the mental and spiritual world as an independent realm of value that is also considered superior to civilization. Its decisive characteristic is the assertion of a universally obligatory, eternally better and more valuable world that must be unconditionally affirmed: a world essentially different from the factual world of the daily struggle for existence, yet realizable by every individual for himself 'from within', without any transformation of the state of fact.[16]

Affirmative culture embodies the promise of tomorrow and thus a critique of today; but it is also a realm we enter in order to be refreshed and renewed to continue with the affairs of today; 'a realm of apparent unity and apparent freedom was constructed within culture in which the antagonistic relations of existence were supposed to be stabilised and pacified. Culture affirms and conceals the new conditions of social life'.[17] The promises made with the emergence of capitalism out of feudalism, of a society based on equality, justice and progress, were increasingly relegated from the world of the everyday to the realm of culture. Nevertheless, the high culture of the early bourgeois period 'nourished the belief that all previous history had been only the dark and tragic prehistory of a coming existence'.[18] 'Authentic' culture maintains a 'subversive negativity' in its creation and occupation of a 'second dimension' of social reality. The culture industry flattens out what remains of

> the antagonism between culture and social reality through the obliteration of the oppositional, alien, and transcendent elements in the higher culture by virtue of which it constituted

*another dimension* of reality. This liquidation of *two-dimensional* culture takes place not through the denial and rejection of the 'cultural values', but through their wholesale incorporation into the established order, through their reproduction and display on a massive scale.[19]

The better future promised by 'authentic' culture is no longer in contradiction with the unhappy present – a spur to make the better future; culture now confirms that this is the better future – here and now – the only better future. It offers 'fulfilment' instead of the promotion of 'desire'. There is some hope that the 'most advanced images and positions' of 'authentic' culture may resist 'absorption' and 'continue to haunt the consciousness with the possibility of their rebirth' in a better future.[20] Like Marx on religion, Marcuse argues that culture makes an unbearable condition bearable by dulling the pain of existence. To make a society without need of such a culture is to transform society into one where such a culture is unnecessary:

> One of the decisive social tasks of affirmative culture is based on this contradiction between the insufferable mutability of a bad existence and the need for happiness in order to make such an existence bearable. Within this existence the resolution can be only illusory. And the possibility of a solution rests precisely on the character of artistic beauty as *illusion*. . . . But this illusion has a real effect, producing satisfaction . . . [in] the service of the status quo.[21]

'Authentic' culture displays 'the defeated possibilities, the hopes unfulfilled, and the promises betrayed'.[22] Marcuse believes that one day those on the margins of society, 'the outcasts and outsiders'[23] out of reach of the full grasp of the culture industry, will undo the defeats, fulfil the hopes, and make capitalism keep all its promises in a world beyond capitalism. Or, as Horkheimer claims,

> One day we may learn that in the depths of their hearts, the masses . . . secretly knew the truth and disbelieved the lie, like catatonic patients who make known only at the end of their trance that nothing had escaped them. Therefore it may not be entirely senseless to continue speaking a language that is not easily understood.[24]

But, as Adorno points out, mass culture is a difficult system to challenge:

Today anyone who is incapable of talking in the prescribed fashion, that is of effortlessly reproducing the formulas, conventions and judgments of mass culture as if they were his own, is threatened in his very existence, suspected of being an idiot or an intellectual.[25]

The culture industry, in its search for profits and cultural homogeneity, deprives 'authentic' culture of its critical function, its mode of negation – '[its] Great Refusal'.[26] Commercialization devalues 'authentic' culture, making it too accessible by turning it into yet another cultural commodity:

The neo-conservative critics of leftist critics of mass culture ridicule the protest against Bach as background music in the kitchen, against Plato and Hegel, Shelley and Baudelaire, Marx and Freud in the drugstore. Instead, they insist on recognition of the fact that the classics have left the mausoleum and come to life again, 'that people are just so much more educated'. True, but coming to life as classics, they come to life as other than themselves; they are deprived of their antagonistic force, of the estrangement which was the very dimension of their truth. The intent and function of these works have thus fundamentally changed. If they once stood in contradiction to the status quo, this contradiction is now flattened out.[27]

It is not difficult to think of examples of this process (whether or not we read them in quite the same way, leftist or neo-conservative). In the 1960s, a bed-sit without a poster of Che Guevara was hardly furnished at all. Was the poster a sign of a commitment to revolutionary politics or a commitment to the latest fashion (or was it complicated mixture of both)? Bennett provides a telling example of an advertisement inserted in *The Times* in 1974:

an advertisement which consisted of a full page colour reproduction of Matisse's *Le Pont*, below which there appeared the legend: 'Business is our life, but life isn't all business.' Profoundly contradictory, what was ostensibly opposed to economic life was made to become a part of it, what was separate became assimilated since any critical dimension which might have pertained to Matisse's painting was eclipsed by its new and unsolicited function as an advertisement for the wares of finance capital.[28]

We might also think of the way classical music is used to sell anything from bread to expensive motorcars. It is difficult, for example, to hear the second movement from Dvorak's *New World Symphony*, without conjuring up an image of Hovis bread.

It is not that Marcuse or the other members of the Frankfurt School object to the 'democratization' of culture, only that they believe that the culture industry's 'assimilation is historically premature; it establishes cultural equality while preserving domination'.[29] In short, the democratization of culture results in the blocking of the demand for full democracy; it stabilizes the prevailing social order.

According to the Frankfurt School, work and leisure under capitalism form a compelling relationship: the effects of the culture industry are guaranteed by the nature of work; the work process secures the effects of the culture industry. The function of the culture industry is therefore, ultimately, to organize leisure time in the same way as industrialization has organized work time. Work under capitalism stunts the senses; the culture industry continues the process: 'the escape from everyday drudgery which the whole culture industry promises . . . [is a] paradise . . . [of] the same old drudgery. . . escape . . . [is] predesigned to lead back to the starting point. Pleasure promotes the resignation which it ought to help to forget.'[30] In short, work leads to mass culture; mass culture leads back to work. Similarly, art or 'authentic' culture circulated by the culture industry operates in the same way. Only 'authentic' culture operating outside the confines of the culture industry could break the cycle.

To make these general points more concrete, I will now examine a specific example of the Frankfurt School's approach to popular culture – Adorno's essay, 'On popular music'. In the essay he makes three specific claims about popular music. First, he claims that it is 'standardized'. 'Standardization' as Adorno points out, 'extends from the most general features to the most specific ones'.[31] Once a musical and/or lyrical pattern has proved successful it is exploited to commercial exhaustion, culminating in 'the crystallization of standards'.[32] Moreover, details from one popular song can be interchanged with details from another. Unlike the organic structure of 'serious music', where each detail expresses the whole, popular music is mechanical in the sense that a given detail can be shifted from one song to another without any real effect on the structure as a whole. In order to conceal standardization, the music industry engages in what Adorno calls 'psuedo-individualization':

Standardization of song hits keeps the customers in line by doing their listening for them, as it were. Psuedo-individualization, for its part, keeps them in line by making them forget that what they listen to is already listened to for them, or 'pre-digested'.[33]

Adorno's second claim is that popular music promotes passive listening. As already noted, work under capitalism is dull and therefore promotes the search for escape, but, because it is also dulling, it leaves little energy for real escape – the demands of 'authentic' culture. Instead refuge is sought in forms such as popular music – the consumption of which is always passive, and endlessly repetitive, confirming *the world as it is*. Whereas 'serious' music (Beethoven, for example) plays to the pleasure of the imagination, offering an engagement with *the world as it could be*, popular music is the 'nonproductive correlate' to life in the office or on the factory floor. The 'strain and boredom' of work lead men and women to the 'avoidance of effort' in their leisure time. Adorno makes it all sound like the hopeless ritual of a heroin addict (as taken from the detective genre he detested so much). Denied 'novelty' in their work time, and too exhausted for it in their leisure time, 'they crave a stimulant' – popular music satisfies the craving.

Its stimulations are met with the inability to vest effort in the ever-identical. This means boredom again. It is a circle which makes escape impossible. The impossibility of escape causes the widespread attitude of inattention toward popular music. The moment of recognition is that of effortless sensation. The sudden attention attached to this moment burns itself out *instanter* and relegates the listener to a realm of inattention and distraction.[34]

Popular music operates in a kind of blurred dialectic: to consume it demands inattention and distraction, while its consumption produces in the consumer inattention and distraction.

Adorno's third point is the claim that popular music operates as 'social cement'.[35] Its 'socio-psychological function' is to achieve in the consumers of popular music 'psychical adjustment' to the needs of the prevailing structure of power.[36] This 'adjustment' manifests itself in 'two major socio-psychological types of mass behaviour . . . the "rhythmically" obedient type and the "emotional" type'.[37] The first type dances in distraction to the rhythm of his or her own exploitation and oppression. The second type wallows in sentimental misery oblivious to the real conditions of existence.

There are a number of points to be made about Adorno's analysis.[38] First of all we must acknowledge that he is writing in 1941. Popular music has changed a great deal since then. However, having said that, Adorno never thought to change his analysis following the changes that occurred in popular music before his death in 1969. Is popular music as monolithic as he would have us believe? For example, does pseudo-individualization really explain the advent of rock'n'roll in 1956, the emergence of the Beatles in 1962, the music of the counterculture in 1965? Does it explain punk rock in 1976, Rock Against Racism in the late 1970s, acid house in 1986, indie pop in the 1980s, rave in the 1990s? Moreover, is the consumption of popular music as passive as Adorno claims? Frith provides sales figures which suggest not: 'despite the difficulties of the calculations . . . most business commentators agree that about 10 per cent of all records released (a little less for singles, a little more for LPs) make money'.[39] In addition to this, about another 10 per cent cover their costs.[40] This means that about 80 per cent of records actually lose money. Moreover, Paul Hirsch has calculated that at least 60 per cent of singles released are never played by anyone.[41] This does not suggest the workings of an all-powerful industry, easily able to manipulate its consumers. It sounds more like an industry trying desperately to sell records to a critical and discriminating public. Such figures certainly imply that consumption is rather more active than Adorno's argument suggests. Subcultural use of music is clearly at the cutting edge of such active discrimination, but by no means the only example. Finally, does popular music really function as social cement? Subcultures or music taste cultures, for instance, would appear to consume popular music in a way not too dissimilar to Adorno's ideal mode of serious music consumption.[42]

Walter Benjamin's essay 'The work of art in the age of mechanical reproduction' is much more optimistic about the possibility of a revolutionary transformation of capitalism. He claims that capitalism will 'ultimately . . . create conditions which would make it possible to abolish capitalism itself'.[43] Benjamin believes that changes in the technological reproduction of culture are changing the function of culture in society: 'technical reproduction can put the copy of the original into situations which would be out of reach for the original itself'.[44] Reproduction thus challenges what Benjamin call the 'aura' of cultural texts.

One might generalise by saying: the technique of reproduction detaches the reproduced object from the domain of tradition. By making many reproductions it substitutes a plurality of copies for a unique existence. And in permitting the reproduction to meet the beholder or listener in his own particular situation, it reactivates the object reproduced. These two processes lead to a tremendous shattering of tradition which is the obverse of the contemporary crisis [the rise of fascism] and the renewal of mankind. Both processes are intimately connected with the contemporary mass movements. Their most powerful agent is film. Its social significance, particularly in its most positive form, is inconceivable without its destructive, cathartic aspect, that is, the liquidation of the traditional value of the cultural heritage.[45]

The 'aura' of a cultural text or practice is its sense of 'authenticity', 'authority', 'autonomy' and 'distance'. The decay of the aura detaches the cultural text or practice from the authority and rituals of tradition. It opens them to a plurality of reinterpretation; freeing them to be used in other contexts, for other purposes. No longer embedded in tradition, significance is now open to dispute; meaning becomes a question of consumption, an active (political), rather than a passive (for Adorno: psychological) event. Technological reproduction changes production: 'To an ever greater degree the work of art reproduced becomes the work of art designed for reproducibility.'[46] Consumption is also changed: from its location in religious ritual to its location in the rituals of aesthetics, consumption is now based on the practice of politics. Culture may have become mass culture, but consumption has not become mass consumption:

Mechanical reproduction of art changes the reaction of the masses toward art. The reactionary attitude toward a Picasso painting changes into the progressive reaction toward a Chaplin movie. The progressive reaction is characterized by the direct, intimate fusion of visual and emotional enjoyment with the orientation of the expert.[47]

Questions of meaning and consumption shift from passive contemplation to active political struggle. Benjamin's celebration of the positive potential of 'mechanical reproduction', his view that it begins the process of a move from an 'auratic' culture to a 'democratic' culture in which meaning is no longer seen as unique, but open to question, open to use and mobilization, has had a profound (if often unacknowledged) influence on cultural theory and popular culture. Susan Willis describes Benjamin's essay thus: 'This may well be the single most important essay in the development of Marxist popular culture criticism'.[48] Whereas Adorno locates meaning in the mode of production (how a cultural text is produced determines its consumption and significance), Benjamin suggests that meaning is produced at the moment of consumption; significance is determined by the process of consumption, regardless of the mode of production. As Frith points out, the 'debate'[49] between Adorno and Benjamin – between a sociopsychological account of consumption combined with an insistence on the determining power of production, against the argument that consumption is a matter of politics – continues to be argued in contemporary accounts of popular music: 'Out of Adorno have come analyses of the economics of entertainment . . . [and the] ideological effects of commercial music making. . . . From Benjamin have come subcultural theories, descriptions of the struggle . . . to make their own meanings in their acts of consumption.'[50]

Despite its Marxist sophistication, the approach of the Frankfurt School to popular culture (with the exception of Benjamin) would in some respects fit easily into the 'culture and civilization' tradition discussed in Chapter 2. Like the perspective developed by Arnold, Leavisism and the American mass culture theorists, the Frankfurt School perspective on popular culture is essentially a discourse from above (a discourse of 'us' and 'them') on the culture of other people. It is true that the Frankfurt School is very critical of conservative cultural critics who bemoaned the passing of, or threat to, a 'pure' autonomous culture for its own sake. Adorno, as J. M. Bernstein points out, 'regards the conservative defence of high culture as reflecting an unreflective hypostatization of culture that protects the economic status quo'.[51] Nevertheless, it remains the case that there are certain similarities between the focus of the 'culture and civilization' tradition and that of the Frankfurt School. They condemn the same things, but for different reasons. The 'culture and civilization' tradition attacks mass culture because it threatens cultural standards and social authority; the Frankfurt School attacks mass culture because it threatens cultural standards and depoliticizes the working class, and thus maintains the iron grip of social authority.

**114**

## Althusserianism

The ideas of Louis Althusser had an enormous influence on cultural theory in the 1970s. This can be quickly established by an exploration of some of the key journals of the period: *Working Papers in Cultural Studies, Screen, New Left Review.* all carry articles on Althusserianism, articles by Althusserians, and articles against Althusserianism. As Hall suggests, 'Althusser's interventions and their consequent development are enormously formative for the field of cultural studies.'[52] Althusser's most significant contributions to the field are his different attempts to theorize the concept of ideology. I will therefore restrict discussion to this aspect of his work.

Althusser rejects both the mechanistic interpretation of the base/superstructure formulation and the Hegelian view of the social totality, insisting instead on the concept of the social formation (a particular theorization of 'society'). A social formation consists of three practices: the economic, the political and the ideological. The relationship between the base and the superstructure is not one of expression, i.e. the superstructure being an expression or passive reflection of the base, but rather the superstructure is seen as necessary to the existence of the base. The model allows for the relative autonomy of the superstructure. Determination remains, but it is determination in the last instance. This operates through what he calls the 'structure in dominance'; that is, although the economic is always determinant, this does not mean that in a particular historical conjuncture it will necessarily be dominant. Under feudalism, for example, the political was the dominant level. Nevertheless, the practice which is dominant in a particular social formation will depend on the specific form of economic production. What he means by this is that the economic contradictions of capitalism never take a pure form: 'the lonely hour of the last instance never comes'.[53] Determination remains but as 'overdetermination': the structured articulation of a number of contradictions and determinations. The economic is determinant in the last instance, not because the other instances are its epiphenomena, but because it determines which practice is dominant. In volume one of *Capital,* Marx makes a similar point in response to criticisms claiming definite limits to the Marxist analysis of social formations:

[Marxism] is all very true for our own time, in which material interests are preponderant, but not for the Middle Ages, dominated by Catholicism, nor for Athens and Rome, dominated by politics. . . . One thing is clear: the Middle Ages could not live on Catholicism, nor could the ancient world on politics. On the contrary, it is the manner in which they gained their livelihood which explains why in one case politics, in the other case Catholicism, played the chief part. . . . And then there is Don Quixote, who long ago paid the penalty for wrongly imagining that knight errantry was compatible with all economic forms of society.[54]

Althusser's theorizations of ideology have had a major influence on cultural studies. In all he produced three definitions, two of which have proved particularly fruitful for the student of popular culture. The first definition, which overlaps in some ways with the second, is the claim that it is through ideology that men and women live their relations to the real conditions of existence. Althusser's notion of determination in the last instance means that other practices in the social formation are relatively autonomous with a certain specific effectivity. Ideology 'a system (with its own logic and rigour) of representations (images, myths, ideas or concepts)'[55] in this formulation is never simply an expression of the economic base, but a practice: 'By practice in general I shall mean any process of transformation of a determinate given raw material into a determinate product, a transformation effected by a determinate human labour, using determinate means (of "production").'[56] He argues that as the economic, the historically specific mode of production, transforms certain raw materials into products by determinate means of production, involving determinate relations of production, so political practice, in the same way, transforms social relations, and, in the same way, ideological practice is the transformation of an individual's lived relations to the social formation. In this definition, ideology exists to dispel contradictions in lived experience. It accomplishes this by offering false, but seemingly true, resolutions to real problems. This is not a 'conscious' process; ideology 'is profoundly unconscious'[57] in its mode of operation:

In ideology men . . . express, not the relation between them and their conditions of existence, but the way they live the relation between them and their conditions of existence: this presupposes both a real relation and an 'imaginary', 'lived' relation. Ideology . . . is the expression of the relation between men and their 'world', that is, the (overdetermined) unity of the real relation and the imaginary relation between them and their real conditions of existence.[58]

The relationship is both real and imaginary in the sense that ideology is the way we live our relationship to the real conditions of existence at the level of representations (myths, concepts, ideas, images, discourses): there are real conditions and there are the ways we represent these conditions to ourselves and to others. This applies to both dominant and subordinate classes; ideologies do not just convince oppressed groups that all is well with the world, they also convince ruling groups that exploitation and oppression are really something quite different, acts of universal necessity. Only a 'scientific' discourse (Althusser's Marxism) can see through ideology to the real conditions of existence.

Because ideology is for Althusser a closed system, it can only ever set itself such problems as it can answer; that is, to remain within its boundaries (a mythic realm without contradictions) it must stay silent on questions that threaten to take it beyond these boundaries. This formulation leads Althusser to the concept of the 'problematic'. He first uses the concept to explain the 'epistemological break' which he claims occurs in Marx's work in 1845. Marx's problematic, 'the objective internal reference system . . . the system of questions commanding the answers given',[59] determines not only the questions and answers he is able to bring into play, but also the absence of problems and concepts in his work. A problematic is the theoretical (and ideological) structure which both frames and produces the repertoire of crisscrossing and competing discourses out of which a text or practice is materially organized. The problematic of a text relates to its moment of historical existence as much by what it excludes as by what it includes. In this way, it encourages a text to answer questions posed by itself, but at the same time, it generates the production of 'deformed' answers to the questions it attempts to exclude. Thus a problematic is structured as much by what is absent (what is not said/what is not done) as by what is present (what is said/what is done). The task of an Althusserian critical practice is to deconstruct the problematic: to perform what Althusser (borrowing from Freud) calls a 'symptomatic reading'.

In *Reading Capital*, Althusser characterizes Marx's method of reading the work of Adam Smith as 'symptomatic' in that it divulges the undivulged event in the text it reads, and in the same movement relates it to a *different text*, present as a necessary absence in the first. Like his first reading, Marx's second reading presupposes the existence of *two texts*, and the measurement of the first against the second. But what distinguishes this new reading from the old is the fact that in the new one the second text is articulated with the lapses in the first text.[60]

By a symptomatic reading of Smith, Marx is able to measure 'the problematic initially visible in his writings against the invisible problematic contained in the paradox of *an answer which does not correspond to any question posed'*.[61] Therefore to read a text symptomatically is to perform a double reading: reading first the manifest text, and then, through the lapses, distortions, silences and absences (the 'symptoms' of a problem struggling to be posed) in the manifest text, to produce and read the latent text. For example, a symptomatic reading of the film *Taxi Driver* would reveal a problematic in which answers are posed to questions it can hardly name: 'How does the Veteran return home to America after the imperialist horrors of Vietnam?' At the heart of the film's problematic are questions relating to real historical problems, albeit deformed and transformed into a fantasy quest and a bloody resolution. A symptomatic reading of *Taxi Driver*, reading the 'symptoms' for evidence of an underlying *dis-ease*, would construct from the film's contradictions, its evasions, its silences, its inexplicable violence, its fairy-tale ending, the central and structuring absence – *Vietnam.*

Pierre Macherey's *A Theory of Literary Production* is undoubtedly the most sustained attempt to apply the technique of the Althusserian symptomatic reading to cultural texts. Although, as the book's title implies, Macherey's main focus is on literary production, the approach developed in the book is of great interest to the student of popular culture. For example, he discusses at some length the work of the French science fiction writer Jules Verne. He demonstrates how Verne's work *stages* the contradictions of late-nineteenth century French imperialism. To explain this further we need to outline Macherey's elaboration of Althusser's method of symptomatic reading. Macherey rejects what he calls 'the interpretative fallacy': the view that a text has a single meaning which it is the task of criticism to uncover. For him the text is not a puzzle which conceals a meaning; it is a construction with a multiplicity of meanings. To 'explain' a text is to recognize this. To do so it is necessary to break with the idea that a text is an harmonious unity; spiralling forth from a moment of creation, a moment of supreme intentionality; at the text's core, the heart of meaning. Against this, he claims that the literary text is 'decentred'; it is incomplete in itself. To say this does not mean that something needs to be added in order to make it whole. His point is that all literary texts are 'decentred' (not centred on an authorial intention) in the specific sense that they consist of a confrontation between several discourses: explicit, implicit, silent and absent. The task of critical practice is not therefore the attempt to measure and evaluate a text's coherence, its harmonious totality, its aesthetic unity, but instead to explain the disparities in the text which point to a conflict of meanings.

> This conflict is not the sign of an imperfection; it reveals the inscription of an otherness in the work, through which it maintains a relationship with that which it is not, that which happens at its margins. To explain the work is to show that, contrary to appearances, it is not independent, but bears in its material substance the imprint of a determinate absence which is also the principle of its identity. The book is furrowed by the allusive presence of those other books against which it is elaborated; it circles about the absence of that which it cannot say, haunted by the absence of certain repressed words which make their return. The book is not the extension of a meaning; it is generated from the incompatibility of several meanings, the strongest bond by which it is attached to reality, in a tense and ever renewed confrontation.[62]

It is this conflict of several meanings which structures a text: it displays this conflict but cannot speak it. Traditionally, criticism has seen its role as making explicit what is implicit in the text; to make audible that which is merely a whisper (i.e. a single meaning). For Macherey, it is not a question of making what is there speak with more clarity so as to be finally sure of the text's meaning. Because a text's meanings are 'both interior and absent',[63] simply to repeat the text's self-knowledge is to fail to explain the text properly. The task of a fully competent critical practice is not to make a whisper audible, nor to complete what the text leaves unsaid, but to produce a new knowledge of the text: one that explains the ideological necessity of its silences, its absences, its structuring incompleteness – the *staging* of that which it cannot speak:

The act of knowing is not like listening to a discourse already constituted, a mere fiction which we have simply to translate. It is rather the elaboration of a new discourse, the articulation of a silence. Knowledge is not the discovery or reconstruction of a latent meaning, forgotten or concealed. It is something newly raised up, an addition to the reality from which it begins.[64]

Borrowing from Freud's work on dreams, Macherey contends that in order for something to be said, other things must be left unsaid. It is the reason(s) for these absences, these silences, within a text which must be interrogated. 'What is important in the work is what it does not say.'[65] Again, like Freud, who believed that the meanings of his patients' problems were not hidden in their conscious discourse, but repressed in the turbulent discourse of the unconscious, necessitating a subtle form of analysis acute to the difference between what is said and what is shown, Macherey's approach dances between the different nuances of *telling* and *showing*. This leads him to the claim that there is a 'gap', an 'internal distanciation', between what a text wants to say and what a text actually says. To explain a text it is necessary to go beyond it, to understand what it 'is compelled to say in order to say what it wants to say'.[66] It is here that the text's 'unconscious' is constituted. And it is in a text's unconscious that its relationship to the ideological and historical conditions of its existence is revealed. It is in the absent centre, hollowed out by conflicting discourses, that the text is related to history. It is important not to misunderstand this relationship (a double relationship: to history and to ideological versions of history). The text's unconscious does not reflect historical contradictions; rather, it evokes, stages and displays them; allowing us, not a 'scientific' knowledge of ideology, but an awareness of 'ideology in contradiction with itself';[67] breaking down before questions it cannot answer: failing to do what ideology is supposed to do: 'ideology exists precisely in order to efface all trace of contradiction'.[68]

In a formal sense, a text always begins by positing a problem that is to be solved. The text then exists as a process of unfolding: the narrative movement to the final resolution of the problem. Macherey contends that between the problem posed and the resolution offered, rather than continuity, there is always a rupture. It is by examining this rupture that we discover the text's relationship with ideology and history: 'We always eventually find, at the edge of the text, the language of ideology, momentarily hidden, but eloquent by its very absence.'[69] All narratives contain an ideological project; that is, they promise to tell the 'truth' about something. Information is initially withheld on the promise that it will be revealed. Narrative constitutes a movement towards disclosure. It begins with a truth promised and ends with a truth revealed. To be rather schematic, Macherey divides the text into three instances: the ideological project (the 'truth' promised), the realization (the 'truth' revealed) and the unconscious of the text (produced by an act of symptomatic reading): the return of the repressed historical 'truth'. 'Science', he claims, 'does away with ideology, obliterates it; literature challenges ideology by using it. If ideology is thought of as a non-systematic ensemble of significations, the work proposes a *reading* of these significations, by combining them as signs. Criticism teaches us to read these signs.'[70] In this way, Machereyan critical practice seeks to explain the way in which, by giving ideology form, the literary text displays ideology in contradiction with itself.

To return to Verne's science fantasy adventure stories, Macherey argues that the ideological project of Verne's work is the *fantastic* staging of the adventures of French imperialism: its colonizing conquest of the earth. Each adventure concerns the hero's conquest of Nature (a mysterious island, the moon, the bottom of the sea, the centre of the earth). In telling these stories, Verne is 'compelled' to tell another: each voyage of conquest becomes a voyage of rediscovery, as Verne's heroes discover that others have either been there before or are there already. The significance of this, for Macherey, lies in the disparity he perceives between 'representation' (what is intended: the subject of the narrative) and 'figuration' (how it is realized: its inscription in narrative): Verne 'represents' the ideology of French imperialism, while at the same time, through the act of 'figuration' (making material in *the form* of a fiction), undermines one of its central *myths* in *the* continual staging of the fact that the lands are always already occupied (similarly, the first edition of this book was written in the middle of a discursive avalanche of media – and other – claims that America was *discovered* in 1492). 'In the passage from the level of representation to that of figuration, ideology undergoes a complete *modification* . . . perhaps because no ideology is sufficiently consistent to survive the test of figuration.'[71] Thus by giving fictional form to the ideology of imperialism, Verne's work ('to read it against the grain of its intended meaning')[72] stages the contradictions between the myth and the reality of imperialism. The stories do not provide us with a 'scientific' denunciation ('a knowledge in the strict sense') of imperialism, but by an act of symptomatic reading 'which dislodges the work internally',[73] they 'make us see', 'make us perceive', 'make us feel', the terrible contradictions of the ideological discourses from which each text is constituted: 'from which it is born, in which it bathes, from which it detaches itself . . . and to which it alludes'.[74] Verne's science fiction shows us – though not in the way intended – the ideological and historical conditions of their existence.

In Althusser's second formulation, ideology is still a representation of the imaginary relationship of individuals to the real conditions of existence, only now ideology is no longer seen only as a body of ideas, but as a lived, material practice – rituals, customs, patterns of behaviour, ways of thinking taking practical form – reproduced through the practices and productions of the Ideological State Apparatuses (ISAs): education, organized religion, the family, organized politics, the media, the culture industries, etc. According to this second definition, 'all ideology has the function (which defines it) of "constructing" concrete individuals as subjects'.[75] Ideological subjects are produced by acts of 'hailing' or 'interpellation'. Althusser uses the analogy of a police officer hailing an individual: 'Hey, you there!' When the individual hailed turns in response, he or she has been interpellated, has become a subject of the police officer's discourse. In this way, ideology is the creation of subjects who are thus subjected to the material practices of ideology.

Althusser's second definition of ideology has had a significant effect on the field of cultural studies, and the study of popular culture. Throughout the 1970s, Althusser's influence on cultural theory, especially on the study of visual culture, was profound.[76] Judith Williamson, for example, deploys Althusser's second definition of ideology in her influential study of advertising, *Decoding Advertisements*.[77] She argues that advertising is ideological in the sense that it represents an imaginary relationship to our real conditions of existence. Instead of class distinctions based on our role in the process of production, advertising continually suggests that what really matters are distinctions based on the consumption of particular goods. Thus social identity becomes a question of what we consume rather than what we produce. Like all ideology, advertising functions by interpellation: it creates subjects who in turn are subjected to its meanings and its patterns of consumption. The consumer is interpellated to make meaning and ultimately to purchase and consume and purchase and consume again. For example, when I am addressed in terms such as 'people like you' are turning to this or that product, I am interpellated as one of a group, but crucially as an individual 'you' of that group. I am addressed as an individual who can recognize myself in the imaginary space opened up by the pronoun 'you'. Thus I am invited to become the imaginary 'you' spoken to in the advertisement. But such a process is for Althusser an act of ideological 'misrecognition'. First, in the sense that in order for the advert to work it must attract many others who also recognize themselves in the 'you' (each one thinking they are the real 'you' of its discourse). Second, it is a misrecognition in another sense: the 'you' I recognize in the advert is in fact a 'you' created by the advertisement. Advertising, according to this perspective, flatters us into thinking we are the special 'you' of its discourse and in so doing we become subjects of and subjected to its material practices: acts of consumption. Advertising is thus both ideological in the way it functions and in the effects it produces.

One of the problems with Althusser's second model of ideology, and its application in cultural theory, is that it seems to work too well. Men and women are always successfully reproduced with all the necessary ideological habits required by the capitalist mode of production; there is no sense of failure, let alone any notion of conflict, struggle or resistance. In terms of popular culture, do advertisements, for example, always successfully interpellate us as consuming subjects? It was against this background of concerns that many working within the field of cultural studies turned to the work of the Italian Marxist Antonio Gramsci.

## Neo-Gramscian cultural studies

Central to the cultural studies appropriation of Gramsci is the concept of hegemony. Hegemony is for Gramsci a political concept developed to explain (given the exploitative and oppressive nature of capitalism) the absence of socialist revolutions in the Western capitalist democracies. The concept of hegemony is used by Gramsci to refer to a *condition in process* in which a dominant class (in alliance with other classes or class fractions) does not merely *rule* a society but *leads* it through the exercise of moral and intellectual leadership. In this sense, the concept is used to suggest a society in which, despite oppression and exploitation, there is a high degree of consensus, a large measure of social stability; a society in which subordinate groups and classes appear to support and subscribe to values, ideals, objectives, cultural and political meanings, which bind them to, and 'incorporate' them into, the prevailing structures of power. For example, throughout most of the course of the twentieth century, general elections in Britain have been contested by what are now the two main political parties, Labour and Conservative. On each occasion the contest has circled around the question, 'who best can administer capitalism?' (usually referred to by the less politically charged term 'the economy') – less nationalization, more nationalization; less taxation, more taxation, etc. And on each occasion, the mainstream media have concurred. In this sense, the parameters of the election debate are ultimately dictated by the needs and interests of capitalism, manifested as the interests and needs of society in general. This is clearly an example of a situation in which the interests of one powerful section of society have been 'universalized' as the interests of the society as a whole. The situation seems perfectly natural; virtually beyond serious contention. But it was not always like this. Capitalism's hegemony is the result of profound political, social, cultural and economic changes that have taken place over a period of at least three hundred years. Until as late as the second part of the nineteenth century, capitalism's position was still uncertain.[78] It is only in the twentieth century that the system seems to have won, or at least be winning, especially with the political and economic collapse of the Soviet Union and Eastern Europe. Capitalism is now, more or less, internationally hegemonic.

Although hegemony implies a society with a high degree of consensus, it should not be understood to refer to a society in which all conflict has been removed. What the concept is meant to suggest is a society in which (class) conflict is contained and channelled into ideologically safe harbours. That is, hegemony is maintained (and must be continually maintained: it is an ongoing process) by dominant groups and classes 'negotiating' with, and making concessions to, subordinate groups and classes. For example, consider the historical case of British hegemony in the Caribbean. One of the ways in which Britain attempted to secure its control over the indigenous population, and the African men, women and children it had transported there as slaves, was by means of the imposition of a version of British culture (a standard practice for colonial regimes everywhere): part of the process was to institute English as the official language. In linguistic terms, the result was not the imposition of English, but, for the majority of the population, the creation of a new language. The dominant element of this new language is English, but the language itself is not simply English. What emerged was a transformed English; with new stresses, and new rhythms; with some words dropped, and new words introduced (from African languages and elsewhere). The new language is the result of a 'negotiation' between dominant and subordinate cultures; a language marked by both 'resistance' and 'incorporation'; that is, not a language imposed from above, nor a language which spontaneously had arisen from below, but a language that is the result of a hegemonic struggle between two language cultures, involving both 'resistance' and 'incorporation'.

Hegemony is 'organized' by those whom Gramsci designates 'organic intellectuals'. According to Gramsci, intellectuals are distinguished by their social function. That is to say, all men and women have the capacity for intellectual endeavour, but only certain men and women have in society the function of intellectuals. Each class, as Gramsci explains, creates 'organically' its own intellectuals:

> one or more strata of intellectuals which give it homogeneity and an awareness of its own function not only in the economic sphere but also in the social and political fields. The capitalist entrepreneur [for example] creates alongside himself the industrial technician, the specialist in political economy, the organisers of a new culture, of a new legal system, etc.[79]

Organic intellectuals function as class organizers (in the broadest sense of the term). It is their task to 'determine and to organise the reform of moral and intellectual life'.[80] I have argued elsewhere[81] that Matthew Arnold is best understood as an organic intellectual, what Gramsci identifies as one of 'an élite of men of culture, who have the function of providing leadership of a cultural and general ideological nature'.[82]

Gramsci tends to speak of organic intellectuals as individuals, but the way the concept has been mobilized in cultural studies, following Althusser's barely acknowledged borrowings from Gramsci, is in terms of collective organic intellectuals – the so-called 'ideological state apparatuses' of the family, television, the mass media, education, organized religion, the culture industries, etc.

Because hegemony is always the result of 'negotiations' between dominant and subordinate groups, it is a process marked by both 'resistance' and 'incorporation'; it is never simply power imposed from above. There are of course limits to such negotiations and concessions. As Gramsci makes clear, they can never be allowed to challenge the economic fundamentals of class power. Moreover, in times of crisis, when moral and intellectual leadership is not enough to secure continued authority, the processes of hegemony are replaced, temporarily, by the coercive power of the 'repressive state apparatus': the army, the police, the prison system, etc.

Using a neo-Gramscian analysis, popular culture is what men and women make from their active consumption of the texts and practices of the culture industries. Youth subcultures are perhaps the most spectacular example of this process. Dick Hebdige offers a clear and convincing explanation of the process ('bricolage') by which youth subcultures appropriate for their own purposes and meanings the commodities commercially provided. Products are combined or transformed in ways not intended by their producers; commodities are rearticulated to produce oppositional meanings. In this way, and through patterns of behaviour, ways of speaking, taste in music, etc., youth subcultures engage in symbolic forms of resistance to both dominant and parent cultures. Youth cultures, according to this model, always move from originality and opposition to commercial incorporation and ideological defusion as the culture industries eventually succeed in marketing subcultural resistance for general consumption and profit. As Hebdige explains: 'Youth cultural styles may begin by issuing symbolic challenges, but they must end by establishing new sets of conventions; by creating new commodities, new industries or rejuvenating old ones.'[83]

The concept of hegemony allows the student of popular culture to free him- or herself from the disabling analysis of many of the previous approaches to the subject. Popular culture is no longer a history-stopping, imposed culture of political manipulation (the Frankfurt School); nor is it the sign of social decline and decay (the 'culture and civilization' tradition); nor is it something emerging spontaneously from below (some versions of culturalism); nor is it a meaning-machine imposing subjectivities on passive subjects (some versions of structuralism). Instead of these and other approaches, hegemony theory allows us to think popular culture as a 'negotiated' mix of intentions and counter-intentions; both from 'above' and from 'below', both 'commercial' and 'authentic'; a shifting balance of forces between resistance and incorporation. This can be analyzed in many different configurations: gender, generation, race, region, etc. From this perspective, popular culture is a contradictory mix of competing interests and values: neither middle nor working class, neither racist nor non-racist, neither sexist nor non-sexist, neither homophobic nor homophilic . . . but always a shifting balance between the two (what Gramsci calls 'a compromise equilibrium'). The commercially provided culture of the culture industries is redefined, re-shaped and redirected in strategic acts of selective consumption and productive acts of reading and articulation, often in ways not intended or even foreseen by its producers.

An interesting example of this process is the reggae music of Rastafarian culture. Bob Marley, for example, had international success with songs articulating the values and beliefs of Rastafari. This success can be viewed in two ways. On the one hand, it signals the expression of the message of his religious convictions to an enormous audience world-wide; undoubtedly for many of his audience the music had the effect of enlightenment, understanding and perhaps even conversion to, or bonding for those already convinced of, the principles of the faith. On the other hand, the music has made and continues to make enormous profits for the music industry, promoters, Island Records, etc. What we have is a paradox in which the anti-capitalist politics of Rastafari are being 'articulated' in the economic interests of capitalism: the music is lubricating the very system it seeks to condemn; and yet the music *is* an expression of an oppositional (religious) politics, and may produce certain political and cultural effects. But it is also true that the politics of Rastafari are expressed in a form that is ultimately of financial benefit to the dominant culture (i.e. as a commodity which circulates for profit). Therefore, Rastafarian reggae is a force for change which paradoxically stabilizes (at least economically) the very forces of power it seeks to overthrow. Another example, in some ways more compelling than that of reggae, is the music of the West Coast counterculture. It inspired people to resist the draft and to organize against *Amerika*'s war in Vietnam; yet, at the same time, it made profits (over which it had no control) that could be used to support the war effort in Vietnam. The more Jefferson Airplane sang 'All your private property/Is target for your enemy/And your enemy/Is *We*', the more money RCA Records made. The proliferation of Jefferson Airplane's anticapitalist politics increased the profits of their capitalist record company. Again, this is an example of the process of hegemony; the way in which dominant groups in society attempted to 'negotiate' oppositional voices on to a terrain which secures for the dominant groups a continued position of leadership. West Coast rock was not denied expression, but its expression was 'articulated' in the economic interests of the war-supporting capitalist music industry.[84]

'Articulation' is a key term in neo-Gramscian cultural studies. Stuart Hall has developed the concept to explain the processes of ideological struggle (Hall's use of 'articulation' plays on the term's double meaning: to express and to join together).[85] He argues that cultural texts and practices are not inscribed with meaning, guaranteed once and for all by the intentions of production; meaning is always the result of an act of 'articulation'. Hall also draws on the work of the Russian theorist Valentin Volosinov.[86] Volosinov argues that meaning is determined by the discursive location and social context. He argues that cultural texts and practices are 'multiaccentual'; that is, they can be 'spoken' with different 'accents' by different people in different discourses and social contexts for different politics. When, for example, a rap group uses the word 'nigger' to attack institutional racism, it is 'spoken' with an 'accent' very different from the 'accent' given the word in, say, the racist discourse of a neo-Nazi. This is, of course, not simply a question of linguistic struggle – a conflict over semantics – but a sign of political struggle about who can claim the power and the authority to define social reality.

From this perspective, the cultural field is marked by a struggle to articulate, disarticulate and rearticulate cultural texts and practices for particular ideologies, particular politics. As Hall points out, 'Meaning is a social production, a practice. The world has to be *made to mean*'.[87] Therefore, because different meanings can be ascribed to the same cultural text or practice, meaning is always the site and the result of struggle. A key question for cultural studies is: 'Why do particular meanings get regularly constructed around particular cultural texts and practices and thereby achieve the status of "common sense", acquire a certain taken-for-granted quality?' Although this is a recognition that the culture industries are a major site of ideological production, constructing powerful images, descriptions, definitions, frames of reference for understanding the world, neo-Gramscian cultural studies rejects the view that 'the people' who consume these productions are 'cultural dupes', victims of 'an up-dated form of the opium of the people'. As Hall insists,

> That judgment may make us feel right, decent and self-satisfied about our denunciations of the agents of mass manipulation and deception – the capitalist cultural industries: but I don't know that it is a view which can survive for long as an adequate account of cultural relationships; and even less as a socialist perspective on the culture and nature of the working class. Ultimately, the notion of the people as a purely passive, outline force is a deeply unsocialist perspective.[88]

Neo-Gramscian cultural studies is informed by the proposition that people *make* popular culture from the repertoire of commodities supplied by the culture industries. *Making* popular culture ('production in use') can be empowering to subordinate and resistant to dominant understandings of the world. But this is not to say that popular culture is always empowering and resistant. To deny the passivity of consumption is not to deny that sometimes consumption is passive; to deny that the consumers of popular culture are not cultural dupes is not to deny that the culture industries may seek to manipulate. But it is to deny that popular culture is little more than a degraded landscape of commercial and ideological manipulation, imposed from above in order to make profit and secure social control. Neo-Gramscian cultural studies insists that to decide these matters requires vigilance and attention to the details of the production, distribution and consumption of culture. These are not matters that can be decided once and for all (outside the contingencies of history and politics) with an élitist glance and a condescending sneer. Nor can they be read off from the moment of production (locating meaning, pleasure, ideological effect, the probability of incorporation, the possibility of resistance, in, variously, the intention, the means of production or the production itself): these are only aspects of the contexts for 'production in use'; and it is, ultimately, in 'production in use' that questions of meaning, pleasure, ideological effect, incorporation or resistance, can be (contingently) decided.

## Popular culture as carnivalesque

The concept of the carnivalesque derives from the work of the Russian critic Mikhail Bakhtin.[89] To understand what cultural critics mean when they refer to popular culture as carnivalesque it is best to begin with Bakhtin's understanding of the actual carnivals which dominated European popular culture throughout the Middle Ages.

In the carnivals of the Middle Ages, he claims, there were no division between performers and spectators. To speak of performers at all is inaccurate. 'Carnival is not contemplated and, strictly speaking, not even performed; its participants live in it, they live by its laws as long as those laws are in effect; that is they live a *carnivalistic* life'.[90]

> The laws, prohibitions, and restrictions that determine the structure and order of ordinary, that is noncarnival, life are suspended during carnival: what is suspended first of all is hierarchical structure and all the forms of terror, reverence, piety, and etiquette connected with it – that is, everything resulting from socio-hierarchical inequality or any other form of inequality among people (including age). All *distance* between people is suspended, and a special carnival category goes into effect: *free and familiar contact among people*.[91]

Carnival works like a dress rehearsal for better times. It allows 'the latent sides of human nature to reveal and express themselves'.[92] In doing this carnival breaks down barriers. As he explains, it 'combines the sacred with the profane, the lofty with the low, the great with the insignificant, the wise with the stupid'.[93] A feature of all medieval carnivals – often misunderstood, according to Bakhtin – is the mock crowning and decrowning of a king. This does not celebrate the office of kingship but the 'joyful relativity' of change itself. What it celebrates is 'the shift itself, the very process of replaceability, and not the precise item that is replaced'.[94] Carnival's 'grotesque realism' works in much the same way. By drawing attention to bodily functions – copulation, birth, growth, eating, drinking, defecation – it celebrates human processes ('unfinished becoming'), against the stasis of non-carnival time. In a similar way, carnival laughter – 'ridicule fused with rejoicing' – is said to articulate a particular view of the world in opposition to the 'monolithically serious' view of the forces of officialdom:

> The serious aspects of class culture are official and authoritarian; they are combined with violence, prohibitions, limitations and always contain an element of fear and of intimidation. These elements prevailed in the Middle Ages. Laughter, on the contrary, overcomes fear, for it knows no inhibitions, no limitations. Its idiom is never used by violence and authority.[95]

Carnival offered, according to Bakhtin, a temporary refusal of the official world. But, as he insists, carnival was not just a retreat from medievalism, it offered the Utopian promise of a better life, one of equality, abundance and freedom. It temporarily removed the hierarchies of inherited distinction and reversed established hierarchies:

> It could be said (with certain reservations, of course) that a person of the Middle Ages lived, as it were, *two lives*: one was the *official* life, monolithically serious and gloomy, subjugated to a strict hierarchical order, full of terror, dogmatism, reverence, and piety; the other was the *life of the carnival square*, free and unrestricted, full of ambivalent laughter, blasphemy, the profanation of everything sacred, full of debasing and obscenities, familiar contact with everyone and everything. Both these lives were legitimate, but separated by strict temporal boundaries.[96]

His view of carnival can summarized in a series of oppositions:

| Carnival culture | Official culture |
| --- | --- |
| Laughter | Seriousness |
| Body | Mind |
| Profane | Spiritual |
| Unofficial | Official |
| Horizontal | Vertical |
| Open | Dogmatic |
| Contingent | Immutable |

| | |
|---|---|
| Movement | Stasis |
| Abundance | Scarcity |
| Intensity | Control |
| Transparency | Opaqueness |

John Docker argues that 'carnivalesque as a cultural mode still strongly influences twentieth-century mass culture, in Hollywood film, popular literary genres, television, music: a culture that in its exuberance, range, excess, internationalism, and irrepressible vigour and inventiveness perhaps represents another summit in the history of popular culture, comparable to that of early modern Europe'.[97]

John Fiske uses carnival to explain the pleasures of wrestling on TV. He describes it as a carnival of bodies, of rule-breaking, of grotesquerie, of degradation and spectacle; it is marked by excess, exaggeration and grotesqueness. In this way, he claims, wrestling on TV can be seen to share certain features with Bakhtin's notion of carnival. For example, wrestling on TV is a form of spectacle, rather than a sport. Its pleasures are the complicated pleasures of looking and participation. Little distinction is made between audience and wrestlers. Audience verbally and physically join in and the camera pans the crowd almost as much as the match itself. The spectators are clearly part of (and intended to be part of) the spectacle. Like carnival, wrestling revels in transgression of rules, presenting a world turned upside down – an inversion of the official world of sport. Managers fight, wrestlers not involved in the match fight; the separation between ring and audience is continually breached. And like carnival, it is a form of inversion. 'The rules of the "game" exist only to be broken, the referee only to be ignored.'[98]

Wrestling on TV presents a travesty of justice; to play fair is to be taken advantage of; the good lose more times than they win:

> 'Natural' justice, enshrined in social law, is inverted; the deserving and the good lose more frequently than they win. It is the evil, the unfair, who triumph in a reversal of most dramatic conflict on television. There is a 'grotesque realism' here that contrasts with the idealized 'prevailing truth' of the social order: despite the official ideology, the experience of many of the subordinate is that the unfair and the ugly *do* prosper, and the 'good' go to the wall.[99]

Like carnival, wrestling on TV revels in a 'festive liberation of laughter' – laughter aimed at authority. Fiske cites the example of a regular character on the American programme *Rock 'n' Wrestling*, Lord Alfred Hayes. 'His name, his dress, and his accent all parody the traditional English aristocrat; he is a carnivalesque metaphor of social power and status who is there to be laughed at.'[100] Fiske contends that wrestling on TV articulates the politics of carnival:

> The sporting values of fairness and equality for all its players, of respect for the loser and proper celebration of the winner, represent the dominant ideology by which democratic capitalism values itself. The grotesque realism of the ugly, distorted body is therefore opposed semiotically and politically to the dominant. It is an appropriate means of articulating the social experience of many subordinate and oppressed groups in capitalism whose everyday sense of the social system is not one of fairness and equality: positioned as they are as 'losers', the subordinated (whether by class, gender, or race) have little sense of being 'respected' by the winners, nor do they necessarily feel admiration for the socially successful. The carnival is both a product and a celebration of the yawning gap between the interests and experiences of the dominant and the subordinate in white patriarchal capitalism.[101]

Fiske's claims about the connection between wrestling on TV and carnival can be summarized in a series of binary oppositions:

| *Sport* | *Wrestling* |
| --- | --- |
| Play by the rules | Rules to be broken |
| Fair play | Unfair play |
| Play to win | Play to be seen |
| Performance | Display |
| Skill | Ritual |
| Fans | Participants |

What Bakhtin presents as a Utopian space, others have characterized as ideological manipulation in the form of an officially sanctioned disruption of the social order, licensed to protect it – a safety valve.[102] Fiske's response to such claims is to argue that 'we must not write carnival off as merely a safety valve that ultimately allows social control to work more effectively: rather it is a recognition of the strength and endurance of those oppositional, disruptive, popular forces'.[103] Docker makes much the same point:

> Carnivalesque . . . offers an ongoing challenge, to the narrowly conceived forms of reason of the 'public sphere', as well as to modernism desiring to legislate, in an equally imperial way,

single standards for all culture; what's good for the modernist avant-garde is good for the world. In relation to both, carnivalesque remains an always dangerous supplement, challenging, destabilising, relativising, pluralising single notions of true culture, true reason, true broadcasting, true art.[104]

## Further reading

Michèle Barrett, *The Politics of Truth: From Marx to Foucault*, Cambridge: Polity Press, 1991. An interesting introduction to 'post-Marxism'.

Tony Bennett, *Formalism and Marxism*, London: Methuen, 1979. Contains helpful chapters on Althusser and Macherey.

Tony Bennett, Colin Mercer and Janet Woollacott (eds), *Culture, Ideology and Social Process*, London: Batsford, 1981. Section 4 consists of extracts from Gramsci and three essays informed by hegemony theory. The book also contains similar sections on culturalism and structuralism.

Dick Hebdige, *Subculture: The meaning of style*, London: Methuen, 1979. The seminal account of youth subcultures: an excellent introduction to hegemony theory and popular culture.

Dave Laing, *The Marxist Theory of Art: An introductory survey*, Hemel Hempstead: Harvester Wheatsheaf, 1978. A very readable introduction to Marxist theories of culture. Contains an interesting section on popular culture.

Karl Marx and Frederick Engels, *On Literature and Art*, St Louis: Telos, 1973. A useful selection of the writings of Marx and Engels on matters cultural.

Pam Morris (ed.), *The Bakhtin Reader: Selected writings of Bakhtin, Medvedev, Volosinov*, London: Edward Arnold, 1994. An excellent introduction to the full range of Bakhtin's work.

Cary Nelson and Lawrence Grossberg (eds), *Marxism and the Interpretation of Culture*, London: Macmillan, 1988. An interesting collection of recent essays on Marxism and culture.

Anne Showstack Sassoon (ed.), *Approaches to Gramsci*, London: Writers and Readers, 1982. A collection of essays on Gramsci. Contains a useful glossary of key terms.

Roger Simon, *Gramsci's Political Thought: An introduction*, London: Lawrence & Wishart, 1982. A very readable introduction to Gramsci.

Phil Slater, *Origin and Significance of the Frankfurt School: A Marxist perspective*, London: Routledge & Kegan Paul, 1977. The book provides a critical overview of the work of the Frankfurt School. Chapter 5, on the culture industry, is of particular interest to the student of popular culture.

# 6
# FEMINISM

## Feminisms

'One of the most striking changes in the humanities in the 1980s has been the rise of gender as a category of analysis.'[1] This is the opening sentence in Elaine Showalter's introduction to a book on gender and literary studies. There can be no doubt that without the emergence of feminism (the second wave) in the early 1970s this sentence could not have been written. It is feminism that has placed gender on the academic agenda. However, the nature of the agenda has provoked a vigorous debate within feminism. So much so that it is really no longer possible, if it ever was, to talk of feminism as a monolithic body of research, writing and activity; one should really speak of *feminisms*.

There are at least four different feminisms: radical, Marxist, liberal and what Sylvia Walby calls dual systems theory.[2] Each responds to women's oppression in a different way, positing different causes and different solutions. Radical feminists argue that women's oppression is the result of the system of patriarchy, a system of domination in which men as a group have power over women as a group. In Marxist feminist analysis the ultimate source of oppression is capitalism. The domination of women by men is seen as a consequence of capital's domination over labour. Liberal feminism differs from both Marxist and radical feminisms in that it does not posit a system – patriarchy or capitalism – determining the oppression of women. Instead, it tends to see the problem in terms of male prejudice against women, embodied in law or expressed in the exclusion of women from particular areas of life. Dual systems theory represents the coming together of Marxist and radical feminist analysis in the belief that women's oppression is the result of a complex articulation of both patriarchy and capitalism. There are of course other feminist perspectives. Rosemary Tong, for example, lists: liberal, Marxist, radical, psychoanalytic, socialist, existentialist and postmodern.[3]

## Cultural politics

Popular culture has been the object of a great deal of feminist analysis. As Michèle Barrett points out, 'Cultural politics are crucially important to feminism because they involve struggles over meaning'.[4] But, as Tania Modleski suggests, too often feminist work on popular culture is seen as something else. It is as if discussion of popular culture consumed by women is gendered and therefore particular, whereas discussion of popular culture consumed by men is ungendered and therefore universal. Feminist writing on culture has done much to challenge this distinction. Although most of the remainder of this chapter will consist of detailed discussions of five specific examples of feminist work on popular culture, I will first present a brief survey of other significant contributions.

In 1978, the 'Women's Study Group' at the Centre for Contemporary Cultural Studies, University of Birmingham, edited a collection of essays called *Women Take Issue*. The essays look at different aspects of women's experience from a feminist perspective; what the editors call 'a feminist analysis of "how things are"'.[5] Part of the interest of the collection is that it contains early work on popular culture by women who have subsequently gone on to make a significant contribution to a feminist analysis of popular culture: for example, Charlotte Brunsdon, Dorothy Hobson, Angela McRobbie and Janice Winship.

In *Loving with a Vengeance*, Tania Modleski claims that women writing about 'feminine narratives' tend to adopt one of three possible positions: 'dismissiveness; hostility – tending unfortunately to be aimed at the consumers of the narratives; or, most frequently, a flippant kind of mockery'.[6] Against this, she declares: 'It is time to begin a feminist reading of women's reading'.[7] Modleski addresses what she calls 'mass-produced fantasies for women': Harlequin Romances, gothic novels and soap operas. She argues that these popular narratives 'speak to very real problems and tensions in women's lives'.[8] Despite this, she acknowledges that the way in which these narratives resolve problems and tensions will rarely 'please modern feminists: far from it'.[9] However, the reader of fantasies and the feminist reader do have something in common: dissatisfaction with women's lives. For example, she claims, referring to Harlequin Romances: 'What Marx said of religious suffering is equally true of "romantic suffering": it is "at the same time an expression of real suffering and a *protest* against real suffering"'.[10]

Modleski does not condemn the novels or the women who read them. Rather, she condemns 'the conditions which have made them necessary', concluding that 'the contradictions in women's lives are more responsible for the existence of Harlequins than Harlequins are for the contradictions'.[11] She drifts towards, then draws back from, the full force of Marx's position on religion, which would leave her, despite her protests to the contrary, having come very close to the mass culture position of popular culture as opiate. Nevertheless, she notes how 'students occasionally cut their women's studies classes to find out what is going on in their favourite soap opera. When this happens, it is time for us to stop merely opposing soap operas and to start incorporating them, and other mass produced fantasies, into our study of women.'[12]

Rosalind Coward's *Female Desire* is about women's pleasure in popular culture. The book explores fashion, romance, pop music, horoscopes, soap operas, food, cooking, women's magazines and other texts and practices which involve women in an endless cycle of pleasure and guilt ('guilt – it's our speciality'[13]). Coward does not approach the material as an 'outsider . . . a stranger to [pleasure and] guilt. The pleasures I describe are often my pleasures. . . . I don't approach these things as a distant critic but as someone examining myself, examining my own life under a microscope.'[14] Her position is in marked contrast to that, say, of the 'culture and civilization' tradition or the perspective of the Frankfurt School. Popular culture is not looked down on from an Olympian height as the disappointing, but rather predictable, culture of other people. This is a discourse about 'our' culture. Furthermore, she refuses to see the cultural practices and cultural representations of popular culture (the discourse of female desire) 'as the forcible imposition of false and limiting stereotypes'.[15]

> Instead I explore the desire presumed by these representations, the desire which touches feminist and non-feminist women alike.

> But nor do I treat female desire as something unchangeable, arising from the female condition. I see the representations of female pleasure and desire as *producing* and sustaining feminine positions. These positions are neither distant roles imposed on us from outside which it would be easy to kick off, nor are they the essential attributes of femininity. Feminine positions are produced as responses to the pleasures offered to us; our subjectivity and identity are formed in the definitions of desire which encircle us. These are the experiences which make change such a difficult and daunting task, for female desire is constantly lured by discourses which sustain male privilege.[16]

Coward's interest in romantic fiction is in part inspired by the intriguing fact that 'over the past decade, the rise of feminism has been paralleled almost exactly by a mushroom growth in the popularity of romantic fiction'.[17] She believes two things about romantic novels. First, that 'they must still satisfy some very definite needs'. And second, that they offer evidence of, and contribute to, 'a very powerful and common fantasy'.[18] She claims that the fantasies played out in romantic fiction are 'pre-adolescent, very nearly preconscious'.[19] She believes them to be 'regressive' in two key respects. On the one hand, they adore the power of the male in ways reminiscent of the very early child–father relationship, while on the other, they are regressive because of the attitude taken to female sexual desire – passive and without guilt, as the responsibility for sexual desire is projected on to the male. In other words, sexual desire is something men have and to which women merely respond. In short, romantic fiction replays the girl's experience of the Oedipal drama; only this time without its conclusion in female powerlessness; this time she does marry the father and replace the mother. Therefore there is a trajectory from subordination to position of power (as the mother figure). But, as Coward points out,

> Romantic fiction is surely popular because it . . . restores the childhood world of sexual relations and suppresses criticisms of the inadequacy of men, the suffocation of the family, or the damage inflicted by patriarchal power. Yet it simultaneously manages to avoid the guilt and fear which might come from that childhood world. Sexuality is defined firmly as the father's responsibility, and fear of suffocation is overcome because women achieve a sort of power in romantic fiction. Romantic fiction promises a secure world, promises that there will be safety with dependence, that there will be power with subordination.[20]

*The Female Gaze* is a collection of essays by women on popular culture. As the title of the collection implies, it is a book about how women look at popular culture, and, more importantly, how women can establish ways to 'inscribe a female gaze into the heart of our cultural life'.[21] As its editors, Lorraine Gamman and Margaret Marshment, point out, the struggle to inscribe a female gaze is a struggle over meaning 'within capitalism, and within patriarchy'.[22] Popular culture is seen as a terrain or site of struggle, 'where many of these meanings are determined and debated'. Moreover,

> It is not enough to dismiss popular culture as merely serving the complementary systems of capitalism and patriarchy, peddling 'false consciousness' to the duped masses. It can also be seen as a site where meanings are contested and where dominant ideologies can be disturbed.[23]

The book advocates a cultural politics of intervention: 'we cannot afford to dismiss the popular by always positioning ourselves outside it'.[24] It is from popular culture

> that most people in our society get their entertainment and their information. It is here that women (and men) are offered the culture's dominant definitions of themselves. It would therefore seem crucial to explore the possibilities and pitfalls of intervention in popular forms in order to find ways of making feminist meanings a part of our pleasures.[25]

## Popular film, cine-psychoanalysis and cultural studies

Laura Mulvey's essay 'Visual pleasure and narrative cinema' is perhaps the classic statement on popular film from the perspective of feminist psychoanalysis. The essay is concerned with how popular cinema produces and reproduces what she calls the 'male gaze'. Mulvey describes her approach as 'political psychoanalysis'. Psychoanalytic theory is 'appropriated . . . as a political weapon [to demonstrate] the way the unconscious of patriarchal society has structured film form'.[26]

The inscription of the image of woman in this system is twofold: (1) she is the object of male desire, and (2) she is the signifier of the threat of castration. In order to challenge popular cinema's 'manipulation of visual pleasure', Mulvey calls for what she describes as the 'destruction of pleasure as a radical weapon'.[27] She is uncompromising on this point: 'It is said that analysing pleasure, or beauty, destroys it. This is the intention of this article'.[28]

So what are the pleasures that must be destroyed? She identifies two. First, there is scopophilia, the pleasure of looking. Citing Freud, she suggests that it is always more than just the pleasure of looking: scopophilia involves 'taking other people as objects, subjecting them to a controlling gaze'.[29] The notion of the controlling gaze is crucial to her argument. But so is sexual objectification: scopophilia is also sexual; 'using another person as an object of sexual stimulation through sight'.[30] Although it clearly presents itself to be seen, Mulvey argues that the conventions of popular cinema are such as to suggest a 'hermetically sealed world which unwinds magically, indifferent to the presence of the audience'.[31] The audience's 'voyeuristic phantasy' is encouraged by the contrast between the darkness of the cinema and the changing patterns of light on the screen.

Popular cinema promotes and satisfies a second pleasure: 'developing scopophilia in its narcissistic aspect'.[32] Here Mulvey draws on Lacan's account of the 'mirror phase' (see Chapter 4 above) to suggest that there is an analogy to be made between the constitution of a child's ego and the pleasures of cinematic identification. Just as a child recognizes and mis-recognizes itself in the mirror, the spectator recognizes and mis-recognizes itself on the screen. She explains it thus:

> The mirror phase occurs at a time when the child's physical ambitions outstrip his motor capacity, with the result that his recognition of himself is joyous in that he imagines his mirror image to be more complete, more perfect than he experiences his own body. Recognition is thus overlaid with mis-recognition: the image recognised is conceived as the reflected body of the self, but its misrecognition as superior projects this body outside itself as an ideal ego, the alienated subject, which, re-introjected as an ego ideal, gives rise to the future generation of identification with others.[33]

Her argument is that popular cinema produces two contradictory forms of visual pleasure. The first invites scopophilia; the second promotes narcissism. The contradiction arises because in film terms, one implies a separation of the erotic identity of the subject from the object on the screen (active scopophilia), the other demands identification of the ego with the object on the screen through the spectator's fascination with and recognition of his like.[34]

In Freudian terms, the separation is between 'scopophilic instinct (pleasure in looking at another person as an erotic object)' and 'ego libido (forming identification processes)'.[35] But in a world structured by 'sexual imbalance', the pleasure of the gaze has been separated into two distinct positions: men look and women exhibit '*to-be-looked-at-ness*' – both playing to and signifying male desire.[36] Women are therefore crucial to the pleasure of the (male) gaze:

> Traditionally, the woman displayed has functioned on two levels: as erotic object for the characters within the screen story, and as erotic object for the spectator within the auditorium, with a shifting tension between the looks on either side of the screen.[37]

She gives the example of the showgirl who can be seen to dance for both looks. When the heroine removes her clothes, it is for the sexual gaze of both the hero in the narrative and the spectator in the auditorium. It is only when they subsequently make love that a tension arises between the two looks.

Popular cinema is structured around two moments: moments of narrative and moments of spectacle. The first is associated with the active male, the second with the passive female. The male spectator fixes his gaze on the hero ('the bearer of the look') to satisfy ego formation, and through the hero to the heroine ('the erotic look'), to satisfy libido. The first look recalls the moment of recognition/mis-recognition in front of the mirror. The second look confirms women as sexual objects. The second look is made more complex by the claim that

> Ultimately, the meaning of woman is sexual difference. . . . She connotes something that the look continually circles around but disavows: her lack of a penis, implying a threat of castration and hence unpleasure. . . . Thus the woman as icon, displayed for the gaze and enjoyment of men, the active controllers of the look, always threatens to evoke the anxiety it originally signified.[38]

To salvage pleasure and escape an unpleasurable re-enactment of the original castration complex, the male unconscious can take two routes to safety. The first means of escape is through detailed investigation of the original moment of trauma, usually leading to 'the devaluation, punishment or saving of the guilty object'.[39] She cites the narratives of film noir as typical of this method of anxiety control. The second means of escape is through 'complete disavowal of castration by the substitution of a fetish object or turning the represented figure itself into a fetish so that it becomes reassuring rather than dangerous'.[40] She gives the example of 'the cult of the female star . . . [in which] fetishistic scopophilia builds up the physical beauty of the object, transforming it into something satisfying in itself'.[41] This often leads to the erotic look of the spectator no longer being borne by the look of the male protagonist; producing moments of pure erotic spectacle as the camera holds the female body (often fragmented) for the unmediated erotic look of the spectator.

Mulvey concludes her argument by suggesting that the pleasure of popular cinema must be destroyed in order to liberate women from the exploitation and oppression of being the '(passive) raw material for the (active) male gaze'.[42] She proposes what amounts to a Brechtian revolution in the making of films. To produce a cinema no longer 'obsessively subordinated to the neurotic needs of the male ego',[43] it is necessary to break with illusionism, making the camera material, and producing in the audience: 'dialectics, passionate detachment'.[44] Moreover, 'Women, whose image has continually been stolen and used for this end [objects of the male gaze], cannot view the decline of the traditional film form with anything much more than sentimental regret'.[45]

Mulvey's analysis is impressive and telling throughout and, despite the fact that it is made in an essay of fewer than thirteen pages, its influence has been enormous. Jane Gaines has calculated that, with its inclusion in Mulvey's own collection of essays, *Visual and Other Pleasures*, the essay has now been reprinted seven times.[46] Since Gaines's calculation, the essay has been reprinted in at least two more collections.[47] However, having noted the essay's power and influence, it has to be said that her 'solution' is somewhat less telling than her analysis of the 'problem'. As an alternative to popular cinema, Mulvey calls for an avant-garde cinema 'which is radical in both a political and an aesthetic sense and challenges the basic assumptions of the mainstream film'.[48] This leaves Mulvey vulnerable to charges of élitist left-vanguardism.[49]

**142**

Some feminists have begun to doubt what they call its 'universal validity',[50] questioning whether 'the gaze is always male', or whether it is 'merely "dominant"' among a range of different ways of seeing, including the female gaze.[51] Many of the essays in *The Female Gaze* are critical of what they see as Mulvey's formalism and her uncritical use of psychoanalysis.[52]

Jackie Stacey's *Star Gazing: Hollywood and Female Spectatorship*[53] rejects the universalism and the textual determinism of much psychoanalytic work on female audiences. Her analysis begins with the audience in the cinema rather than the audience constructed by the text. Her approach takes her from the traditions of film studies to the theoretical concerns of cultural studies. Here is her diagram of the differences marking out the two paradigms:[55]

| *Film studies* | *Cultural studies* |
| --- | --- |
| Spectatorship positioning | Audience readings |
| Textual analysis | Ethnographic methods |
| Meaning as production-led | Meaning as consumption-led |
| Passive viewer | Active viewer |
| Unconscious | Conscious |
| Pessimistic | Optimistic |

Stacey's study is based on an analysis of responses she received from a group of white British women, mostly aged over 60, and mostly working class, who had been keen cinema-goers in the 1940s and 1950s. On the basis of letters and completed questionnaires, she organized her analysis in terms of three discourses generated by the responses themselves, *escapism, identification* and *consumption*.

*Escapism* is one of the most frequently cited reasons given by the women for going to the cinema. Seeking to escape its pejorative connotations, Stacey uses Richard Dyer's[55] argument for the Utopian sensibility of much popular entertainment, to construct an account of the Utopian possibilities of Hollywood cinema for British women in the 1940 and 1950s. Dyer deploys a set of binary oppositions to reveal the relationship between the social problems experienced by audiences and the textual solutions played out in the texts of popular entertainment.

| *Social problems* | *Textual solutions* |
| --- | --- |
| Scarcity | Abundance |
| Exhaustion | Energy |

| Dreariness | Intensity |
|---|---|
| Manipulation | Transparency |
| Fragmentation | Community |

For Dyer, entertainment's Utopian sensibility is a property of the text. Stacey extends his argument to include the social context in which entertainment is experienced. The letters and completed questionnaires made it clear that the pleasures of cinema were always more than the visual and aural pleasures of the cinema text – they included the ritual of attending a screening, the shared experience and imagined community of the audience, the comfort and comparative luxury of the cinema building. It was never a simple matter of enjoying the glamour of Hollywood. As Stacey explains,

> The physical space of the cinema provided a transitional space between everyday life outside the cinema and the fantasy world of the Hollywood film about to be shown. Its design and decor facilitated the processes of escapism enjoyed by these female spectators. As such, cinemas were dream palaces not only in so far as they housed the screening of Hollywood fantasies, but also because of their design and decor which provided a feminised and glamorised space suitable for the cultural consumption of Hollywood films.[56]

Escapism is always a historically specific two-way event. Stacey's women were not only escaping into the luxury of the cinema and the glamour of Hollywood film, they were also escaping *from* the hardships, the dangers and the restrictions of wartime Britain. It is this mix of Hollywood glamour, the relative luxury of the cinema interiors, experienced in a context of war and its aftermath of shortages and sacrifice, which generates 'the multi-layered meanings of escapism'.[57]

*Identification* is Stacey's second focus. She is aware of how it often functions in psychoanalytic criticism to point to the way in which film texts are said to position female spectators in the interests of patriarchy. According to this argument, identification is the means by which women collude and become complicit in this process. However, by shifting the focus from the female spectator constructed within the film text to the actual female audience in the cinema, she claims that identification can be shown often to work quite differently. Her respondents continually draw attention

**144**

to the way in which stars can generate fantasies of power, control and self-confidence.

Her third category is *consumption*. Again, she rejects the rather monolithic position which figures consumption as entangled in an always-successful relationship of domination, exploitation and control. She insists instead that 'consumption is a site of negotiated meanings, of resistance and of appropriation as well as of subjection and exploitation'.[58] Much work in film studies, she claims, has tended to be production-led, fixing its critical gaze on 'the ways in which the film industry produces cinema spectators as consumers of both the film and the [associated] products of other industries'.[59] Such analysis is never able to pose theoretically (let alone discuss in concrete detail) how audiences actually use and make meanings from the commodities they consume. She argues that her respondents' accounts reveal a more contradictory relationship between audiences and what they consume. For example, she highlights the ways in which 'American feminine ideals are clearly remembered as transgressing restrictive British femininity and thus employed as strategies of resistance'.[60] Many of the letters and completed questionnaires reveal the extent to which Hollywood stars represented an alternative femininity, exciting and transgressive. In this way, Hollywood stars, and the cultural commodities associated with them, could be *used* as a means to negotiate with and extend the boundaries of what was perceived as restrictive British femininity.

She is careful not to argue that these women were free to construct through consumption entirely new feminine identities. Similarly, she does not deny that such forms of consumption may pander to the patriarchal gaze. The key to her position is the question of excess. As she explains, 'the consumption of Hollywood stars and other [associated] commodities for the transformation of self-image produces something in excess of the needs of dominant culture'.[61]

She contends that

> Paradoxically, whilst commodity consumption for female spectators in mid to late 1950s Britain concerns producing oneself as a desirable object, it also offers an escape from what is perceived as the drudgery of domesticity and motherhood which increasingly comes to define femininity at this time. Thus, consumption may signify an assertion of self in opposition to the self-sacrifice associated with marriage and motherhood in 1950s Britain.[62]

Stacey's work represents something of a rebuke to the universalistic claims of much cine-psychoanalysis. By studying the audience, 'female spectatorship might be seen as a process of negotiating the dominant meanings of Hollywood cinema, rather than one of being passively positioned by it'.[63] From this perspective, Hollywood's patriarchal power begins to look less monolithic, less seamless, its success never guaranteed.

## Janice Radway: *Reading the Romance*

Janice Radway begins her study of romance reading with the observation that the increased popularity of the genre can be in part explained by the 'important changes in book production, distribution, advertising and marketing techniques'.[64] Taking issue with earlier accounts, Radway points out that the increasing success of romances may have as much to do with the sophisticated selling techniques of publishers, making romances more visible, more available, as with any simple notion of women's increased need for romantic fantasy. Although her primary interest is the act of romance reading, she feels it is important not to lose sight of the context of production. Nevertheless, at the core of Radway's study is research she carried out in 'Smithton', involving a group of forty-two romance readers (mostly married with children). The women are all regular customers at the book shop where 'Dorothy Evans' works. It was in fact Dot's reputation which attracted Radway to Smithton. Out of her own enthusiasm for the genre, Dot publishes a newsletter ('Dorothy's diary of romance reading') in which romances are graded in terms of their romantic worth. The newsletter, and Dot's general advice to customers, has in effect created what amounts to a small but significant symbolic community of romance readers. It is this symbolic community which is the focus of Radway's research. Research material was compiled through individual questionnaires, open-ended group discussions, face-to-face interviews, some informal discussions and by observing the interactions between Dot and her regular customers at the book shop. Radway supplemented this by reading the titles brought to her attention by the Smithton women.

The influence of Dot's newsletter, its suggested selections and rejections, on the purchasing patterns of readers, alerted Radway to the inadequacy of a methodology that attempts to draw conclusions about the genre from a sample of current titles. She discovered that in order to understand the cultural significance of romance reading, it is necessary to pay attention to popular discrimination ('the singularity of readers'),[65] to the process of selection and rejection which finds some titles satisfying and others not. She also encountered the actual extent of romance reading. The majority of the women she interviewed read every day, spending eleven to fifteen hours a week on romance reading. At least a quarter of the women informed her that, unless prevented by domestic and family demands, they prefer to read a romance from start to finish in one sitting. Consumption varies from one to fifteen books a week. Four informants claimed to read between fifteen and twenty-five romances a week.[66]

According to the Smithton women, the ideal romance is one in which an intelligent and independent woman with a good sense of humour is overwhelmed, after much suspicion and distrust, and some cruelty and violence, by the love of an intelligent, tender and good-humoured man, who in the course of their relationship is transformed from an emotional pre-literate to someone who can *care* for her and *nurture* her in ways that traditionally we would expect only from a woman to a man. As Radway explains: 'The romantic fantasy is . . . not a fantasy about discovering a uniquely interesting life partner, but a ritual wish to be cared for, loved, and validated in a particular way.'[67] It is a fantasy about reciprocation; the wish to believe that men can bestow on women the care and attention women are expected regularly to bestow on men. But the romantic fantasy offers more than this; it recalls a time when the reader was in fact the recipient of an intense 'maternal' care.

Drawing on the work of Nancy Chodorow,[68] Radway claims that romantic fantasy is a form of regression in which the reader is imaginatively and emotionally transported to a time 'when she was the center of a profoundly nurturant individual's attention'.[69] Romance reading, she argues, is a fantasy in which the hero is eventually the source of care and attention not experienced by the reader since she was an Oedipal child. Romance reading is therefore a means by which women can vicariously – through the hero–heroine relationship – experience the emotional succour which they themselves are expected to provide to others without adequate reciprocation for themselves in their everyday existence.

She also takes from Chodorow the notion of the female self as a self-in-relation to others, and the male self as a self autonomous and independent. Chodorow argues that this results from the different relations that a girl and boy have with their mother. Radway sees a correlation between the psychological events described by Chodorow and the narrative pattern of the ideal romance: in the journey from identity in crisis to identity restored, 'the heroine successfully establishes by the end of the ideal narrative . . . the now familiar female self, the self-in-relation'.[70] Radway also takes from Chodorow the belief that women emerge from the Oedipus complex with a 'triangular psychic structure intact'. The result is that 'not only do they need to connect themselves with a member of the opposite sex, but they also continue to require an intense emotional bond with someone who is reciprocally nurturant and protective in a maternal way.'[71] In order to experience this regression to maternal emotional fulfilment, she has three options: lesbianism, a relationship with a man, or to seek fulfilment by other means. The homophobic nature of our culture limits the first; the nature of masculinity limits the second; romance reading may be an example of the third. Radway suggests that it is:

> the fantasy that generates the romance originates in the oedipal desire to love and be loved by an individual of the opposite sex and in the continuing pre-oedipal wish that is part of a woman's inner-object configuration, the wish to regain the love of the mother and all that it implies – erotic pleasure, symbiotic completion, and identity confirmation.[72]

The resolution to the ideal romance provides perfect triangular satisfaction: 'fatherly protection, motherly care, and passionate adult love'.[73]

The failed romance is unable to provide these satisfactions because on the one hand, it is too violent, and on the other, it concludes sadly, or with an unconvincing happy ending. This highlights in an unpleasurable way the two structuring anxieties of all romances. The first is the fear of male violence. In the ideal romance, this is contained by revealing it to be not the fearful thing it appears to be; either an illusion or benign. The second anxiety is the 'fear of an awakened female sexuality and its impact on men'.[74] In the failed romance, female sexuality is not confined to a permanent and loving relationship; nor is male violence convincingly brought under control. Together they find form and expression in the violent punishment inflicted on women who are seen as sexually promiscuous. In short, the failed romance is unable to produce a reading experience in which emotional fulfilment is satisfied through the vicarious sharing of the heroine's journey from a crisis of identity to an identity restored in the arms of a nurturing male. Whether a romance is good or bad is ultimately determined by the kind of relationship the reader can establish with the heroine.

> If the events of the heroine's story provoke too intense feelings such as anger at men, fear of rape and violence, worry about female sexuality, or worry about the need to live with an unexciting man, that romance will be discarded as a failure or judged to be very poor. If, on the other hand, those events call forth feelings of excitement, satisfaction, contentment, self-confidence, pride, and power, it matters less what events are used or how they are marshalled. In the end, what counts most is the reader's sense that for a short time she has become other and been elsewhere. She must close that book reassured that men and marriage really do mean good things for women. She must also turn back to her daily round of duties, emotionally reconstituted and replenished, feeling confident of her worth and convinced of her ability and power to deal with the problems she knows she must confront.[75]

Radway claims that by engaging in this process of popular discrimination, the Smithton women are taking emotional benefits for themselves, where other critics see only financial benefits for the publishing industry. The Smithton women 'partially reclaim the patriarchal form of the romance for their own use'.[76] The principal 'psychological benefits' derive from 'the ritualistic repetition of a single, immutable cultural myth'.[77] The fact that 60 per cent of the Smithton readers find it occasionally necessary to read the ending first, to ensure that the experience of the novel will not counteract the satisfactions of the underlying myth, suggests quite strongly that it is the underlying myth of the nurturing male that is ultimately of most importance in the Smithton women's experience of romance reading.

Following a series of comments from the Smithton women, Radway was forced to the conclusion that if she really wished to understand their view of romance reading she must relinquish her preoccupation with the text, and consider also the very *act* of romance reading itself. In conversations it became clear that when the women used the term 'escape' to describe the pleasure of romance reading, the term was operating in a double but related sense. As we have seen, it can be used to describe the process of identification between the reader and the heroine–hero relationship. But it became clear that the term was also used 'literally to describe the act of denying the present, which they believe they accomplish each time they begin to read a book and are drawn into its story'.[78] Dot revealed to Radway that men often found the very act of women reading threatening. It is seen as time reclaimed from the demands of family and domestic duties. Many of the Smithton women describe romance reading as 'a special gift' they give themselves. To explain this, Radway cites Chodorow's view of the patriarchal family as one in which 'There is a fundamental asymmetry in daily reproduction . . . men are socially and psychologically reproduced by women, but women are reproduced (or not) largely by themselves.'[79] Romance reading is therefore a small but not insignificant contribution to the emotional reproduction of the Smithton women: 'a temporary but literal denial of the demands women recognize as an integral part of their roles as nurturing wives and mothers'.[80] And, as Radway suggests, 'Although this experience is vicarious, the pleasure it induces is nonetheless real.'[81]

> I think it is logical to conclude that romance reading is valued by the Smithton women because the experience itself is *different* from ordinary existence. Not only is it a relaxing release from the tension produced by daily problems and responsibilities, but it creates a time or a space within which a woman can be entirely on her own, preoccupied with her personal needs, desires, and pleasure. It is also a means of transportation or escape to the exotic or, again, to that which is different.[82]

The conclusion *Reading the Romance* finally comes to is that it is at present very difficult to draw absolute conclusions about the cultural significance of romance reading. To focus on the act of reading or to focus on the narrative fantasy of the texts produces different, contradictory answers. The first suggests that 'romance reading is oppositional because it allows the women to refuse momentarily their self-abnegating social role.'[83] The second suggests that 'the romance's narrative structure embodies a simple

recapitulation and recommendation of patriarchy and its constitu-
ent social practices and ideologies.'[84] It is this difference, 'between
the meaning of the act and the meaning of the text as read',[85] that
must be brought into tight focus if we are to understand the full
meaning of romance reading.

On one thing Radway is clear: women do not read romances
out of a sense of contentment with patriarchy. Romance reading
contains an element of Utopian protest, a longing for a better
world. But against this, the narrative structure of the romance
appears to suggest that male violence and male indifference are
really expressions of love waiting to be decoded by the right
woman. This suggests that patriarchy is only a problem until
women learn how to read it properly. It is these complexities and
contradictions which Radway refuses to ignore or pretend to resolve. Her only certainty is that it is too soon to know if romance
reading can be cited simply as an ideological agent of the patriarchal social order:

> I feel compelled to point out . . . that neither this study nor any
> other to date provides enough evidence to corroborate this argu-
> ment fully. We simply do not know what practical effects the
> repetitive reading of romances has on the way women behave
> after they have closed their books and returned to their normal,
> ordinary round of daily activities.[86]

Therefore we must continue to acknowledge the activity of readers
– their selections, purchases, interpretations, appropriations, uses,
etc. – as an essential part of the cultural process and complex
practice of making meaning. By paying attention in this way we
increase the possibility of 'articulating the differences between the
repressive imposition of ideology and oppositional practices that,
though limited in their scope and effect, at least dispute or contest
the control of ideological forms'.[87] The ideological power of romances may be great, but where there is power there is always
resistance. The resistance may be confined to selective acts of consumption – dissatisfactions momentarily satisfied by the articulation of limited protest and Utopian longing – but as feminists

> . . . We should seek it out not only to understand its origins and
> its utopian longing but also to learn how best to encourage it and
> bring it to fruition. If we do not, we have already conceded the
> fight and, in the case of the romance at least, admitted the

impossibility of creating a world where the vicarious pleasure supplied by its reading would be unnecessary.[88]

Charlotte Brunsdon calls *Reading the Romance* 'the most extensive scholarly investigation of the act of reading', crediting Radway with having installed in the classroom 'the figure of the ordinary woman'.[89] In a generally sympathetic review of the British edition of *Reading the Romance,* Ien Ang makes a number of criticisms of Radway's approach. She is unhappy with the way in which Radway makes a clear distinction between feminism and romance reading: 'Radway, the researcher, is a feminist and not a romance fan, the Smithton women, the researched, are romance readers and not feminists.'[90] Ang sees this as producing a feminist politics of 'them' and 'us' in which non-feminist women play the role of an alien 'them' to be recruited to the cause. In her view, feminists should not set themselves up as guardians of the true path. This is what Radway does in her insistence, as Ang sees it, that ' "real" social change can only be brought about . . . if romance readers would stop reading romances and become feminist activists instead'.[91] As we shall see shortly, in my discussion of *Watching Dallas,* Ang does not believe that one (romance reading) excludes the other (feminism). Radway's 'vanguardist . . . feminist politics' leads only to 'a form of political moralism, propelled by a desire to make "them" more like "us" '.[92] What is missing from Radway's analysis, according to Ang, is a discussion of 'pleasure as pleasure'. Pleasure is discussed, but always in terms of its unreality – its vicariousness, its function as compensation, its falseness. Ang's complaint is that such an approach focuses too much on the effects, rather than the mechanisms of pleasure. Ultimately, for Radway, it always becomes a question of 'the ideological function of pleasure'.[93] Against this, Ang argues for seeing pleasure as something which can 'empower' women and not as something which always works 'against their own "real" interests'.[94]

Radway has reviewed this aspect of her work and concluded,

Although I tried very hard not to dismiss the activities of the Smithton women and made an effort to understand the act of romance reading as a positive response to the conditions of everyday life, my account unwittingly repeated the sexist assumption that has warranted a large portion of the commentary on romance. It was still motivated, that is, by the assumption that someone ought to worry responsibly about the effect of fantasy on women readers. . . . [Repeating] the familiar pattern whereby the commentator distances herself as knowing analyst from those who, engrossed and entranced by fantasy, cannot know. . . . Despite the fact that I wanted to claim the romance for feminism, this familiar opposition between blind fantasy and perspicacious knowing continued to operate within my account. Thus I would now link it [*Reading the Romance*], along with Tania Modleski's *Loving with a Vengeance*, with the first early efforts to understand the changing genre, a stage in the debate that was characterized most fundamentally, I believe, by suspicions about fantasy, daydream, and play.[95]

She cites with approval Alison Light's[96] point that feminist 'cultural politics must not become "a book-burning legislature", nor should feminists fall into the traps of moralism or dictatorship when discussing romances. "It is conceivable . . . that Barbara Cartland could turn you into a feminist.[97] Reading is never simply a linear con job but a . . . process which therefore remains dynamic and open to change." '[98]

## Ien Ang: *Watching Dallas*

*Watching Dallas* was originally published in the Netherlands in 1982. The version under discussion here is the revised edition translated into English in 1985. The context for Ang's study is the emergence of the American 'prime time soap' *Dallas* as an international success (watched in over ninety countries) in the early 1980s. In the Netherlands, *Dallas* was regularly watched by 52 per cent of the population. With its spectacular success, *Dallas* soon gathered around itself a whole discourse of activity – from extensive coverage in the popular press to souvenir hats reading 'I Hate JR'. It also attracted critics who, like Jack Lang, the French Minister of Culture, viewed it as the latest example of 'American cultural imperialism'.[99] Whether cause of pleasure or threat to 'national identity', *Dallas* made an enormous impact world-wide in the early 1980s. It is in this context that Ang placed the following advertisement in *Viva*, a Dutch women's magazine: 'I like watching the TV serial *Dallas*, but often get odd reactions to it. Would anyone like to write and tell me why you like watching it too, or dislike it? I should like to assimilate these reactions in my university thesis. Please write to . . .'[100]

Following the advertisement she received forty-two letters (thirty-nine from women or girls), from both lovers and haters of *Dallas*. These form the empirical basis of her study of the pleasure(s) of watching *Dallas* for its predominantly female audience. She is not concerned with pleasure understood as the satisfaction of an already pre-existent need, but 'the mechanisms by which pleasure is aroused'.[101] Ang writes as 'an intellectual and a feminist', but also as someone who has 'always particularly liked watching soap operas like *Dallas*'.[102] Again, we are a long way from the *view from above* which has so often characterized the relations between cultural theory and popular culture:

> The admission of the reality of this pleasure [her own] . . . formed the starting point for this study. I wanted in the first place to understand this pleasure, without having to pass judgment on whether *Dallas* is good or bad, from a political, social or aesthetic view. Quite the contrary; in my opinion it is important to emphasize how difficult it is to make such judgments – and hence to try to formulate the terms for a progressive cultural politics – when pleasure is at stake.[103]

Instead of the question: 'What are the effects of pleasure?' she poses the question: 'What is the mechanism of pleasure; how is it produced and how does it work?' For Ang's letter-writers the pleasures or displeasures of *Dallas* are inextricably linked with questions of 'realism'. The extent to which a letter-writer finds the programme 'good' or 'bad' is determined by whether they find it 'realistic' (good) or 'unrealistic' (bad). Critical of both 'empiricist realism' (a text is considered realistic to the extent to which it adequately reflects that which exists outside itself)[104] and 'classic realism' (Colin MacCabe's claim that realism is an illusion created by the extent to which a text can successfully conceal its constructedness),[105] she contends that *Dallas* is best understood as an example of what she calls 'emotional realism'. *Dallas* can be read on two levels: the level of denotation and the level of connotation. The level of denotation refers to the literal content of the programme, general storyline, character interactions, etc. The level of connotation(s) refers to the associations, implications, which resonate from the storyline and character interactions, etc. (see Chapter 4):

It is striking; the same things, people, relations and situations which are regarded at the denotative level as unrealistic, and unreal, are at the connotative level apparently not seen at all as unreal, but in fact as 'recognizable'. Clearly, in the connotative reading process the denotative level of the text is put in brackets.[106]

Viewing *Dallas*, like any other programme, is a selective process, reading across the text from denotation to connotation; weaving our sense of self in and out of the narrative. As one letter-writer says: 'Do you know why I like watching it? I think it's because those problems and intrigues, the big and little pleasures and troubles occur in our own lives too . . . . In real life I know a horror like JR, but he's just an ordinary builder.'[107] It is this ability to connect our own lives with the lives of a family of Texan millionaires which gives the programme its emotional realism. We may not be rich, but we have other fundamental things in common: relationships and broken relationships, happiness and sadness, illness and health. Those who find it realistic shift the focus of attention from the particularity of the narrative to the generality of its themes.

Ang uses the term a 'tragic structure of feeling'[108] to describe the way in which *Dallas* plays with the emotions in an endless musical chairs of happiness and misery. As one letter-writer told her: 'Sometimes I really enjoy having a good cry with them. And why not? In this way my other bottled up emotions find an outlet.'[109] Viewers who 'escape' in this way are not so much engaging in

a denial of reality as playing with it . . . [in a] game that enables one to place the limits of the fictional and the real under discussion, to make them fluid. And in that game an imaginary participation in the fictional world is experienced as pleasurable.[110]

Whatever else is involved, part of the pleasure(s) of *Dallas* is quite clearly connected to the amount of fluidity viewers are able or willing to establish between its fictional world and the world of their day-to-day existence. In order to activate Dallas's tragic structure of feeling the viewer must have the necessary cultural capital to occupy a 'reading formation'[111] informed by what she calls, following Peter Brooks,[112] the 'melodramatic imagination'. The melodramatic imagination is the articulation of a way of seeing that finds in ordinary day-to-day existence, with its pain and triumphs, its victories and defeats, a world as profoundly meaningful and significant as the world of classical tragedy. In a world cut loose from the certainties of religion, the melodramatic imagination offers a means of organizing reality into meaningful contrasts and conflicts. As a narrative form committed to melodrama's emphatic contrasts, conflicts and emotional excess, *Dallas* is well placed to give sustenance to, and make manifest, the melodramatic imagination. For those who see the world in this way (Ang claims that it demands a cultural competence most often shared by women),[113] 'the pleasure of *Dallas* . . . is not a *compensation* for the presumed drabness of daily life, nor a flight from it, but a *dimension* of it.'[114] The melodramatic imagination activates Dallas's tragic structure of feeling, which in turn produces the pleasure of emotional realism. However, because the melodramatic imagination is an effect of a specific reading formation, it follows that not all viewers of *Dallas* will activate the text in this way.

On the basis of the letters, Ang is able to separate the viewers into four reading positions: (i) those who hate the programme, (ii) ironical viewers, (iii) fans, and (iv) populists. The first three are reading positions made from within what she calls 'the ideology of mass culture'.[115] The ideology *articulates* (in the Gramscian sense discussed in Chapter 5) the view that popular culture is the product of capitalist commodity production and is therefore subject to the laws of the capitalist market economy; the result of which is the seemingly endless circulation of degraded commodities, whose only real significance is that they make a profit for their producers. She quite rightly sees this as a distorted and one-sided version of Marx's analysis of capitalist commodity production, in that it allows 'exchange value' to mask 'use value' completely (see Chapter 8). Against this, she insists, as would Marx, that it is not possible to read how a product might be consumed from the means by which it was produced. The ideology of mass culture, like any ideological discourse, works by interpellating individuals into specific subject positions (see discussion of Althusser in Chapter 5).

Those letter-writers who claim to hate *Dallas* draw most clearly on the ideology. They use it in two ways. First, to locate the programme negatively as an example of mass culture. Second, as a means to account for and support their dislike of the programme. As Ang puts it, 'their reasoning boils down to this: "*Dallas* is obviously bad because it's mass culture, and that's why I dislike it"'.[116] In this way, the ideology both comforts and reassures: 'it makes a search for more detailed and personal explanations super-fluous, because it provides a finished explanatory model that con-vinces, sounds logical and radiates legitimacy'.[117] This is not to say that it is wrong to dislike *Dallas*, only that professions of dislike are often made without thinking; in fact with a confidence born of uncritical thought.

It is possible to like *Dallas* and still subscribe to the ideology of mass culture. The contradiction is resolved by 'mockery and irony'.[118] *Dallas* is subjected to an ironizing and mocking commen-tary in which it 'is transformed from a seriously intended melo-drama to the reverse: a comedy to be laughed at. Ironizing viewers therefore do not take the text as it presents itself, but invert its preferred meaning through ironic commentary'.[119] In this con-struction the pleasure of *Dallas* derives from the fact that it is *bad* – pleasure and bad mass culture are reconciled in an instant. As one of the letter-writers puts it: 'Of course *Dallas* is mass culture and therefore bad, but precisely because I am so well aware of that I can really enjoy watching it and poke fun at it'.[120] For both the ironizing viewer and the hater of *Dallas*, the ideology of mass culture operates as a bedrock of common sense, making judgements obvious and self-evident. Although both operate within the normative standards of the ideology, the difference between them is marked by the question of pleasure. On the one hand, the ironizers can have plea-sure without guilt, in the sure and declared knowledge that they know mass culture is bad. On the other hand, the haters, although secure in the same knowledge, can, nevertheless, suffer 'a conflict of feelings if, *in spite of this*, they cannot escape its seduction'.[121]

Thirdly, there are the fans, those who love *Dallas*. For the viewers who occupy the previous two positions, to like *Dallas* with-out resort to irony is to be identified as someone duped by mass culture. As one letter-writer puts it: 'The aim is simply to rake in money, lots of money. And people try to do that by means of all these things – sex, beautiful people, wealth. And you always have people who fall for it.'[122] The claim is presented with all the confi-dence of having the full weight of the ideology's discursive sup-port. Ang analyzes the different strategies the fans of *Dallas* must use to deal consciously and unconsciously with such condescen-sion. The first strategy is to 'internalize' the ideology; to acknowl-edge the 'dangers' of *Dallas*, but to declare one's ability to deal with them in order to derive pleasure from the programme. It is a little like the heroin user in the early 1990s British drugs awareness campaign, who, against the warnings of impending addiction, declares: 'I can handle it.' A second strategy used by fans is to confront the ideology of mass culture as one letter-writer does: 'Many people find it worthless or without substance. But I think it does have substance.'[123] But, as Ang points out, the writer remains firmly within the discursive constraints of the ideology as she attempts to relocate *Dallas* in a different relationship from the binary oppositions – with substance/without substance, good/bad. 'This letter-writer "negotiates" as it were within the discursive space created by the ideology of mass culture, she does not situate herself outside it and does not speak from an opposing ideological position'.[124] A third strategy of defence deployed by fans against the normative standards of the ideology of mass culture is to use irony. These fans are different from Ang's second category of viewer, the ironist, in that the strategy involves the use of 'surface irony' to justify what is in all other respects a form of non-ironic pleasure. Irony is used to condemn the characters as 'horrible' people, while at the same time demonstrating an intimate knowledge of the programme and a great involvement in its narrative development and character interactions. The letter-writer who uses this strategy is caught between the dismissive power of the ideology and the pleasure she obviously derives from watching *Dallas*. Her letter seems to suggest that she adheres to the former when viewing with friends, and to the latter when viewing alone (and perhaps secretly when viewing with friends). As Ang explains: 'irony is here a defence mechanism with which this letter-writer tries to fulfil the social norms set by the ideology of mass culture, while secretly she "really" likes *Dallas*'.[125]

As Ang shows, the fans of *Dallas* find it necessary to locate their pleasure in relation to the ideology of mass culture; they 'internalize' the ideology; they 'negotiate' with the ideology; they use 'surface irony' to defend their pleasure against the withering dismissal of the ideology. What all these strategies of defence reveal is that 'there is no clear cut ideological alternative which can be employed against the ideology of mass culture – at least no alternative that offsets the latter in power of conviction and coherence.'[126] The struggle therefore, as so far described, between those who like *Dallas* and those who dislike it, is an unequal struggle between those who argue from within the discursive strength and security of the ideology of mass culture, and those who resist from within (for them) its inhospitable confines. 'In short, these fans do not seem to be able to take up an effective ideological position – an identity – from which they can say in a positive way and independently of the ideology of mass culture: "I like *Dallas* because . . .".'[127]

The final viewing position revealed in the letters, one that might help these fans, is a position informed by the ideology of populism. At the core of this ideology is the belief that one person's taste is of equal value to another person's taste. As one letter-writer puts it: 'I find the people who react oddly rather ludicrous – they can't do anything about someone's taste. And anyway they might find things pleasant that you just can't stand seeing or listening to'.[128] The ideology of populism insists that as taste is an autonomous category, continually open to individual inflection, it is absolutely meaningless to pass aesthetic judgements on other people's preferences. Given that this would seem to be an ideal discourse from which to defend one's pleasure in *Dallas*, why do so few of the letter-writers adopt it? Ang's answer is to point to the ideology's extremely limited vocabulary. After one has repeated 'there's no accounting for taste' a few times, the argument begins to appear somewhat bankrupt. Compared with this, the ideology of mass culture has an extensive and elaborate range of arguments and theories. Little wonder, then, that when invited to explain why they like or dislike *Dallas*, the letter-writers find it difficult to escape the normative discourse of the ideology of mass culture.

However, according to Ang, there are ways to escape: it is the very 'theoretical' nature of the discourse which restricts its influence 'to people's opinions and rational consciousness, to the discourse people use when *talking* about culture. These opinions and rationalizations need not, however, necessarily prescribe people's cultural *practices*.'[129] This would in part explain the contradictions experienced by some letter-writers: confronted by both 'the intellectual dominance of the ideology of mass culture and the "spontaneous", practical attraction of the populist ideology'.[130] The difficulty with adopting the populist ideology for a radical politics of popular culture is that it has already been appropriated by the culture industries for its own purposes of profit maximization. However, drawing on the work of Bourdieu, Ang argues that populism is related to the 'popular aesthetic', in which the moral categories of middle class taste are replaced by an emphasis on contingency, on pluralism, but above all, on pleasure (see Chapter 8). Pleasure, for Ang, is the key term in a transformed feminist cultural politics. Feminism must break with 'the paternalism of the ideology of mass culture . . . [in which w]omen are . . . seen as the passive victims of the deceptive messages of soap operas . . . [their] pleasure . . . totally disregarded'.[131] Even when pleasure is considered, it is there only to be condemned as an obstruction to the feminist goal of women's liberation. The question Ang poses is: Can pleasure through identification with the women of 'women's weepies' or the emotionally masochistic women of soap operas, 'have a meaning for women which is relatively independent of their political attitudes'?[132] Her answer is yes: fantasy and fiction do not

> function in place of, but beside, other dimensions of life (social practice, moral or political consciousness). It . . . is a source of pleasure because it puts 'reality' in parentheses, because it constructs imaginary solutions for real contradictions which in their fictional simplicity and their simple fictionality step outside the tedious complexity of the existing social relations of dominance and subordination.[133]

Of course this does not mean that significations of women do not matter. They can still be condemned for being reactionary in an ongoing cultural politics. But to experience pleasure from them is a completely different issue: 'it need not imply that we are also bound to take up these positions and solutions in our relations to our loved ones and friends, our work, our political ideals, and so on'.[134]

> Fiction and fantasy, then, function by making life in the present pleasurable, or at least livable, but this does not by any means exclude radical political activity or consciousness. It does not follow that feminists must not persevere in trying to produce new fantasies and fight for a place for them. . . . It does, however, mean that, where cultural consumption is concerned, no fixed standard exists for gauging the 'progressiveness' of a fantasy. The personal may be political, but the personal and the political do not always go hand in hand.[135]

In a somewhat hostile review of *Watching Dallas*, Dana Polan accuses Ang of simplifying questions of pleasure by not bringing into play psychoanalysis. He also claims that Ang's attack on the ideology of mass culture simply reverses the valuations implicit and explicit in the high culture/popular culture divide. Instead of the consumer of high culture imagining 'high taste as a kind of free expression of a full subjectivity always in danger of being debased by vulgar habits', Ang is accused of presenting 'the fan of mass culture as a free individual in danger of having his/her open access to immediate pleasure corrupted by artificial and snobbish values imposed from on high'.[136] Polan claims that Ang is attacking 'an antiquarian and anachronistic approach to mass culture'; and that she is out of touch with the new postmodern sensibility, still clinging, 'to mythic notions of culture as tragedy, culture as meaning'.[137] The idea that the ideology of mass culture is antiquated and anachronistic might be true in the fantasy realms of American academic psychoanalytic cultural criticism, but it is still very much alive in the conscious/unconscious world of everyday culture.

## Janice Winship: *Inside Women's Magazines*

In the Preface to *Inside Women's Magazines,* Janice Winship explains how she has been doing research on women's magazines since 1969. It was also around the same time that she began to regard herself as a feminist. Integrating the two, she admits, has sometimes proved difficult; often it was hinted that she should research 'something more important politically'.[138] But she insists that the two must be integrated: 'to simply dismiss women's magazines was also to dismiss the lives of millions of women who read and enjoyed them each week. More than that, I still enjoyed them, found them useful and escaped with them. And I knew I couldn't be the only feminist who was a "closet" reader.'[139] As Winship continues: this did not mean she was not (and still is) critical of women's magazines, but what is crucial to a feminist cultural politics is this dialectic of 'attraction and rejection'.[140]

> Many of the guises of femininity in women's magazines contribute to the secondary status from which we still desire to free ourselves. At the same time it is the dress of femininity which is both source of the pleasure of being a woman – and not a man – and in part the raw material for a feminist vision of the future. . . . Thus for feminists one important issue women's

magazines can raise is how *do* we take over their feminine ground
to create new untrammelled images of and for ourselves?[141]

Part of the aim of *Inside Women's Magazines* is, 'then, to explain the
appeal of the magazine formula and to critically consider its limitations and potential for change'.[142] Since their inception in the late
eighteenth century, women's magazines have offered their readers
a mixture of advice and entertainment. Regardless of politics,
women's magazines continue to operate as survival manuals, providing their readers with practical advice on how to survive in a
patriarchal culture. This might take the form of an explicit feminist politics, as in *Spare Rib*, for example; or stories of women
triumphing over adversity, as, for example, in *Woman's Own*. The
politics may be different, but the formula is much the same.

Women's magazines have always had two audiences: the
women who buy the magazines, and the advertisers who place their
advertisements in the magazines. Without the latter, most magazines would have to double their cover price. Often, then, a magazine will aim not so much at attracting a particular section of the
female population, as at attracting a particular segment of the
advertising market. Therefore, although it is true that readers attract advertising, it is also true that particular readers attract particular advertising and advertising revenue. For a magazine to
survive it has to ensure a complex combination of the right readership for the right advertising. This can mean identifying first the
source of advertising revenue and then shaping the magazine to
recruit the right readership for the advertisements. In this way the
pressures of the market can determine to a large extent not only
the range of magazines available, but also their actual contents.
This often leads to women being 'caught up in defining their own
femininity, inextricably, through consumption'.[143]

Women's magazines appeal to their readers by means of a
combination of entertainment and useful advice. This appeal,
according to Winship, is organized around a range of 'fictions'.
These can be the visual fictions of advertisements, or items on
fashion, cookery or family and home. They can also be actual
fictions: romantic serials, five-minute stories, for example. There
are also the stories of the famous and reports of events in the lives
of 'ordinary' women and men. Each in its different way attempts to
draw the reader into the world of the magazine, and ultimately
into a world of consumption. But pleasure is not totally dependent

on purchase. Winship recalls how in the hot July in which she wrote the book, without any intention of buying the product, she gained enormous visual pleasure from a magazine advertisement showing a woman diving into an ocean surrealistically continuous with the tap-end of a bath.

> We recognise and relish the vocabulary of dreams in which ads deal; we become involved in the fictions they create; but we know full well that those commodities will not elicit the promised fictions. It doesn't matter. Without bothering to buy the product we can vicariously indulge in the good life through the image alone. This is the compensation for the experience you do not and cannot have.[144]

Magazine advertisements, like the magazines themselves, therefore provide a terrain on which to dream. In this way, they generate a desire for fulfilment (through consumption). Paradoxically, this is deeply pleasurable *because* it also always acknowledges the existence of the labours of the everyday:

> They would not offer quite the same pleasure, however, if it were not expected of women that they perform the various labours around fashion and beauty, food and furnishing. These visuals acknowledge those labours while simultaneously enabling the reader to avoid doing them. In everyday life 'pleasure' for women can only be achieved by accomplishing these tasks; here the image offers a temporary substitute, as well as providing an (allegedly) easy, often enjoyable pathway to their accomplishment.[145]

Desire is generated for something more than the everyday, yet it can only be accomplished by what is for most women an everyday activity – shopping. What is ultimately being sold in the fictions of women's magazines, in editorials or advertisements, fashion and home furnishing items, cookery and cosmetics, is successful and therefore *pleasurable* femininity. Follow *this* practical advice or buy *this* product and be a better lover, a better mother, a better wife, a better woman. The problem with all this from a feminist perspective is that it is always constructed around a mythical individual woman, existing outside powerful social and cultural structures and constraints.

Women's magazines also construct 'fictional collectivities'[146] of women. This can be seen in the insistent 'we' of editorials; but it is also there in the reader–editor interactions of the letters page.

Here we often find women making sense of the everyday world through a mixture of optimism and fatalism. Winship identifies this tension as an expression of women being 'ideologically bound to the personal terrain and in a position of relative powerlessness about public events'.[147] Like the so-called 'triumph over tragedy' stories, the readers' letters and editorial responses often reveal a profound commitment to the 'individual solution'. Both 'teach' the same parable: individual effort will overcome all odds. The reader is interpellated as admiring subject (see discussion of Althusser in Chapter 5), her own problems put in context; able to carry on. Short stories work in much the same way. What links these different 'fictions' is 'that the human triumphs they detail are emotional and not material ones'.[148] In many ways this is essential for the continued existence of the magazines' imagined communities; for to move from the emotional to the material is to run the risk of encountering the divisive presence of class and race:

> Thus the 'we women' feeling magazines construct is actually comprised of different cultural groups; the very notion of 'we' and 'our world', however, constantly undercuts those divisions to give the semblance of a unity – inside magazines. Outside, when the reader closes her magazine, she is no longer 'friends' with Esther Rantzen and her ilk; but while it lasted it has been a pleasant and reassuring dream.[149]

This is perhaps even more evident on the problem page. Although the problems are personal, and therefore seek personal solutions, Winship argues that 'unless women have access to knowledge which explains personal lives in social terms . . . the onus on "you" to solve "your" problem is likely to be intimidating or . . . only lead to frustrated "solutions".'[150] She gives the example of a letter about a husband (with a sexual past) who cannot forget or forgive his wife's sexual past. As Winship points out, a personal solution to this problem cannot begin to tackle the social and cultural heritage of the sexual double standard. To pretend otherwise is to mislead:

> Agony aunties (and magazines) act as 'friends' to women – they bring women together in their pages and yet by not providing the knowledge to allow women to see the history of their common social condition, sadly and ironically, they come between women, expecting, and encouraging, them to do alone what they can only do together.[151]

At the centre of Winship's book are three chapters, which in turn discuss, the individual and family values of *Woman's Own*, the (hetero)sexual liberation ideology of *Cosmopolitan* and the feminist politics of *Spare Rib*. I have space only to make one point with reference to these chapters. Discussing *Spare Rib*'s reviews of popular film and television, Winship responds with comments which echo through much recent 'post-feminist' analysis (and much of the work discussed in this chapter) on popular culture:

> These reviews . . . bolster the reviewer's position and raise feminism and feminists to the lofty pedestal of 'having seen the light', with the consequent dismissal not only of a whole range of cultural events but also of many women's pleasurable and interested experiences of them. Whether intentionally or not, feminists are setting themselves distinctly apart: 'us' who know and reject most popular cultural forms (including women's magazines); 'them' who remain in ignorance and continue to buy *Woman's Own* or watch *Dallas*. The irony, however, is that many of 'us' feel like 'them': closet readers and viewers of this fare.[152]

Winship's comments bring us to the complex question of postfeminism. Does the term imply that the moment of feminism has been and gone; that it is now a movement of the past? Certainly, there are those who would wish to suggest that this is the case. According to Winship, 'if it means anything useful', the term refers to the way in which the 'boundaries between feminists and non-feminists have become fuzzy'.[153] This is to a large extent due to the way in which 'with the "success" of feminism some feminist ideas no longer have an oppositional charge but have become part of many people's, not just a minority's, common sense'.[154] Of course this does not mean that all feminist demands have been met (far from it), and that feminism is now redundant. On the contrary, 'it suggests that feminism no longer has a simple coherence around a set of easily defined principles . . . but instead is a much richer, more diverse and contradictory mix than it ever was in the 1970s.'[155]

## The other gender: men's studies and masculinity

Feminism has brought into being many things. But one which some feminists have already disowned is men's studies. Despite

Peter Schwenger's concern that for a man 'to think about masculinity is to become less masculine oneself. . . . The real man thinks about practical matters rather than abstract ones and certainly does not brood upon himself or the nature of his sexuality',[156] many men have thought, spoken and written about masculinity. As Antony Easthope writes in *What a Man's Gotta Do*, 'It is time to try to speak about masculinity, about what it is and how it works.'[157] He analyzes the way masculinity is represented across a range of popular cultural texts: pop songs, popular fiction, films, television and newspapers, and concludes:

> Clearly men do not passively live out the masculine myth imposed by the stories and images of the dominant culture. But neither can they live completely outside the myth, since it pervades the culture. Its coercive power is active everywhere – not just on screens, hoardings and paper, but inside our own heads.[158]

Whilst feminists have always encouraged men to examine their masculinity, many feminists are less than impressed with men's studies. Joyce Canaan and Christine Griffin declare:

> While feminist understandings of patriarchy would undoubtedly be wider if we had access to men's understandings of how they construct and transform this pervasive system of relationships, we nevertheless fear that such research might distort, belittle, or deny women's experiences with men and masculinity. Feminists therefore must be even more insistent about conducting research on men and masculinity at a time when a growing number of men are beginning to conduct apparently 'comparable' research.[159]

## Feminism as reading

Feminism, like Marxism (discussed in Chapter 5), is always more than a body of academic texts and practices. It is also, and perhaps more fundamentally so, a political movement concerned with women's oppression and the ways and means to empower women – what the African-American critic bell hooks describes as 'finding a voice':

> As a metaphor for self-transformation . . . ['finding a voice'] . . . has been especially relevant for groups of women who have previously never had a public voice, women who are speaking and

writing for the first time, including many women of color. Feminist focus on finding a voice may sound cliched at times. . . . However, for women within oppressed groups . . . coming to voice is an act of resistance. Speaking becomes both a way to engage in active self-transformation and a rite of passage where one moves from being object to being subject. Only as subjects can we speak.[160]

Feminism is not, as Eagleton says of Marxism (see Chapter 5), just another way of reading texts. Nevertheless, it has proved an incredibly productive way of reading:

There is an optical illusion which can be seen as either a goblet or two profiles. The images oscillate in their tension before us, one alternately superseding the other and reducing it to meaningless background. In the purest feminist literary theory we are similarly presented with a radical alteration of our vision, a demand that we see meaning in what has previously been empty space. The orthodox plot recedes, and another plot, hitherto submerged in the anonymity of the background, stands out in bold relief like a thumb print.[161]

What Showalter claims for feminist literary criticism can equally be claimed for feminist work on popular culture.

## Further reading

Ien Ang, *Living Room Wars: Rethinking media audiences for a postmodern world*, London: Routledge, 1995. An excellent collection of essays from one of the leading intellectuals in the field.

Michèle Barrett, *Women's Oppression Today: Problems in Marxist feminist analysis*, London: Verso, 1980. The book is of general interest to the student of popular culture in its attempt to synthesize Marxist and feminist modes of analysis; of particular interest is Chapter 3, 'Ideology and the cultural production of gender'.

Rosalind Brunt and Caroline Rowan (eds), *Feminism, Culture and Politics*, London: Lawrence & Wishart, 1982. A collection of essays illustrative of feminist modes of analysis. See especially: Michèle Barrett, 'Feminism and the definition of cultural politics'.

Antony Easthope, *What a Man's Gotta Do: The masculine myth in popular culture*, London: Paladin, 1986. A useful and entertaining account of the ways in which masculinity is represented in contemporary popular culture.

Sarah Franklin, Celia Lury and Jackie Stacey (eds), *Off Centre: Feminism and cultural studies*, London: HarperCollins, 1991. An excellent collection of feminist work in cultural studies.

Christine Geraghty, *Women and Soap Opera: A study of prime time soaps*, Cambridge: Polity Press, 1991. A comprehensive introduction to feminist analysis of soap operas.

Susan Jeffords, *The Remasculinization of America: Gender and the Vietnam War*, Bloomington and Indianapolis: Indiana University Press, 1989. The book explores representations of masculinity across a range of popular texts to argue that following the crisis of defeat in Vietnam strenuous attempts have been made to remasculinize American culture.

Angela McRobbie, *Feminism and Youth Culture*, London: Macmillan, 1991. A selection from the work of one of the leading figures in feminist analysis of popular culture.

Deidre E. Pribram (ed.), *Female Spectators: Looking at film and television*, London: Verso, 1988. A useful collection of essays looking at different aspects of filmic and televisual popular culture.

Sue Thornham, *Feminism and Film Theory*, London: Edward Arnold, 1997. An excellent introduction to the contribution of feminism to the study of film.

Susan Willis, *A Primer for Daily Life*, London: Routledge, 1991. An interesting investigation of the cultural landscape of everyday life.

# 7

# POSTMODERNISM

## The postmodern condition

Postmodernism is a term current inside and outside the academic study of popular culture. It has entered discourses as diverse as pop music journalism and Marxist debates on the cultural conditions of late or multinational capitalism. As a concept it shows little sign of slowing down its colonial proliferation. Here is Dick Hebdige's 1988 list of the ways in which the term is being used.

> When it becomes possible for people to describe as 'postmodern' the decor of a room, the design of a building, the diegesis of a film, the construction of a record, or a 'scratch' video, a television commercial, or an arts documentary, or the 'intertextual' relations between them, the layout of a page in a fashion magazine or critical journal, an anti-teleological tendency within epistemology, the attack on the 'metaphysics of presence', a general attenuation of feeling, the collective chagrin and morbid projections of a post-War generation of baby boomers confronting disillusioned middle age, the 'predicament' of reflexivity, a group of rhetorical tropes, a proliferation of surfaces, a new phase in commodity fetishism, a fascination for images, codes and styles, a process of cultural, political, or existential fragmentation and/or crisis, the 'de-centring' of the subject, an 'incredulity towards metanarratives', the replacement of unitary power axes by a plurality of power/discourse formations, the 'implosion of meaning', the collapse of cultural hierarchies, the dread engendered by the threat of nuclear self-destruction, the decline of the university, the functioning and effects of the new miniaturised technologies, broad societal and economic shifts into a 'media', 'consumer' or 'multinational' phase, a sense (depending on who you read) of 'placelessness' or the abandonment of placelessness ('critical regionalism') or

(even) a generalised substitution of spatial for temporal coordinates: when it becomes possible to describe all these things as 'postmodern' (or more simply, using a current abbreviation, as 'post' or 'very post') then it's clear we are in the presence of a buzzword.[1]

For the purposes of this discussion I will consider postmodernism only as it relates to the study of popular culture. To facilitate this I will focus on the development of postmodern theory from its beginnings in the United States and Britain in the 1950s and 1960s, through its theorization in the work of Jean-François Lyotard, Jean Baudrillard and Fredric Jameson. This will be followed by a discussion of two examples of postmodern culture: pop music and television.

## Postmodernism in the 1960s

Although the term postmodern had been in cultural circulation since the 1870s,[2] it is only in the late 1950s and early 1960s that we see the beginnings of what is now understood as postmodernism. In the work of Susan Sontag and Leslie Fiedler[3] we encounter the celebration of what Sontag calls a 'new sensibility'[4] – a sensibility which had broken 'with the Matthew Arnold notion of culture, finding it historically and humanly obsolescent':[5]

> One important consequence of the new sensibility (with its abandonment of the Matthew Arnold idea of culture) [is] that the distinction between 'high' and 'low' culture seems less and less meaningful.[6]

It is also a sensibility in revolt against the cultural élitism of modernism. This is a sensibility in which, say, a painting by Robert Rauschenberg might be discussed in the same way as a song by the Supremes.[7] Paradoxically, it is also a sensibility in revolt against the canonization of modernism's avant-garde revolution; it attacks modernism's official status, its canonization in the museum and the academy, as the high culture of the modern capitalist world. It laments the passing of the scandalous and bohemian power of modernism, its ability to shock and disgust the middle class. Instead of outraging from the critical margins of bourgeois society, the work of Pablo Picasso, James Joyce, T. S. Eliot, Bertolt Brecht,

Igor Stravinsky and others has not only lost the ability to shock and disturb, it has become central, classical: in a word – canonized. Modernist culture has become bourgeois culture. Its subversive power has been drained by the academy and the museum. It is now the canon against which an avant-garde must struggle. As Fredric Jameson points out,

> This is surely one of the most plausible explanations for the emergence of postmodernism itself, since the younger generation of the 1960s will now confront the formerly oppositional modern movement as a set of dead classics, which 'weigh like a nightmare on the brains of the living', as Marx once said in a different context.[8]

Jameson argues that postmodernism was born out of

> the shift from an oppositional to a hegemonic position of the classics of modernism, the latter's conquest of the university, the museum, the art gallery network and the foundations, the assimilation . . . of the various high modernisms, into the 'canon' and the subsequent attenuation of everything in them felt by our grandparents to be shocking, scandalous, ugly, dissonant, immoral and antisocial.[9]

One response to modernism's incorporation was a re-evaluation of popular culture. Modernism, despite its often quoting of popular culture, is marked by a deep suspicion of all things popular. Its entry into the museum and the academy was undoubtedly made easier (despite its declared antagonism to bourgeois philistinism) by its appeal to, and homologous relationship with, the élitism of class society. The postmodernism of the 1960s was therefore in part a populist attack on the élitism of modernism. It signalled a refusal of what Andreas Huyssen calls 'the great divide . . . [a] discourse which insists on the categorical distinction between high art and mass culture'.[10] Moreover, according to Huyssen, 'To a large extent, it is by the distance we have travelled from this "great divide" between mass culture and modernism that we can measure our own cultural postmodernity'.[11] Nevertheless, in much of the theory which follows, postmodernism signifies a culture of kitsch, when measured against the 'real' culture of modernism.

Hal Foster distinguishes between 'a postmodernism which seeks to deconstruct modernism and resist the status quo and a postmodernism which repudiates the former to celebrate the latter: a postmodernism of resistance and a postmodernism of reaction'.[12] He adds that the postmodernism of resistance not only attacks modernism, but also reactionary postmodernism. Together with the positive cultural discourse of Fiedler, Sontag and Ihab Hassan, there was the negative cultural discourse of George Steiner, Irving Howe, Harry Levin and Daniel Bell. Western societies and cultures were seen to be in decline, and part of the problem was the combative nature of contemporary popular culture.

> Both the positive and negative theorists were responding to developments in contemporary capitalism – though rarely conceptualizing them as such – which was going through an expansionist cycle and producing new commodities, abundance, and a more affluent lifestyle. Its advertising, credit plans, media, and commodity spectacles were encouraging gratification, hedonism, and the adoption of new habits, cultural forms, and lifestyles which would later be termed postmodern. Some theorists were celebrating the new diversity and affluence, while others were criticizing the decay of traditional values or increased powers of social control. . . . Thus, by the 1980s, the postmodern discourses were split into cultural conservatives decrying the new developments and avant-gardists celebrating them.[13]

The American and British pop art of the 1950s and the 1960s also rejected the distinction between popular and high culture. It rejected Arnold's definition of culture as 'the best that has been thought and said'; preferring instead Williams's anthropological definition of culture as 'a whole way of life'. The term pop art was first coined by the British artist Richard Hamilton in the 1950s.[14] Pop art was then developed by the Independent Group of artists and critics who met at the London Institute of Contemporary Arts in the 1950s. It was a movement which dreamed of America from the grey deprivation of 1950s Britain.[15] Lawrence Alloway was the movement's first theorist:

> The area of contact was mass produced urban culture: movies, advertising, science fiction, pop music. We felt none of the dislike of commercial culture standard among most intellectuals, but accepted it as a fact, discussed it in detail, and consumed it enthusiastically. One result of our discussions was to take Pop culture out of the realm of 'escapism', 'sheer entertainment', 'relaxation', and to treat it with the seriousness of art.[16]

Andy Warhol was a key figure in the theorizing of American pop art. He refused the distinction between commercial and non-commercial art. He saw 'commercial art as real art and real art as commercial art'[17] and claimed that

> 'real' art is defined simply by the taste (and wealth) of the ruling class of the period. This implies not only that commercial art is just as good as 'real' art its value simply being defined by other social groups, other patterns of expenditure.[18]

We can of course object that Warhol's merging of high and popular culture is a little misleading. Whatever the source of his ideas and material, once located in an art gallery the context determines them as art and thus high culture. John Rockwell argues that this was not the intention or the necessary outcome. Art, he argues, is what you perceive as art:

> A Brillo box isn't suddenly art because Warhol puts a stacked bunch of them in a museum. But by putting them there he encourages you to make your every trip to the supermarket an artistic adventure, and in so doing he has exalted your life. Everybody's an artist if they want to be.[19]

Huyssen claims that the full impact of the relationship between pop art and popular culture can only be fully understood when located within the larger cultural context of the American counterculture and the British underground scene:

> Pop in the broadest sense was the context in which a notion of the postmodern first took shape, and from the beginning until today, the most significant trends within postmodernism have challenged modernism's relentless hostility to mass culture.[20]

Postmodernism was thus born out of a generational refusal of the categorical certainties of high modernism. The insistence on an absolute distinction between high and popular culture came to be regarded as the 'un-hip' assumption of an older generation. One sign of this collapse was the merging of art and pop music. For example, Peter Blake designed the Beatles' *Sergeant Pepper's Lonely Hearts Club Band* album; Richard Hamilton designed their 'white album'; Andy Warhol designed the Rolling Stones' album, *Sticky Fingers*.

Huyssen sees a clear relationship between the American postmodernism of the 1960s and certain aspects of an earlier European avant-garde; seeing the American counterculture – its opposition to the war in Vietnam, its support for black civil rights, its rejection of the élitism of high modernism, its birthing of the second wave of feminism, its cultural experimentalism, its alternative theatre, its happenings, its love-ins, its celebration of the everyday, its psychedelic art, its acid rock, its 'acid perspectivism' (Hebdige) – 'as the closing chapter in the tradition of avantgardism'.[21] That is, 'an American avantgarde and the endgame of international avantgardism'.[22]

By the late 1970s the debate about postmodernism crossed the Atlantic. The next three sections will consider the responses of two French cultural theorists to the debate on the 'new sensibility', before returning to America and Fredric Jameson's account of postmodernism as the cultural dominant of late capitalism.

## Jean-François Lyotard

Jean-François Lyotard's principal contribution to the debate on postmodernism is *The Postmodern Condition*, published in France in 1979, translated into English in 1984. The influence of this book on the debate has been enormous. In many respects it was this book which introduced the term postmodernism into 'general' circulation.

For Lyotard the postmodern condition is marked by a crisis in the status of knowledge in Western societies. This is expressed as 'incredulity towards metanarratives' and 'the obsolescence of the metanarrative apparatus of legitimation'.[23] This refers to the supposed contemporary rejection of all overarching and totalizing thought: Marxism, liberalism, Christianity, for example, that tell universalist stories (metanarratives), which organize and justify the everyday practices of a plurality of different stories (narratives). According to Lyotard, metanarratives operate through inclusion and exclusion, as homogenizing forces, marshalling heterogeneity into ordered realms; silencing and excluding other discourses, other voices in the name of universal principles and general goals. Postmodernism is said to signal the collapse of all universalist metanarratives with their privileged truth to tell, and to witness instead the increasing sound of a plurality of voices from the margins, with their insistence on difference, on cultural diversity, and the claims of heterogeneity over homogeneity.

**174**

Lyotard's particular focus is the function 'of narrative within scientific discourse and knowledge. His interest is not so much in scientific knowledge and procedures as such, as in the forms by which such knowledge and procedures gain or claim legitimacy.'[24] Science is important for Lyotard because of the role assigned to it by the Enlightenment. Its task, through the accumulation of scientific knowledge, is to play a central role in the gradual emancipation of humankind. In this way, science assumes the status of a metanarrative, organizing and validating other narratives on the royal road to human liberation. However, since the Second World War, Lyotard claims, the legitimizing force of science's status as metanarrative has waned considerably; there has occurred, as we have already noted, what he calls an 'incredulity towards metanarratives'. Science is no longer seen to be slowly making progress on behalf of humankind towards absolute knowledge and absolute freedom. It has lost its way – its 'goal is no longer truth, but performativity'.[25] Similarly, higher education is 'called upon to create skills, and no longer ideals'.[26] Knowledge is no longer seen as an end in itself, but as a means to an end. Like science, education will be judged by its performativity. More and more will it be shaped to the demands of power. No longer will it respond to the question, 'Is it true?', it will hear only, 'What use is it?', 'How much is it worth?' and 'Is it saleable?'[27] (Postmodern pedagogy would teach how to use knowledge as a form of cultural capital without recourse to concern or anxiety about whether what is taught is true or false.)[28] This has produced a situation in which

> scientists no longer look to prescriptive philosophies of science to warrant their procedures of inquiry. Rather, they themselves problematize, modify, and warrant the constitutive norms of their practice even as they engage in it. Instead of hovering above, legitimation descends to the level of practice and becomes immanent in it. There are no special tribunals set apart from the sites where inquiry is practised. Rather, practitioners assume responsibility for legitimizing their own practice.[29]

In other words, and simplifying somewhat, science has become less philosophical and more pragmatic. If we shift this argument from science to the study of popular culture, it should be clear that such a change in perspective can only assist popular culture studies, in that it should remove the overarching metanarrative of the categorical distinction between high and popular culture which

**175**

continually calls into question the point and purpose of studying popular culture in the first place. This is the end of the Arnoldian metanarrative, with its privileged binary opposition – high culture ('culture') and popular culture ('anarchy').

Before leaving Lyotard, it is worth noting his own less than favourable response to this collapse. The popular culture ('contemporary general culture') of the postmodern condition is for Lyotard an 'anything goes' culture, a culture of 'slackening', where taste is irrelevant, and money the only sign of value.[30] The only relief is Lyotard's view that postmodernist culture is not the end of the much superior culture of modernism, but the sign of the advent of a new modernism. Postmodernism is that which breaks with one modernism to form a new modernism: 'A work can become modern only if it is first postmodern. Postmodernism thus understood is not modernism at its end but in the nascent state, and this state is constant.'[31]

Steven Connor suggests that *The Postmodern Condition* may be read 'as a disguised allegory of the condition of academic knowledge and institutions in the contemporary world'. Lyotard's 'diagnosis of the postmodern condition is, in one sense, the diagnosis of the final futility of the intellectual'. Lyotard is himself aware of what he calls the contemporary intellectual's 'negative heroism'. Intellectuals have, he argues, been losing their authority since 'the violence and critique mounted against the academy during the sixties'.[32] Michel Foucault's distinction between the 'specific intellectual' and the 'universal intellectual' is useful here.[33] The specific intellectual is the postmodern intellectual; the universal intellectual is the man (they are mostly men) who speaks for all, with the confidence of knowing that he stands at the shoreline of history watching the waves break upon the beach. Postmodernism suggests instead a micropolitics, a politics of the particular, a politics of difference. For universal intellectuals, with an insistence on the primacy of macropolitics, this is not, as Iain Chambers points out, a welcomed prospect:

> the debate over postmodernism can . . . be read as the symptom of the disruptive ingression of popular culture, its aesthetics and intimate possibilities, into a previously privileged domain. Theory and academic discourses are confronted by the wider, unsystemized, popular networks of cultural production and knowledge. The intellectual's privilege to explain and distribute knowledge is threatened; his authority, for it is invariably 'his',

redimensionalized. This in part explains both the recent defensiveness of the modernist, particularly Marxist, project, and the cold nihilism of certain notorious strands in postmodernism.[34]

Postmodernism has enfranchised a new body of intellectuals; voices from the margins speaking from positions of difference: ethnic, gender, class, sexual preference – those whom Angela McRobbie refers to as 'the new generation of intellectuals' (often black, female or working class).[35] As Kobena Mercer points out,

> While the loudest voices in the culture announced nothing less than the end of everything of any value, the emerging voices, practices and identities of dispersed African, Caribbean and Asian peoples crept in from the margins of postimperial Britain to dislocate commonplace certainties and consensual 'truths' and thus open up new ways of seeing, and understanding, the peculiarities of living in the twilight of an historic interregnum in which 'the old is dying and the new cannot be born' (Gramsci).[36]

## Jean Baudrillard

Jean Baudrillard, according to Steven Best and Douglas Kellner, 'has achieved guru status throughout the English speaking world'.[37] They claim that 'Baudrillard has emerged as one of the most high profile postmodern theorists'.[38] His presence has not been confined to the world of academia; articles and interviews have appeared in many popular magazines.

Baudrillard claims that we have reached a stage in social and economic development in which 'it is no longer possible to separate the economic or productive realm from the realms of ideology or culture, since cultural artifacts, images, representations, even feelings and psychic structures have become part of the world of the economic'.[39] This is partly explained, he claims, by the fact that there has been a historical shift in the West, from a society based on the production of things to one based on the production of information. In *For a Critique of the Political Economy of the Sign*, he describes this as 'the passage from a metallurgic into a semiurgic society'.[40] However, for Baudrillard, postmodernism is not simply a culture of the sign, rather it is a culture of the 'simulacrum'.

A simulacrum is an identical copy without an original. In Chapter 5, we examined Benjamin's claim that mechanical reproduction had destroyed the 'aura' of the work of art; Baudrillard argues that the very distinction between original and copy has itself now been destroyed. He calls this process 'simulation'. So, for example, although one can see copies of, say, the 'Mona Lisa' in different forms and in different places, to see the original painting one must go to Paris. However, when someone buys a copy of Steve Earle's single 'Johnny Too Bad', it makes little sense to speak of having purchased the original. In the same way, it would make no sense for someone having seen *Dead Man Walking* in Newcastle to be told by someone having seen the film in Nashville or Sydney that he had seen the original and she had not. Both would have witnessed an exhibition of a copy without an original. In both cases, film and record, we see or hear a copy without an original. Similarly, a film is a construction made from editing together film footage shot in a different sequence and at different times. In the same way, a recording is a construction made from editing together sounds recorded in a different sequence and at different times. Neither is a copy of an original continuous performance.

Baudrillard calls simulation 'the generation by models of a real without origins or reality: a hyperreal'.[41] Hyperrealism is the characteristic mode of postmodernity. In the realm of the hyperreal, the distinction between simulation and the 'real' implodes; the 'real' and the imaginary continually collapse into each other. The result is that reality and simulation are experienced as without difference – operating along a roller-coaster continuum. Simulations can often be experienced as more real than the real itself – 'even better than the real thing' (U2). Think of the way in which *Apocalypse Now* has become the mark against which to judge the realism of representations of America's war in Vietnam. 'Does it have the "look" of *Apocalypse Now?*' is virtually the same as asking 'is it realistic?'.

The evidence for hyperrealism is said to be everywhere. For example, we live in a society in which people write letters addressed to characters in soap operas, making them offers of marriage, sympathizing with their current difficulties, offering them new accommodation, or just writing to ask how they are coping with life. Television villains are regularly confronted in the street and warned about the possible future consequences of not altering their behaviour. Television doctors, television lawyers and television detectives regularly receive requests for advice and help. I saw an

American tourist on television enthusing about the beauty of the English Lake District. Searching for suitable words of praise, he said, 'It's just like Disneyland'. The Northumbria Police Force have introduced 'cardboard police cars' in an attempt to keep motorists within the law. I recently visited an Italian restaurant in Morpeth, Northumberland, in which a painting of Marlon Brando as the 'Godfather' is exhibited as a mark of the restaurant's genuine Italianicity. The riots, following the acquittal of the four Los Angeles police officers captured on video physically assaulting the black motorist Rodney King, were headlined in two British newspapers as 'LA Lawless', and in another as 'LA War' – the story anchored not by a historical reference to similar demonstrations in Watts, Los Angeles in 1965, or to the implications of the words – 'No justice no peace' – chanted by demonstrators during the riots; the editors chose instead to locate the story within the fictional world of the American television series *LA Law*. Baudrillard calls this 'the dissolution of TV into life, the dissolution of life into TV'.[42] Politicians increasingly play on this, relying on the conviction politics of the 'photo-opportunity' to win the hearts and minds of voters.

In New York in the mid-1980s the City Arts Workshop and Adopt a Building commissioned artists to paint murals on a block of abandoned buildings. After consultations with local residents it was agreed to depict images of what the community lacked: grocery store, newsstand, laundromat and record shop.[43] What the story demonstrates is something similar to the Northumbria Police story – the substitution of an image for the real thing; instead of police cars, the illusion of police cars; instead of enterprise, the illusion of enterprise. Simon Frith and Howard Horne's rather patronizing account of working class youth out on the weekend illustrates much the same point:

> What made it all real for them: the TAN. The tan courtesy of the sun bed. No one here had been on a winter break (this is the Tebbit generation); they'd bought their look across the counter of the hairdresser, the beauty parlour and the keep fit centre. And so every weekend they gather in dreary, drizzly York and Birmingham and Crewe and act not as if they were on holiday but as if they were in an advertisement for holidays. Shivering. A simulation, but for real.[44]

John Fiske claims that the postmodern media no longer provide 'secondary representations of reality; they affect and produce the reality that they mediate'.[45] He is aware that to make an event a media event is not simply in the gift of the media. For something to become a media event it must successfully articulate (in the Gramscian sense discussed in Chapter 5) the concerns of both public and media. The relationship between media and public is complex, but what is certain in our postmodern world is that all events that 'matter' are media events. He cites the example of the arrest of O. J. Simpson:

> Local people watching the chase on TV went to O. J.'s house to be there at the showdown, but took their portable TVs, with them in the knowledge that the live event was not a substitute for the mediated one but a complement to it. On seeing themselves on their own TVs, they waved to themselves, for postmodern people have no problem in being simultaneously and indistinguishably livepeople and mediapeople.

These people knew implicitly that the media do not simply report or circulate the news, they produce it. In order to be part of the news of O. J. Simpson's arrest it was not enough to be there, one had to be there on television. In the hyperreal world of the postmodern there is no longer a clear distinction between a 'real' event and its media representation. O. J. Simpson's trial cannot be neatly separated into a 'real' event that television then represented as media event. Anyone who watched the proceedings unfold on TV knows that the trial was conducted for the television audience at least as much as for those present in the court. Without the presence of the cameras this would have been a very different event indeed.[46]

Baudrillard's own example of hyperrealism is Disneyland: he calls it 'a perfect model of all the entangled orders of simulation'.[47] He claims that the success of Disneyland is not due to its ability to allow Americans a fantasy escape from reality, but because it allows them an unacknowledged concentrated experience of 'real' America:

> Disneyland is there to conceal the fact that it is the 'real' country, all of 'real' America, which *is* Disneyland (just as prisons are there to conceal the fact that it is the society in its entirety, in its banal omnipresence, which is carceral). Disneyland is presented as imaginary in order to make us believe that the rest is real, when in fact all of Los Angeles and the America surrounding it are no longer real, but of the order of the hyperreal and of

simulation. It is no longer a question of a false representation of reality (ideology), but of concealing the fact that the real is no longer real.[48]

He explains this in terms of Disneyland's social 'function': 'It is meant to be an infantile world, in order to make us believe that the adults are elsewhere, in the "real" world, and to conceal the fact that real childishness is everywhere.'[49] He argues that the reporting of 'Watergate' operated in much the same way. It had to be reported as a scandal in order to conceal the fact that it was a commonplace of American political life. This is an example of what he calls 'a simulation of a scandal to regenerative ends'.[50] It is an attempt 'to revive a moribund principle by simulated scandal . . . a question of proving the real by the imaginary; proving truth by scandal'.[51] In the same way, it could be argued that recent revelations about the activities of certain businessmen operating in the financial markets of London had to be reported as a scandal in order to conceal what Baudrillard calls capitalism's 'instantaneous cruelty; its incomprehensible ferocity; its fundamental immorality'.[52]

Baudrillard's general analysis supports Lyotard's central point about postmodernism, the collapse of certainty, the dissolution of the metanarrative of 'truth'. God, nature, science, the working class, all have lost their authority as centres of authenticity and truth; evidence on which to rest one's case. The result is not a retreat from the 'real', but the collapse of the real into hyperrealism. As he says, 'When the real is no longer what it used to be, nostalgia assumes its full meaning. There is a proliferation of myths of origin and signs of reality . . . a panic stricken production of the real and the referential.'[53] This is an example of the second historical shift identified by Baudrillard. Modernity was the era of what he calls the 'hermeneutics of suspicion', the search for meaning in the underlying reality of appearances. Marx and Freud are cited as examples of this mode of thinking. Hyperreality thus calls into question the claims of representation: both political and cultural. If there is no real behind the appearance, no beyond or beneath, what can be called with validity a representation? For example, given this line of argument, Rambo does not represent a type of American thinking on Vietnam, it *is* a type of American thinking on Vietnam. Representation does not stand at one remove from reality, to conceal or distort, it *is* reality. The revolution proposed by postmodern theory is a revolution against latent meaning and the foundations for ideological analysis.

Baudrillard is ambivalent about these changes. On the one hand, he appears to celebrate them. On the other, he suggests they signal a form of cultural exhaustion: all that remains is endless cultural repetition. I suppose the truth of Baudrillard's position is a kind of resigned celebration. Lawrence Grossberg calls it 'celebration in the face of inevitability, an embracing of nihilism without empowerment, since there is no real possibility of struggle'.[54] John Docker is more critical,

> Baudrillard offers a classic modernist narrative, history as a linear, unidirectional story of decline. But whereas the early twentieth-century high literary modernists could dream of an avant-garde or cultural élite that might preserve the values of the past in the hope of a future seeding and regrowth, no such hope surfaces in Baudrillard's vision of a dying, entropic world. It's not even possible to write in a rational argumentative form, for that assumes a remaining community of reason.[55]

## Fredric Jameson

Fredric Jameson is an American Marxist cultural critic who has written a number of very influential essays on postmodernism. Like Lyotard and Baudrillard, Jameson believes that there has been a fundamental break: 'The point is that we are within the culture of postmodernism to the point where its facile repudiation is as impossible as any equally facile celebration of it is complacent and corrupt.'[56] Where Jameson differs from other theorists is in his insistence that this break can best be theorized from within a Marxist or neo-Marxist framework. In 'Postmodernism and consumer society', Jameson points to

> the erosion of the older distinction between high culture and so-called mass or popular culture. This is perhaps the most distressing development of all from an academic standpoint, which has traditionally had a vested interest in preserving a realm of high or elite culture against the surrounding environment of philistinism, of schlock and kitsch, of TV series and *Reader's Digest* culture, and in transmitting difficult and complex skills of reading, listening and seeing to its initiates.[57]

It is interesting, and perhaps revealing, that in the revised version of this argument, 'Postmodernism, or the cultural logic of

late capitalism', Jameson changes the above formulation in significant ways. For example, popular culture is replaced by 'commercial culture', the surrounding environment of philistinism is
replaced by 'this whole "degraded" landscape'. In 'The politics of
theory: ideological positions in the postmodernism debate': 'the
surrounding environment of philistinism, of schlock and kitsch, of
commodification and of *Reader's Digest* culture' is more or less
repeated.[58] It seems that the more he thinks about it, the more
reliant he becomes on the standard Frankfurt School critique of
popular culture. Again, in a piece of classic Frankfurt School rhetoric, he writes of

> the older kinds of folk and genuinely 'popular' culture which
> flourished when the older social classes of a peasantry and an
> urban artisanat still existed and which, from the mid-nineteenth
> century on, have gradually been colonized and extinguished by
> commodification and the market system.[59]

Jameson is of course aware of the ways in which the makers of high
modernism mobilized popular culture to high cultural ends. What
has changed is that the texts and practices of high culture have
become intermixed with the texts and practices of popular culture,
'to the point where the line between high art and commercial
forms seems increasingly difficult to draw'.[60]

For Jameson, postmodernism is more than just a particular
cultural style, it is above all a 'periodizing concept'.[61] Postmodernism is 'the cultural dominant' of late or multinational capitalism.
His argument is informed by Ernest Mandel's[62] characterization of
capitalism's three-stage development: 'market capitalism', 'mono-
poly capitalism' and 'late or multinational capitalism'. Capitalism's
third stage 'constitutes . . . the purest form of capital into hitherto
uncommodified areas'.[63] He matches Mandel's tripartite schema
with his own tripartite schema of cultural development: 'realism',
'modernism' and 'postmodernism'.[64] His argument also borrows
from Williams's influential claim that a given social formation will
always consist of three cultural moments ('dominant', 'emergent'
and 'residual').[65] It is on the basis of this claim that Jameson
argues that postmodernism is 'the cultural dominant' of late or
multinational capitalism (modernism is the residual; it is unclear
what is the emergent). Williams's argument is that the move from
one historical moment to another does not usually involve the

complete collapse of one cultural mode and the installation of another. What marks the cultural difference is the place of cultural modes in a sociocultural hierarchy. It is therefore possible to isolate certain features of postmodernist culture within modernity, and certain features of modernist culture in postmodernity.

What is being argued is that within each social formation, other cultural modes will exist but that only one will be dominant. It therefore follows that although postmodernism is the cultural dominant within Western capitalist societies, it is by no means the only form of cultural production and consumption. The formulation prevents cultural analysis from having to make a choice between cultural homogeneity (absolute cultural determinancy) or cultural heterogeneity (random cultural difference). More than this, Jameson insists that 'every position on postmodernism in culture – whether apologia or stigmatization – is also at one and the same time, and necessarily, an implicitly or explicitly political stance on the nature of multinational capitalism today.'[66] It is because of this insistence on the political dimension of the debate that Jameson sees it as 'essential to grasp postmodernism not as a style, but rather as a cultural dominant'.[67] Having said this, Jameson is nevertheless concerned to identify the constitutive features of postmodernism.

First of all, postmodernism is a culture of pastiche: the 'complacent play of historical allusion'.[68] Pastiche is often confused with parody; both involve imitation and mimicry. However, whereas parody has an 'ulterior motive', to mock a divergence from convention or a norm, pastiche is a 'blank parody' or 'empty copy', which has no sense of the very possibility of there being a norm or a convention from which to diverge. As he explains,

> In this situation, parody finds itself without a vocation; it has lived, and that strange new thing pastiche slowly comes to take its place. Pastiche is, like parody, the imitation of a peculiar mask, speech in a dead language: but it is a neutral practice of such mimicry, without any of parody's ulterior motives, amputated of the satiric impulse, devoid of laughter and of any conviction that alongside the abnormal tongue you have momentarily borrowed, some healthy linguistic normality still exists. Pastiche is thus blank parody.[69]

He is aware that modernism itself often 'quoted' from other cultures and other historical moments, but he insists that there is a difference: postmodern cultural texts do not just quote other cultures, other historical moments, they actually incorporate them to the point where any sense of critical distance threatens to collapse. This is particularly true of the relationship between high and popular culture. The producers of postmodern culture are accused of the dissolution of the distinction between high and popular culture. This is then related to the claim that postmodernism marks the 'death of the subject', the end of individualism. Jameson claims that 'the disappearance of the individual subject, along with its formal consequences, the increasing unavailability of the personal style, engender the well nigh universal practice today of what may be called pastiche.'[70] In one sense this means the end of the private and unique vision which is said to have informed the aesthetic thinking and cultural practices of high modernism. As he points out, there are two ways of seeing this. On the one hand, we can agree that the moment of individual style has passed. On the other, we can say with post-structuralism that such individualism was a myth, a construct. It does not really matter on which we decide; according to Jameson, both lead us to the world of pastiche: 'a world in which stylistic innovation is no longer possible, all that is left is to imitate dead styles, to speak through the masks and with the voices of the styles in the imaginary museum.'[71] Rather than a culture of pristine creativity, postmodern culture is a culture of quotations, a culture of 'intertextuality'. Rather than original cultural production, we have cultural production born out of other cultural production. In short, according to Jameson, it is a culture which 'involve[s] the necessary failure of art and the aesthetic, the failure of the new, the imprisonment in the past'.[72] It is therefore a culture 'of flatness or depthlessness, a new kind of superficiality in the most literal sense'.[73] A culture of images and surfaces, without 'latent' possibilities, it derives its hermeneutic force from other images, other surfaces, the interplay of intertextuality. The result is what he calls 'the waning of affect'[74] in postmodern cultural texts and practices. Lawrence Grossberg suggests that the situation is more complicated than this: it is not that there has been a waning of affect, rather that there has been a separation between affect and meaning.[75]

The supposed collapse of high culture into the domain of popular culture produces again what sounds remarkably like the standard Frankfurt School dismissal of popular culture. We are a long way from Chambers' and McRobbie's celebration of the new intellectual. Grossberg makes the point with economy:

> For Jameson . . . we need new 'maps' to enable us to understand the organization of space in late capitalism. The masses, on the other hand, remain mute and passive, cultural dopes who are deceived by the dominant ideologies, and who respond to the leadership of the critic as the only one capable of understanding ideology and constituting the proper site of resistance. At best, the masses succeed in representing their inability to respond. But without the critic, they are unable even to hear their own cries of hopelessness. Hopeless they are and shall remain, presumably until someone else provides them with the necessary maps of intelligibility and critical models of resistance.[76]

Jameson takes as an example of the practice of pastiche in this new culture what he calls the 'nostalgia film'. The category could include a number of films from the 1980s and 1990s: *Back to the Future I* and *II, Peggy Sue Got Married, Rumble Fish, Angel Heart, Blue Velvet.* He argues that the nostalgia film sets out to recapture the atmosphere and stylistic peculiarities of America in the 1950s. He claims that 'for Americans at least, the 1950s remain the privileged lost object of desire – not merely the stability and prosperity of a *pax Americana,* but also the first naive innocence of the counter-cultural impulses of early rock and roll and youth gangs.'[77] He also insists that the nostalgia film is not just another name for the historical film. This is clearly demonstrated by the fact that his own list includes *Star Wars.* Now it might seem strange to suggest that a film about the future can be nostalgic for the past, but as Jameson explains, '[*Star Wars*] is metonymically a . . . nostalgia film . . . it does not reinvent a picture of the past in its lived totality; rather, by reinventing the feel and shape of characteristic art objects of an older period'.[78]

Films such as *Raiders of the Lost Ark* and *Robin Hood, Prince of Thieves* operate in a similar way to evoke metonymically a sense of the narrative certainties of the past. Therefore, according to Jameson, the nostalgia film works in one or/and two ways: it recaptures and represents the atmosphere and stylistic features of the past; and it recaptures and represents certain styles of viewing of the past. What is of absolute significance for Jameson is that such films do not attempt to recapture or represent the 'real' past, but always make do with certain cultural myths and stereotypes about the past. They offer what he calls 'false realism', films about other films, representations of other representations (what Baudrillard calls simulations: see discussion above). History is effaced by 'historicism . . . the random cannibalisation of all the styles of the past, the play of random stylistic allusion'.[79] Here we might cite films such as *True Romance* and *Pulp Fiction.* More than this, Jameson insists that our awareness of the play of stylistic allusion 'is now a constitutive and essential part'[80] of our experience of the post-modern film. Moreover, it is an example of a culture 'in which the history of aesthetic styles displaces "real" history'.[81] This relates to a second stylistic feature Jameson identifies, what he calls schizophrenia. He uses the term in the sense developed by Lacan to signify a language disorder, a failure of the temporal relationship between signifiers. The schizophrenic experiences time not as a continuum (past–present–future), but as a perpetual present which is only occasionally marked by the intrusion of the past or the possibility of a future. The 'reward' for the loss of conventional selfhood (the sense of self as always located within a temporal continuum) is an intensified sense of the present, probably what Hebdige means by 'acid perspectivism'. Jameson explains it thus:

> Note that as temporal continuities break down, the experience of the present becomes powerfully, overwhelmingly vivid and 'material': the world comes before the schizophrenic with heightened intensity, bearing a mysterious and oppressive charge of affect, glowing with hallucinatory energy. But what might for us seem a desirable experience – an increase in our perceptions, a libidinal or hallucinogenic intensification of our normally humdrum and familiar surroundings – is here felt as loss, as 'unreality'.[82]

To call postmodern culture schizophrenic is to claim that it has lost its sense of history (and its sense of a future different from the present). It is a culture suffering from 'historical amnesia', locked into the discontinuous flow of perpetual presents. The temporal culture of modernism has given way to the spatial culture of postmodernism.

Jameson's final point, implicit in his claim that postmodernism is the 'cultural dominant' of late or multinational capitalism, is the claim that postmodernism is a hopelessly commercial culture. Unlike modernism, which taunted the commercial culture of capitalism, postmodernism, rather than resisting, 'replicates and reproduces – reinforces – the logic of consumer capitalism'.[83] Postmodern culture 'does more than merely replicate the logic of late capitalism; it reinforces and intensifies it'.[84] It forms the principal part of a process in which 'aesthetic production . . . has become integrated into commodity production generally'.[85] Culture is no longer ideological, disguising the economic activities of capitalist society, it is itself an economic activity, perhaps the most important economic activity of all. Culture's changed situation can have a significant effect on cultural politics. No longer is it credible to see culture as ideological representation, an immaterial reflection of the hard economic reality. Rather, what we now witness is not just the collapse of the distinction between high and popular culture, but the collapse of the distinction between the realm of culture and the realm of economic activity.

According to Jameson, when compared with 'the Utopian "high seriousness" of the great modernisms', postmodern culture is marked by an 'essential triviality'.[86] More than this, it is a culture which blocks 'a socialist transformation of society'.[87] Despite his rejection of a moral critique as inappropriate ('a category mistake'), and regardless of his citing of Marx's insistence on a dialectical approach, which would see postmodern culture as both a positive and a negative development, his argument drifts inexorably to the standard Frankfurt School critique of popular culture. The postmodern collapse of the distinction between high and popular culture has been gained at the cost of modernism's 'critical space'. The destruction of this critical space is not the result of an extinction of culture. On the contrary, it has been achieved by what he calls

> an 'explosion': a prodigious expansion of culture throughout the social realm, to the point at which everything in our social life from economic value and state power to practices and to the very structure of the psyche itself can be said to have become 'cultural' in some original and as yet unauthorized sense.[88]

The thorough 'culturalization' or 'aestheticization' of everyday life is what marks postmodernism off from previous sociocultural moments. Postmodernism is a culture which offers no position of 'critical distance'; it is a culture in which claims of 'incorporation' or 'co-optation' make no sense, as there is no longer a critical space from which to be incorporated or co-opted. This is Frankfurt School pessimism at its most pessimistic.

## Postmodern pop music

I will now draw together the different features of the postmodern condition and postmodern culture and discuss their relationship to the study of popular culture. McRobbie suggests that 'the recent debates on postmodernism possess both a positive attraction and a usefulness to the analyst of popular culture.'[89] Postmodernism heralds 'the coming into being of those whose voices were historically drowned out by the (modernist) metanarratives of mastery, which were in turn both patriarchal and imperialist'.[90]

> Postmodernism has entered into a more diverse number of vocabularies more quickly than most other intellectual categories. It has spread outwards from the realms of art history into political theory and onto the pages of youth culture magazines, record sleeves, and the fashion pages of *Vogue*. This seems to me to indicate something more than the mere vagaries of taste.[91]

A discussion of postmodernism and popular culture might highlight any number of different cultural forms and cultural practices: television, music video, film, pop music. I have space here to consider only two examples, television and pop music.

As Frith and Horne point out, 'Pop songs are the soundtrack of postmodern daily life, inescapable in lifts and airports, pubs and restaurants, streets and shopping centres and sports grounds'.[92] Connor argues that pop music is perhaps 'the most representative of postmodern cultural forms'.[93] Pop music continually recycles its own history: remakes, revivals, cover versions and comebacks. Rapid advances in technology (for example, 'sampling') have democratized this process. Pop music is expansive in terms of both its global market and the welcome it gives to both those on the cultural margins, and to other musics and cultures.

Jameson[94] has distinguished between modernist and postmodernist pop music, making the argument that the Beatles and the Rolling Stones represent a modernist moment, against which punk rock can be seen as postmodernist. Andrew Goodwin[95] has quite correctly argued that for various reasons this does not make sense. Goodwin's own position is to claim that postmodernism has no real explanatory relationship with regard to pop music. My own view is that although Jameson may be wrong, this does not make Goodwin's position right. In virtually all accounts, the moment of postmodernism begins in the late 1950s – the same period as the emergence of pop music. In terms of periodization, pop music and postmodernism are very closely related. This does not necessarily mean that all pop music is postmodern. As Goodwin has shown, this is a very difficult argument to sustain. Jameson's compressed time-span solution (pop music culture's rapid progression through realism, modernism, postmodernism), enabling him to establish a modernist moment against which to mark out a postmodernist response, is not really satisfactory. As Goodwin convincingly argues, the Beatles and the Rolling Stones are as different from each other as together they are different from the Clash and Talking Heads. In fact, it would be much easier to make an argument in which the distinction is made between the 'artifice' of the Beatles and Talking Heads and the 'authenticity' of the Rolling Stones and the Clash.

Perhaps the best way to think the relationship between pop music and postmodernism is historically, using Williams's model of 'dominant', 'emergent' and 'residual' moments of culture.[96] Postmodern pop music can be seen as 'emergent' in the 1960s with the late Beatles, and West Coast rock, as principal examples, and in the 1970s with 'art school' punk, to become in the late 1980s the 'cultural dominant' of pop music. To see the relationship in this way avoids the either/orism of 'it is all postmodern' or 'none of it is postmodern'. This is to envisage the relationship (perhaps in unpostmodern or pre-postmodern terms) as exhibiting a neo-Gramscian 'shifting equilibrium' between emergent and dominant forms. This would allow for the claim that all pop music is in some sense postmodern (potentially so), but that all pop music is not necessarily postmodern (it can be, to borrow Jameson's schema, 'realist' or 'modernist'). Goodwin's very detailed and informed discussion of the pop music/postmodernism relationship leads him to this possibility, but his hostility to postmodernism prevents him from accepting the logic of his own argument.

He considers a number of ways of seeing pop music and pop music culture as postmodernist. Perhaps the most cited aspect is the technological developments which have facilitated the emergence of 'sampling'. He acknowledges that the parallel with some postmodern theorizing is interesting and suggestive, but that is all it is – interesting and suggestive. What is often missed in such claims is the way in which sampling is used:

these critical strategies miss both the historicizing function of sampling technologies in contemporary pop and the ways in which textual incorporation cannot be adequately understood as 'blank parody'. We need categories to add to pastiche, which demonstrate how contemporary pop opposes, celebrates and promotes the texts it steals from.[97]

He also suggests that sampling is often 'used to invoke history and authenticity' and that 'it has often been overlooked that the "quoting" of sounds and styles acts to historicize contemporary culture'.[98]

Rap is perhaps the best example of sampling being used in this way. The African–American cultural theorist Cornel West, when asked to name *the* black means of cultural expression answered, 'music and preaching'. He went on to say,

> rap is unique because it combines the black preacher and the black music tradition, replacing the liturgical ecclesiastical setting with the African polyrhythms of the street. A tremendous *articulateness* is syncopated with the African drumbeat, the African funk, into an American postmodernist product: there is no subject expressing originary anguish here but a fragmented subject, pulling from past and present, innovatively producing a heterogeneous product. The stylistic combination of the oral, the literate, and the musical is exemplary . . . it is part and parcel of the subversive energies of black underclass youth, energies that are forced to take a cultural mode of articulation because of the political lethargy of American society.[99]

One can make similar claims for British rap as postmodern. McRobbie, as we noted earlier, claims that postmodernism appeals 'to what might be called the new generation of intellectuals (often black, female, or working class)'. The Ruthless Rap Assassins (now disbanded) were black and working class: three organic intellectuals articulating their politics with 'a funky North Hulme beat'. They engage in postmodern pla(y)giarism, not as an end in itself, but to construct compelling critiques of the everyday racism of British society. They would certainly reject Jameson's claim that their work is an example of postmodern pastiche (on this point Goodwin is certainly correct). Their intertextual play of quotations is not the result of aesthetic exhaustion, but the telling combination of found fragments from a cultural repertoire which by and large denies their existence. These are not the fragments of

191

modernism shored against aesthetic ruin, but fragments combined to damn those who have sought to deny them a voice within British culture.

It is also possible to see the consumption of pop music and the surrounding pop music culture as in itself postmodern. This is a point made by McRobbie.[100] Fred Pfeil[101] claims that in America at least, postmodernism is a particular style of consumption; the 'structure of feeling' of a specific class fraction: the professional managerial class. Instead of an approach concerned with identifying and analysing the postmodern text or practice, he suggests we look instead for postmodernism in 'the emergence of reading formations which celebrate pastiche, and ahistorical modes of consumption'.[102] The notion of a particular reading formation, people who combine an 'ironic hedonism' with 'a commitment to the weird',[103] is very suggestive. Umberto Eco, using Charles Jencks's notion of 'double coding', identifies a postmodern sensibility exhibited in an awareness of what he calls the 'already said'. He gives the example of a lover who cannot tell his lover 'I love you madly', and says instead: 'As Barbara Cartland would put it, I love you madly.'[104] Seeing the world in inverted commas in this way can be a way of attacking bourgeois taste, but it can also be a means of patronizing those supposedly without taste – those who speak without the inverted commas. Again, there is a postmodernism of resistance and a postmodernism of reaction.

While academics argue about whether postmodernism is best understood as text and practice, or as reading formation, the music industry has not been slow to bring text and consumption into combination. There is now a generic/sales category of pop music called postmodern: perhaps the most notable example of this was MTV's programme *Post Modern MTV* (1988–93). The presenter described the music played on the programme as 'a slightly alternative mix'. This description, and the general content of the programme, suggested that postmodernism is used as perhaps little more than another way to market so-called 'indie pop', or what students and others call 'student music'. This usage has also been taken up by record companies who now market certain performers as postmodern. Goodwin's own conversations with students produced three possible usages: 'first, "art rock", "indie pop" and "college radio" music that is . . . acts who define themselves as existing outside the mainstream of the charts, and whose music is supposed to be taken more seriously than the supposedly disposable sounds of pop';[105] second, pop music which follows chronologically the supposedly dominant sound of the so-called 'modern rock' of the 1980s; third, the music which followed the defeat of punk's politicalism – this is meant to suggest that pop music post-punk is non-political.

Goodwin is particularly unhappy with the claim 'that we are now living in an era where distinctions between art and mass culture have collapsed', because, as he points out, most consumers of pop music insist on a distinction between 'serious' pop music and 'trivial' pop music, and between the 'authentic' and the 'hopelessly commercial'.[106] I remember at school how we argued that the Rolling Stones' cover versions of black rhythm and blues numbers were authentic and in some obscure way anti-commercial, while Herman's Hermits' cover versions of English pop songs were obviously signs of the inauthentic and the commercial. Such distinctions are clearly ideological and mythological. But more importantly, distinctions within popular culture are not the same as distinctions between popular and high culture. The fact that the former exists does not mean that the latter must also exist. It is of course possible to read this in quite a different way. Rather than seeing the collapse of the distinction between high and popular culture, all we are really witnessing is the growth of a new subculture or radical taste culture. In claiming 'authenticity' for its taste and consumption, it does two things: first, it marks itself as different from other forms of popular taste, and second, in doing this, it appears to claim for itself an alignment with the traditional discourse of culture – thus the claim that we are witnessing the collapse of the distinction between high and popular culture, and the counter-claim that the distinction still exists.

## Postmodern television

Television, like pop music, does not have a period of modernism to which it can be 'post'. But, as Jim Collins[107] points out, television is often seen as the 'quintessence' of postmodern culture. This claim can be made on the basis of a number of television's textual and contextual features. If we take a negative view of postmodernism, as the domain of simulations, then television seems an obvious example of the process – with its supposed reduction of the complexities of the world to an ever-changing flow of depthless and banal visual imagery. If, on the other hand, we take a positive view of postmodernism, then the visual and verbal practices of television can be put forward, say, as the knowing play of intertextuality and 'radical eclecticism',[108] encouraging and helping to produce the 'sophisticated bricoleur'[109] of postmodern culture. For example, a television series such as *Twin Peaks* both constitutes an audience as *bricoleurs* and in turn is watched by an audience who celebrate its *bricolage.*

> Postmodernist eclecticism might only occasionally be a preconceived design choice in individual programs, but it is built into the technologies of media sophisticated societies. Thus television, like the postmodern subject, must be conceived as a site – an intersection of multiple, conflicting cultural messages. Only by recognizing this interdependency of bricolage and eclecticism can we come to appreciate the profound changes in the relationship of reception and production in postmodern cultures. Not only has reception become another form of meaning production, but production has increasingly become a form of reception as it rearticulates antecedent and competing forms of representation.[110]

Another divide within the approach to television as postmodern is between textual and 'economic' analysis. Instead of the semiotic sophistication of its intertextual play and radical eclecticism, television is condemned as hopelessly commercial. Collins uses *Twin Peaks* as a means of bringing together the different strands of the relationship between postmodernism and television. *Twin Peaks* is chosen because it 'epitomizes the multiple dimensions of televisual postmodernism'.[111] He argues that the postmodernism of the series is the result of a number of interrelated factors: David Lynch's reputation as a film-maker, the stylistic features of the series, and, finally, its commercial intertextuality (the marketing of related products: for example, *The Secret Diary of Laura Palmer*). At the economic level, *Twin Peaks* represents an attempt by American network television to win back affluent sections of the television audience lost to cable and video. In this sense *Twin Peaks* marks a new era in network television's view of the audience. Instead of seeing the audience as an homogeneous mass, the series was part of a strategy in which the audience is seen as fragmented, consisting of different segments – stratified by age, class, gender, geography and race – of interest to different

**194**

advertisers. Mass appeal now involves attempts to intertwine the different segments to enable them to be sold to different sections of the advertising market. The significance of *Twin Peaks*, at least from this perspective, is that it was marketed to appeal to those most likely to have been tempted away from network television by VCR, cable and cinema: in short, the so-called 'yuppie' generation. Collins demonstrates this by addressing the way the series was promoted. First, there was the intellectual appeal – Lynch as auteur, *Twin Peaks* as avant-garde television. This was followed by *Twin Peaks* as soap opera. Together the two appeals soon coalesced into a postmodern reading formation in which the series was 'valorized as would-be cinema and would-be soap opera'.[112] This was supported and sustained by the polysemic play of *Twin Peaks* itself. The series is, as Collins suggests, 'aggressively eclectic',[113] not only in its use of conventions from Gothic horror, police procedural, science fiction and soap opera, but also in the different ways – from straight to parody – these conventions are mobilized in particular scenes. Collins also notes the play of 'tonal variations . . . within and across scenes'.[114] This has led some critics to dismiss *Twin Peaks* as 'mere camp'. But it is never simply camp – it is never simply anything – moving the audience from moments of parodic distance to other moments of emphatic intimacy, continually playing with our expectations. Although this is a known aspect of Lynch's filmic technique, it is also a characteristic 'reflective of changes in television entertainment and of viewer involvement in that entertainment'.[115]

> That viewers would take a great deal of pleasure in this oscillation and juxtaposition is symptomatic of the 'suspended' nature of viewer involvement in television that developed well before the arrival of *Twin Peaks*. The ongoing oscillation in discursive register and generic conventions describes not just *Twin Peaks* but the very act of moving up and down the televisual scale of the cable box. While watching *Twin Peaks*, viewers may be overtly encouraged to move in and out of an ironic position, but watching other television soap operas (nighttime or daytime) involves for many viewers a similar process of oscillation in which emotional involvement alternates with ironic detachment. Viewing perspectives are no longer mutually exclusive, but set in perpetual alternation.[116]

What makes *Twin Peaks* different from other soap operas is not that it produces shifting viewing positions, but that it 'explicitly acknowledges this oscillation and the suspended nature of television viewing . . . . [It] doesn't just acknowledge the multiple subject positions that television generates; it recognizes that one of the great pleasures of the televisual text is that very suspension and exploits it for its own sake'.[117] In other words, *Twin Peaks* is not a reflection of postmodernism, nor is it an allegory of postmodernism; it is a specific address to the postmodern condition – a postmodern text – and as such it helps to redefine the possibilities of entertainment in the contemporary capitalist world.

## Postmodernism and the pluralism of value

Postmodernism has disturbed many of the old certainties surrounding questions of cultural value. While it is now widely recognized that value and evaluation is everywhere – ignoring it does not make it go away – the cultural studies interest in questions of value does not represent a return to the standard terms of axiology: 'intrinsic', 'objective', 'absolute', 'universal', 'transcendent'. Cultural studies is not impressed with demands to pay homage to the timeless text of fixed value. A cultural text or practice survives its moment of production – becomes canonical – because it is able to meet the needs and desires of people with cultural power. Surviving its moment of production makes it available to meet the (usually different) desires and needs of other generations of people with cultural power.

There are two ways to argue this point. First, we can insist that the cultural texts that are valued and canonized are those that are sufficiently polysemic to sustain multiple and continuous readings.[118] From this perspective, value is always the result of a historically situated encounter between reader and text. The texts that survive their original moment of production are those that are able to bear the weight of further historically-situated encounters between text and reader. The problem with this approach is that it seems to ignore questions of power. It fails to pose the question: 'Who is doing the reading, in what context(s) and with what effects of power?' In short, it is very difficult to see how a process, in which only certain people have the power and cultural authority to ensure the reproduction of cultural texts and practices, can really be described as simply an effect of a text's polysemy.

A second response is to start with power. Like value itself, the canon is a construction. Moreover, as a construction, it is an articulation of particular relations of cultural power. Canons arise from particular interests, located in specific social and historical contexts. They are as much about policing knowledge as they are about organizing terrains of critical inquiry. Therefore, although canon formation may well be an inevitable outcome in encounters between academic discourse and cultural production, it is the attempt to deny agency, power and struggle that must be articulated and resisted.

It is not difficult to demonstrate how canons form and re-form in response to the social and political concerns of those with cultural power. To the less watchful eye, the changes often seem insignificant – changes at the perimeter, relative stability at the core – but even when the canonical texts remain the same, how and why they are valued certainly changes. So much so that they are hardly the same texts from one historical moment to the next.[119] As the Four Tops put it, in a slightly different context: 'It's the same old song/But with a different meaning since you've been gone'. Or to put it in a less danceable discourse, the text is not the issuing source of value, but the site where the construction of value – variable values – can take place.

Of course, when we ascribe value to a cultural text or practice, we are not (or hardly ever) saying this is only of value to me; our evaluation always (or usually always) includes the notion that the cultural text or practice should also be of value to others. The trouble with some forms of evaluation is that they insist that their community of others is an ideal community, with absolute cultural authority over all other valuing communities. It is not that they insist that all others should consume what they value (it is usually better for 'value' if they do not). But they do insist on due deference for their judgements and absolute recognition of their cultural authority to judge (see Chapter 2).

The return to questions of value has witnessed an increased interest in the work of Pierre Bourdieu.[120] As I pointed out in Chapter 1, Bourdieu argues that distinctions of 'culture' (whether understood as text, practice or way of living) are a significant aspect in the struggle between dominant and subordinate groups in society. He shows how arbitrary tastes and arbitrary ways of living are continually transmuted into legitimate taste and the only legitimate way of life. The consumption of culture is thus a means to produce and to legitimize social difference.

Bourdieu's project is to (re-)locate 'value' in the world of everyday experience, to suggest that similar things are happening when I 'value' a holiday destination or a particular mode of dress, as are happening when I 'value' a poem by T. S. Eliot or a song by Otis Redding or a photograph by Cindy Sherman or a piece of music by Gavin Bryars. Such evaluations are never a simple matter of individual taste; cultural value operates both to identify and to maintain social difference and sustain social deference. Distinction is generated by learned patterns of cultural consumption which are internalized as 'natural' cultural preferences and interpreted and mobilized as evidence of 'natural' cultural competences, which are, ultimately, used to justify forms of social domination. The cultural tastes of dominant groups are given institutional form, and then, with deft ideological sleight of hand, their taste for this institutionalized culture (i.e. their own) is held up as evidence of their cultural and, ultimately, their social superiority. The effect of such cultural distinction is to produce and reproduce social distinction, social separation and social hierarchy. It becomes a means of establishing differences between dominated and dominant groups in society. The production and reproduction of cultural space thus produce and reproduce social space.

Bourdieu's purpose is not to prove the self-evident, that different classes have different lifestyles, different tastes in culture, but to identify and interrogate the processes by which the making of cultural distinctions secures and legitimizes forms of power and control rooted in economic inequalities. He is interested not so much in the actual differences, but in how these differences are used by dominant groups as a means of social reproduction. The much-heralded collapse of standards rehearsed (almost weekly) in the the so-called 'quality' media of our postmodern new times, may be nothing more than a perceived sense that the opportunities to use culture to make and mark social distinction are becoming more and more difficult to find, as Pavarotti tops the charts, Gorecki out-sells most of the acts on *Top of the Pops*, and Premier League football becomes, in many instances, as expensive as, say, ballet or opera.

Perhaps the most significant thing about postmodernism for the student of popular culture is the recognition that there is no absolute categorical difference between high and popular culture. This is not to say that one text or practice might not be 'better' (for what/for whom, etc., must always be decided and made clear) than another text or practice. But it is to say that there are no longer any easy reference points, to which we can refer, and which will automatically preselect for us the good from the bad. Some might regard such a situation (or even the description of such a situation) with horror – the end of standards. On the contrary, without easy recourse to fixed categories of value, it calls for rigorous, if always contingent, standards, if our task is to separate the good from the bad, the usable from the obsolete, the progressive from the reactionary. As John Fekete points out,

> By contrast [to modernism], postmodernism may be at last ready – or may, at least, represent the transition to a readiness – unneurotically, to get on without the Good-God-Gold Standards, one and all, indeed without any capitalized Standards, while learning to be enriched by the whole inherited inventory once it is transferred to the lower case. . . . We need to believe and enact the belief that there are better and worse ways to live the pluralism of value. To see all cows as the same colour would truly amount to being lost in the night. But the prospect of learning to be at ease with limited warranties, and with the responsibility for issuing them, without the false security of inherited guarantees, is promising for a livelier, more colourful, more alert, and, one hopes, more tolerant culture that draws enjoyment from the dappled relations between meaning and value.[121]

Fekete's point is not significantly different from the argument made by Susan Sontag at the birth of the '[postmodern] new sensibility':

> The new sensibility is defiantly pluralistic; it is dedicated both to an excruciating seriousness and to fun and wit and nostalgia. It is also extremely history-conscious; and the voracity of its enthusiasms (and of the supercession of these enthusiams) is very high-speed and hectic. From the vantage point of this new sensibility, the beauty of a machine or of the solution to a mathematical problem, of a painting by Jasper Johns, of a film by Jean-Luc Godard, and of the personalities and music of the Beatles is equally accessible.[122]

Postmodernism has changed the theoretical and the cultural basis of the study of popular culture. It raises many questions, not least about the role of the student of popular culture: that is, what is our relationship to our object of study? With what authority, and for whom, do we speak? As Frith and Horne suggest,

> In the end the postmodern debate concerns the source of meaning, not just its relationship to pleasure (and, in turn, to the source of that pleasure) but its relationship to power and authority. Who now determines significance? Who has the right to interpret? For pessimists and rationalists like Jameson the answer is multinational capital – records, clothes, films, TV shows, etc. are simply the results of decisions about markets and marketing. For pessimists and irrationalists, like Baudrillard, the answer is nobody at all – the signs that surround us are arbitrary. For optimists like Iain Chambers and Larry Grossberg the answer is consumers themselves, stylists and subculturalists, who take the goods on offer and make their own marks with them.[123]

The next chapter will consist mostly of an attempt to find answers to some of these questions.


## Further reading

Lisa Appignanesi (ed.), *Postmodernism*, London: ICA, 1986. A collection of essays mostly philosophical on postmodernism. McRobbie's contribution, 'Postmodernism and popular culture' is essential reading.

Steven Best and Douglas Kellner, *Postmodern Theory: Critical interrogations*, London: Macmillan, 1991. An excellent introduction to the debate about postmodernism.

Roy Boyne and Ali Rattansi (eds), *Postmodernism and Society*, London: Macmillan, 1990. A useful collection of essays, with a very good introduction to the main issues in the debate about postmodernism.

Steven Connor, *Postmodernist Culture: An introduction to theories of the contemporary*, Oxford: Basil Blackwell, 1989. A comprehensive introduction to postmodernism: useful discussion of popular culture.

Thomas Docherty (ed.), *Postmodernism: A reader*, Hemel Hempstead: Harvester Wheatsheaf, 1993. An excellent collection of essays, but little on popular culture.

John Docker, *Postmodernism and Popular Culture: A cultural history*, Cambridge: Cambridge University Press, 1994. The aim of the book is to challenge the way a century of modernist theory has understood twentieth century popular culture. Intelligent, polemical and very readable. Essential reading.

Mike Featherstone, *Consumer Culture and Postmodernism*, London: Sage, 1991. An interesting sociological discussion of consumer culture and postmodernism. Essential reading.

Dick Hebdige, *Hiding in the Light*, London: Comedia, 1988. A collection of essays mostly related to questions of postmodernism and popular culture. Essential reading.

Meaghan Morris, *The Pirate's Fiancée: Feminism, reading, postmodernism*, London: Verso, 1988. A collection of essays concerned with both theory and analysis. Essential reading.

Andrew Ross (ed.), *Universal Abandon: The politics of postmodernism*, Minneapolis: University of Minnesota Press, 1988. A useful collection of essays on postmodernism: some interesting discussion of popular culture.

Madan Sarup, *An Introductory Guide to Post-structuralism and Postmodernism*, 2nd edn, Hemel Hempstead: Harvester Wheatsheaf, 1993. An interesting and accessible guide to the field.

# 8

# THE POLITICS OF
# THE POPULAR

I have tried in this book to outline something of the history of
the relationship between cultural theory and popular culture.
In the main I have tended to focus on the theoretical and methodological aspects and implications of the relationship, as
this, in my opinion, is the best way in which to *introduce* the
subject. However, I am aware that this has been largely at
the expense of, on the one hand, the historical conditions
of the production of theory about popular culture and, on the
other, the political relations of its production and reproduction
(these are analytical emphases and not separate and distinct
'moments').

Something I hope I have demonstrated, however, is the
extent to which popular culture is a concept of ideological con-
testation and variability, to be filled and emptied, to be articulated and disarticulated, in a range of different and competing
ways. Even my own truncated and selective history of the study
of popular culture shows that 'studying' popular culture can
be a very serious business indeed – serious political business.
We have seen how popular culture is presented as that which
keeps 'the people' from considered engagement with 'real'
culture; and we have also seen how it is presented as that which
holds 'the people' in thrall to the commercial and ideological
manipulations of the capitalist culture industries. In both instances, popular culture is the debilitating *other* of culture; the
dangerous shadow which haunts and tempts the progress of the
real thing.

## A paradigm crisis in cultural studies

In *Cultural Populism*, Jim McGuigan claims that the study of popular culture within contemporary cultural studies is in the throes of a paradigm crisis. This is nowhere more clearly signalled than in the current polities of cultural populism. McGuigan defines cultural populism as 'the intellectual assumption, made by some students of popular culture, that the symbolic experiences and practices of ordinary people are more important analytically and politically than Culture with a capital C'.[1] On the basis of this definition, I am a cultural populist, and, moreover, so is McGuigan. However, the purpose behind McGuigan's book is not to challenge cultural populism as such, but what he calls 'an *uncritical* populist drift in the study of popular culture', with an increasing fixation on strategies of interpretation at the expense of an adequate grasp of the historical and economic conditions of cultural consumption. He contends that there has been an uncritical drift away from the 'once compelling . . . neo-Gramscian hegemony theory',[2] towards an uncritical populism. In some ways, this was inevitable (he claims) given the commitment of cultural studies to a hermeneutic mode at the expense of the perspective of political economy. He also maintains that cultural studies has narrowed its focus to questions of interpretation without situating such questions within a context of material relations of power. To reverse the trend, he advocates a dialogue between cultural studies and the political economy of culture. He fears that for cultural studies to remain separate is for it to remain politically ineffective as a mode of explanation, and thus for it to remain complicit with the prevailing exploitative and oppressive structures of powers.

> In my view, the separation of contemporary cultural studies from the political economy of culture has been one of the most disabling features of the field of study. The core problematic was virtually premised on a terror of economic reductionism. In consequence, the economic aspects of media institutions and the broader economic dynamics of consumer culture were rarely investigated, simply bracketed off, thereby severely undermining the explanatory and, in effect, critical capacities of cultural studies.[3]

The consumptionist perspective of uncritical populism, according to McGuigan, vastly overestimates the power of consumers, 'falling into an uncritical populism not entirely different from right-wing political economy'.[4] Uncritical populism fails to connect consumption with production. Although neo-Gramscian hegemony theory once cohered the field, 'it has never done so adequately due to the original schism with the political economy of culture'.[5] Can we return to hegemony theory revitalized by political economy? It seems that the answer is no: hegemony theory inevitably leads to an uncritical populism, fixated with consumption at the expense of production. Our only hope is the political economy of culture perspective.

McGuigan also claims that cultural populism's exclusive focus on consumption and a corresponding uncritical celebration of popular reading has produced a 'crisis of qualitative judgment'.[6] What he means by this is that there are no longer absolutist criteria of judgement. What is 'good' and what is 'bad' is now open to dispute. He blames postmodern uncertainty fostered by cultural populism, claiming that 'the reinsertion of aesthetic and ethical judgment into the debate is a vital rejoinder to the uncritical drift of cultural populism and its failure to dispute laissez-faire conceptions of consumer sovereignty and quality.'[7] Clearly unhappy with the intellectual uncertainties of postmodernism, he desires a return to the full authority of the modernist intellectual: always there to make clear and comprehensive that which the ordinary mind is unable to grasp. He seeks a return to the Arnoldian certainties – culture is the best that has been thought and said (and the modernist intellectual will tell us what this is). He seems to advocate an intellectual discourse in which the university lecturer is the guardian of the eternal flame of the cultural, initiating the uninitiated into the glow of its absolute moral and aesthetic value; students assume the role of passive consumers of an already constituted knowledge – fixed, formulated and administered by the professorial guardians of the flame. Cultural populism's refusal to judge a text or practice 'good' or 'bad' is not in my opinion a crisis, but a welcome recognition that there are other, sometimes far more interesting, questions to be asked (see Chapter 7 for a discussion of postmodernism and questions of value). Those who insist on a return to absolute standards are saying little more than that it is too confusing now: I want back my easy and unquestioned authority to tell ordinary people what it is worth and how it is done:

> That ordinary people use the symbolic resources available to them under present conditions for meaningful activity is both

manifest and endlessly elaborated upon by new revisionism. Thus emancipatory projects to liberate people from their alleged entrapment, whether they know they are entrapped or not, are called into question by this fundamental insight. Economic exploitation, racism, gender and sexual oppression, to name but a few, exist, but the exploited, estranged and oppressed cope, and, furthermore, if such writers as John Fiske and Paul Willis are to be believed, they cope very well indeed, making valid sense of the world and obtaining grateful pleasure from what they receive. Apparently, there is so much action in the micro-politics of everyday life that the Utopian promises of a better future, which were once so enticing for critics of popular culture, have lost all credibility.[8]

Most of this is simply untrue. Even Fiske (his prime example) does not celebrate an achieved Utopia, but the active struggle of men and women to make sense and make space in a world based on exploitation and oppression. McGuigan seems to be saying that pleasure (and its identification and celebration) is in some fundamental sense counter-revolutionary. The duty and historical destiny of ordinary men and women is to suffer and be still, until moral leftists like McGuigan reveal what is to be enjoyed on the glorious morning of the long day after the Revolution. The rhetorical vacuousness of this kind of thinking was exposed long ago by feminists unwilling to lie back and think about the economic base. It simply is not the case that claims that audiences produce meaning are in some profound sense a denial of the need for political change. We can celebrate symbolic resistance without abandoning our commitment to radical politics. This is in effect the essence of Ang's point (see Chapter 6). Presented in this way, political economy seems to amount to little more than another (sometimes sophisticated) version of the 'ideology of mass culture'.

Despite my criticisms, I believe McGuigan's is an important argument of some significance to students of popular culture. As he names John Fiske and Paul Willis as perhaps the most 'guilty' of uncritical cultural populists, I shall outline some of the key features of their recent work to explain what is at issue in what is so far a rather one-sided debate. In order to facilitate this, I will introduce two new concepts which have their provenance in the work of Pierre Bourdieu, the 'cultural field' and the 'economic field'.

## The cultural field

John Fiske is generally seen as the epitome of the uncritical drift to cultural populism. 'Fiske's position is . . . indicative of the critical decline of British cultural studies.'[9] According to McGuigan, Fiske continually sacrifices economic and technological determinations to make space for interpretation – a purely hermeneutic version of cultural studies. For example, he is accused of reducing the study of television 'to a kind of subjective idealism'[10] in which the popular reading is king or queen, untroubled by questions of sexism, racism; ungrounded in economic and political relations, and always 'progressive'. In short, Fiske is accused of an uncritical and unqualified celebration of popular culture; he is the classic example of what happened to cultural studies following the supposed collapse of neo-Gramscian hegemony theory and the consequent emergence of what McGuigan calls, following Philip Schlesinger, the 'new revisionism', the reduction of cultural studies to competing hermeneutic models of consumption. New revisionism is the latest moment in the development of cultural studies: its themes are pleasure, empowerment, resistance and popular discrimination. It represents a moment of 'retreat from more critical positions'.[11] In political terms, it is at best an uncritical echo of liberal claims about the 'sovereignty of the consumer', and at worse it is uncritically complicit with prevailing 'free market' ideology. Fiske, however, rejects the view that 'the capitalist culture industries produce only an apparent variety of products whose variety is finally illusory for they all promote the same capitalist ideology.'[12] He also rejects the view 'that "the people" are "cultural dopes" . . . a passive, helpless mass incapable of discrimination and thus at the economic, cultural, and political mercy of the barons of the industry.'[13] He argues that the commodities from which popular culture is made circulate in two simultaneous economies, the financial and the cultural:

> The workings of the financial economy cannot account adequately for all cultural factors, but it still needs to be taken into account in any investigation. . . . But the cultural commodity cannot be adequately described in financial terms only: the circulation that is crucial to its popularity occurs in the parallel economy – the cultural.[14]

Whereas the financial economy is primarily concerned with exchange value, the cultural is primarily focused on use – 'meanings, pleasures, and social identities'.[15] There is, of course, continual interaction between these separate, but related economies. Fiske gives the example of *Hill Street Blues*. The programme was made by MTM and sold to NBC. NBC then sold the audience to Mercedes Benz, which sponsors the programme. This all takes place in the financial economy. In the cultural economy, the series changes from commodity (to be sold to NBC) to producer (of meanings for its audience). And in the same way, the audience changes from commodity (to be sold to Mercedes Benz) to producer (of meanings and pleasures). He argues that 'the power of audiences as producers in the cultural economy is considerable.'[16] It is such assertions that attract the wrath of political economy theorists such as McGuigan. The power of the audience, Fiske contends,

> derives from the fact that meanings do not circulate in the cultural economy in the same way that wealth does in the financial. They are harder to possess (and thus to exclude others from possessing), they are harder to control because the production of meaning and pleasure is not the same as the production of the cultural commodity, or of other goods, for in the cultural economy the role of consumer does not exist as the end point of a linear economic transaction. Meanings and pleasures circulate within it without any real distinction between producers and consumers.[17]

The power of the consumer derives from the failure of producers to predict what will sell. 'Twelve out of thirteen records fail to make a profit, TV series are axed by the dozen, expensive films sink rapidly into red figures (*Raise the Titanic* is an ironic example – it nearly sank the Lew Grade empire)'.[18] In an attempt to offset failures, the culture industries produce 'repertoires' of goods in the hope of attracting an audience. But audiences constantly engage in 'semiotic guerrilla warfare'.[19] Whereas the industries seek to incorporate audiences as commodity consumers, the audience often excorporates the text to its own purposes. Fiske cites the example of the way Australian Aboriginal viewers appropriated Rambo as a figure of resistance, relevant to their own political and cultural struggles. He also cites the example of Russian Jews watching *Dallas* in Israel and reading it as 'capitalism's self-criticism'.[20]

Fiske argues that resistance to the power of the powerful by those without power in Western societies takes two forms, semiotic and social. The first is mainly concerned with meanings, pleasures and social identities; the second with transformations of the socio-economic system. He contends that 'the two are closely related, although relatively autonomous'.[21] Popular culture operates mostly, 'but not exclusively', in the domain of semiotic power. It is involved in 'the struggle between homogenization and difference, or between consensus and conflict'.[22] In this sense, popular culture is a semiotic battlefield in which a conflict is fought out between the forces of incorporation and the forces of resistance, between an imposed set of meanings, pleasures and social identities, and the meanings, pleasures and social identities produced in acts of semiotic resistance. It is a relationship of conflict: 'the hegemonic forces of homogeneity are always met by the resistances of heterogeneity'.[23] In Fiske's semiotic war scenario, the two economies are on opposing sides of the struggle: the financial economy is on the side of the forces of incorporation and homogenization, the cultural economy is on the side of the forces of resistance and difference. Semiotic resistance, he argues, has the effect of undermining capitalism's attempt at ideological homogeneity: dominant meanings are challenged by subordinate meanings; thus, the dominant class's intellectual and moral leadership is challenged. Fiske states his position without apology and with absolute clarity:

> It . . . sees popular culture as a site of struggle, but, while accepting the power of the forces of dominance, it focuses rather upon the popular tactics by which these forces are coped with, are evaded or are resisted. Instead of tracing exclusively the processes of incorporation, it investigates rather that popular vitality and creativity that makes incorporation such a constant necessity. Instead of concentrating on the omnipresent, insidious practices of the dominant ideology, it attempts to understand the everyday resistances and evasions that make that ideology work so hard and insistently to maintain itself and its values. This approach sees popular culture as potentially, and often actually, progressive (though not radical), and it is essentially optimistic, for it finds in the vigour and vitality of the people evidence both of the possibility of social change and of the motivation to drive it.[24]

He is insistent that the struggle in which popular culture is engaged is located not in the field of economic and technological determinations, but in the cultural field in a contest with the claims and counter-claims of high culture. It is a cultural struggle between high or dominant culture and popular culture abstracted from economic and technological determinations, but ultimately overdetermined by them. This is anathema to McGuigan, who sees the struggle in quite different terms: 'It is a curious conception of "the dominant" in the cultural field that confines it to the official terrain of . . . [high or dominant culture] and has no sense of a much more dominant set of market based arrangements.'[25] Fiske would defend himself against this charge by making reference to one of his principal sources, Bourdieu:

> For Bourdieu all societies are characterized by a struggle between groups and/or classes and class fractions to maximize their interests in order to ensure their reproduction. The social formation is seen as a hierarchically organized series of fields within which human agents are engaged in specific struggles to maximize their control over the social resources specific to that field, the intellectual field, the educational field, the economic field etc. . . . The fields are hierarchically organized in a structure over-determined by the field of class struggle over the production and distribution of material resources and each subordinate field reproduces within its own structural logic, the logic of the field of class struggle.[26]

One of the fields of struggle not specifically named here is the cultural field. If we accept Bourdieu's account, then it is clear that Fiske's notion of cultural struggle is perfectly legitimate.

The cultural field is characterized by a division between dominant or official culture and popular culture. The historical creation of a unique space for Culture with a capital C above and beyond the social has for Bourdieu the purpose, or at least the consequence, of reinforcing and legitimizing class power as class cultural/aesthetic difference. The class relations of the cultural field are structured around two divisions: on the one hand, between the dominant classes and the subordinate classes; and on the other, within the dominant classes between those with high economic capital as opposed to high cultural capital, and those with high cultural capital as opposed to high economic capital. The division within the dominant class can be explained thus:

> Broadly Bourdieu sees a historical development whereby the dominant class has divided into two specialized groups, the

dominant one concerned with material reproduction in the sphere of production, the dominated one concerned with the legitimation of material reproduction through the exercise of symbolic power.[27]

Those whose power stems primarily from cultural rather than economic power are engaged in a constant struggle within the cultural field 'to raise the social value of the specific competences involved in part by constantly trying to raise the scarcity of those competences. It is for this reason that . . . they will always resist as a body moves towards cultural democracy.'[28]

As we noted in Chapter 1 (see also Chapter 7), for Bourdieu the category of 'taste' functions as a marker of 'class' (using the word in a double sense to mean both a socio-economic category and a particular level of quality). At the pinnacle of the hierarchy of taste is the 'pure' aesthetic gaze – a historical invention – with its emphasis on form over function. The 'popular aesthetic' reverses this emphasis, subordinating form to function. Accordingly, popular culture is about performance, high culture is about contemplation; high culture is about representation, popular culture is about what is represented. As he explains, 'Intellectuals could be said to believe in the representation – literature, theatre, painting – more than in the things represented, whereas the people chiefly expect representations and the conventions which govern them to allow them to believe "naively" in the things represented.'[29]

Aesthetic distance is in effect the denial of function: it insists on the 'how' and not the 'what'. It is analogous to the difference between judging a meal good because it was economically priced and filling, and judging a meal good on the basis of how it was served, where it was served. . . . The 'pure' aesthetic or cultured gaze emerges with the emergence of the cultural field. One in effect guarantees the other. Bourdieu sees the art museum as the institutionalization of the aesthetic or cultured gaze and the cultural field. Once inside the museum art loses all prior functions (except that of being art) and becomes pure form: 'Though originally subordinated to quite different or even incompatible functions (crucifix and fetish, Pietà and still life), these juxtaposed works tacitly demand attention to form rather than function, technique rather than theme.'[30] For example, an advertisement for soup displayed in an art gallery becomes an example of the aesthetic, whereas the same advertisement in a magazine is an example of commerce. The effect of the distinction is to produce 'a sort of ontological promotion akin to a transubstantiation'.[31] In this way, 'art and cultural consumption are predisposed, consciously and deliberately or not, to fulfil a social function of legitimating social differences'.[32] It is the operation of such distinctions that Bourdieu calls the 'ideology of art', the view that genuine 'appreciation' can only be attained by an instinctively gifted minority armed against the mediocrity of the masses. Ortega y Gasset makes the point with precision: 'art helps the "best" to know and recognize one another in the greyness of the multitude and to learn their mission, which is to be few in number and to have to fight against the multitude.'[33]

As Bourdieu says, 'it is not easy to describe the "pure" gaze without also describing the naive gaze which it defines itself against.'[34] The naive gaze is of course the gaze of the popular aesthetic:

> The affirmation of continuity between art and life, which implies the subordination of form to function . . . a refusal of the refusal which is the starting point of the high aesthetic, i.e., the clear cut separation of ordinary dispositions from the specially aesthetic disposition.[35]

The relations between the pure and the popular/naive are, needless to say, not those of equality, but a relation of dominant and dominated. The popular aesthetic, in its stress on function over form, is necessarily contingent and pluralistic, contrary and, in deference, to the absolute insistence of the transcendent universality of the pure aesthetic. Bourdieu sees the two aesthetics as articulating the two separate, but related, realms of necessity and freedom. Without the required cultural capital to decipher the 'code' of art we are made socially *vulnerable* to the condescension of those who have the required cultural capital. What is social is presented as innate and, in turn, used to justify what is social. Aesthetic relations thus mimic and help reproduce social relations of power:

> Aesthetic intolerance can be terribly violent. . . . The most intolerable thing for those who regard themselves as the possessors of legitimate culture is the sacrilegious reuniting of tastes which taste dictates shall be separated. This means that the games of artists and aesthetes and their struggles for the monopoly of

artistic legitimacy are less innocent than they seem. At stake in
every struggle over art there is also the imposition of an art of
living, that is, the transmutation of an arbitrary way of living into
the legitimate way of life which casts every other way of living into
arbitrariness.[36]

The 'ideology of natural taste' insists that good taste is the property
of two groups: a dominant group, those who *instinctively* know, and
a fortunate subordinate group, those who know only through education, the rules and rituals of taste. Like other ideological strategies, 'The ideology of natural taste owes its plausibility and its
efficacy to the fact that . . . it naturalizes real differences, convert-
ing differences in the mode of acquisition of culture into differences of nature.'[37]

In an argument that draws heavily on the work of Bourdieu,
Paul Willis argues that the aesthetic appreciation of 'art' has un-
dergone an 'internal hyperinstitutionalization' – the dissociation
of art from life, a stress on form over function – in a further
attempt to distance itself and those who 'appreciate' it from the
'uncultured mass'. Part of this process is the denial of its foundations in education: the production and reproduction of the necessary knowledge on which aesthetic appreciation is founded. Instead
aesthetics attempts to present aesthetic appreciation (consumption) as something innate, rather than something learned. This
produces in many people a sense of being 'uncultured'. But rather
than seeing this as a question of non-access to knowledge – they
have not been educated in the necessary code to 'appreciate' the
formal qualities of high culture – they are encouraged to view
'themselves as ignorant, insensitive and without the finer sensibilities of those who really "appreciate". Absolutely certainly
they're not the "talented" or "gifted", the élite minority held to
be capable of performing or creating "art"'.[38] This produces a
situation in which people who make culture in their everyday existence see themselves as uncultured. Against the claims of the 'internal hyperinstitutionalization' of culture, Willis argues the case
for what he calls 'grounded aesthetics':

> This is the creative element in a process whereby meanings are
> attributed to symbols and practices and where symbols and prac-
> tices are selected, reselected, highlighted and recomposed to
> resonate further appropriate and particularized meanings. Such
> dynamics are emotional as well as cognitive. There are as many

aesthetics as there are grounds for them to operate in. Grounded aesthetics are the yeast of common culture.[39]

Grounded aesthetics is the process through which ordinary people make cultural sense of the world: 'the ways in which the received natural and social world is made human to *them* and made, to however small a degree (even if finally symbolic), controllable by them'.[40] Grounded aesthetic value is never intrinsic to a cultural text or practice, a universal quality of its form; it is always inscribed in the 'sensuous/emotive/cognitive'[41] act of consumption (how the text or practice is appropriated and 'used'). This is an argument against those who locate creativity only in the act of production: consumption being merely the recognition or misrecognition of the aesthetic intention. Against this, Willis insists on consumption as a symbolic act of creativity. His 'fundamental point . . . is that "messages" are not now so much "sent" and "received" as *made* in reception. . . . "Sent message" communication is being replaced by "made message" communication.'[42] Cultural communication is ceasing to be a process of listening to the voices of others. Grounded aesthetics is the insistence that popular culture is consumed on the basis of use, rather than on the basis – as with high or dominant culture – of the supposed inherent and ahistorical qualities (textual or authorial) of a text or practice. In the grounded aesthetics of popular culture, meaning is undecidable, always the result of a 'production in use' in terms of relevance (whereas in high or dominant culture, it is always already decided, a question of the correct interpretation arrived at on the basis of aesthetic contemplation). This of course means that a text or practice that is judged to be intrinsically banal and uninteresting may, on the basis of its 'production in use' within specific relations of consumption, be judged to be of great cultural interest and originality. His position is a rebuke to both textualism, which judges on the basis of formal qualities, and the political economy of culture approach, which judges on the basis of the relations of production. The 'symbolic work' of consumption is never a simple repetition of the relations of production, nor is it a simple confirmation of the semiotic certainties of the lecture theatre:

> People bring living identities to commerce and the consumption of cultural commodities as well as being formed there. They bring experiences, feelings, social position and social memberships to their encounter with commerce. Hence they bring a

necessary creative symbolic pressure, not only to make sense of cultural commodities, but partly through them also to make sense of contradiction and structure as they experience them in school, college, production, neighbourhood, and as members of certain genders, races, classes and ages. The results of this necessary symbolic work may be quite different from anything initially coded into cultural commodities.[43]

The French cultural theorist Michel de Certeau[44] also seeks to unpack the term 'consumer', to reveal the activity which lies within the act of consumption or what he prefers to call 'secondary production'. Consumption 'is devious, it is dispersed, but it insinuates itself everywhere, silently and almost invisibly, because it does not manifest itself through its own products, but rather through its ways of using the products imposed by a dominant economic order'.[45] For de Certeau, the cultural field is a site of continual conflict (silent and almost invisible) between the 'strategy' of cultural imposition (production) and the 'tactics' of cultural use (consumption or 'secondary production'). The cultural critic must be alert to 'the difference or similarity between . . . production . . . and . . . secondary production hidden in the process of . . . utilization'.[46] He thus characterizes the active consumption of texts as 'poaching': 'readers are travellers; they move across lands belonging to someone else, like nomads poaching their way across the fields they did not write'.[47] The acts of reader appropriation are always in potential conflict with the 'scriptural economy' of textual producers and those institutional voices (professional critics, academics, etc.) who work, through an insistence on the authority of authorial/textual meaning, to limit and confine the productive proliferation and circulation of 'unauthorized' meanings. De Certeau's notion of 'poaching' is a rejection of this traditional model of reading, in which the purpose of reading is the passive reception of authorial/textual intent; a model in which reading is reduced to a question of being right or wrong.

Many areas of cultural life could be said to illustrate de Certeau's claim but perhaps none more so than the consumption practices of fan culture. Together with youth subcultures, fans are perhaps the most visible part of the audience for popular cultural texts and practices. In recent years fandom has come increasingly under the critical gaze of cultural studies. Traditionally, fans have been treated in one of two ways – ridiculed or pathologized. According to Joli Jenson,[48]

'The literature on fandom is haunted by images of deviance. The fan is consistently characterized (referencing the term's origins) as a potential fanatic. This means that fandom is seen as excessive, bordering on deranged, behaviour.'[49] Jenson suggests two typical types of fan pathology, 'the obsessed individual' (usually male) and 'the hysterical crowd' (usually female). She contends that both figures result from a particular reading and 'unacknowledged critique of modernity' in which fans are viewed 'as a psychological symptom of a presumed social dysfunction'.[50] Fans are presented as one of the dangerous 'others' of modern life. 'We' are sane and respectable; 'they' are obsessed or hysterical.

This is yet another discourse on other people. Fandom is what 'other people' do; 'we' always pursue interests, exhibit tastes and preferences. Moreover, as Jenson points out, this is a discourse which seeks to secure and police distinctions between class cultures. This is clear in the way in which fandom is assigned to the cultural activities of popular audiences, while dominant groups are said to have cultural interests, tastes and preferences. This is confirmed by the object(s) of admiration. Official or dominant culture produces aesthetic appreciation; fandom is only appropriate for the texts and practices of popular culture.[51] Distinction is not just established by the object of admiration but in how the object is said to be admired. Popular audiences are said to display their pleasure to emotional excess, whereas the audience for official or dominant culture are always able to maintain respectable aesthetic distance and control.

Perhaps the most interesting recent account of fan culture from within cultural studies is Henry Jenkins's *Textual Poachers*.[52] In an ethnographic investigation of a fan community (mostly, but not exclusively, white middle class women), he approaches fandom as 'both . . . an academic (who has access to certain theories of popular culture, certain bodies of critical and ethnographic literature) and as a fan (who has access to the particular knowledge and traditions of that community)'.[53]

Fan reading is characterized by an intensity of intellectual and emotional involvement. 'The text is drawn close not so that the fan can be possessed by it but rather so that the fan may more fully possess it. Only by integrating media content back into their everyday lives, only by close engagement with its meanings and materials, can fans fully consume the fiction and make it an active

**215**

resource'.[54] Arguing against textual determinism (the text determines how it will be read and in so doing positions the reader in a particular ideological discourse; see Chapter 4 above), he insists that 'The reader is drawn not into the preconstituted world of the fiction but rather into a world she has created from textual materials. Here, the reader's pre-established values are at least as important as those preferred by the narrative system'.[55]

Fans do not just read texts, they continually reread them. This profoundly changes the nature of the text–reader relationship. Rereading undermines the operations of what Roland Barthes calls the 'hermenuetic code' (the way a text poses questions to generate the desire to keep reading).[56] Rereading thus shifts the reader's attention from 'what will happen' to 'how things happen', to questions of character relations, narrative themes, the production of social knowledges and discourses.

Whereas most reading is a solitary practice, performed in private, fans consume texts as part of a community. Fan culture is about the public display and circulation of meaning production and reading practices. Fans make meanings to communicate with other fans. Without the public display and circulation of these meanings fandom would not be fandom. 'Organized fandom is, perhaps first and foremost, an institution of theory and criticism, a semistructured space where competing interpretations and evaluations of common texts are proposed, debated, and negotiated and where readers speculate about the nature of the mass media and their own relationship to it.'[57]

Fan communities are not just bodies of enthusiastic readers; fan culture is also about cultural production. Jenkins notes ten ways in which fans re-write their favourite television shows:[58]

1. *Recontextualization* – the production of vignettes, short stories and novels which seek to fill in the gaps in broadcast narratives and suggest additional explanations for particular actions.
2. *Expanding the series timeline* – the production of vignettes, short stories, novels which provide background history of characters, etc. not explored in broadcast narratives or suggestions for future developments beyond the period covered by the broadcast narrative.
3. *Refocalization* – this occurs when fan writers move the focus of attention from the main protagonists to secondary figures. For

example, female or black characters are taken from the margins of a text and given centre stage.

4. *Moral realignment* – a version of refocalization in which the moral order of the broadcast narrative is inverted (the villains become the good guys). In some versions the moral order remains the same but the story is now told from the point of view of the villains.

5. *Genre shifting* – characters from broadcast science fiction narratives, say, are relocated in the realms of romance or the Western, for example.

6. *Cross overs* – characters from one television programme are introduced into another. For example, characters from *Dr Who* may appear in the same narrative as characters from *Star Wars*.

7. *Character dislocation* – characters are relocated in new narrative situations, with new names and new identities.

8. *Personalization* – the insertion of the writer into a version of their favourite television programme. For example, I could write a short story in which I am recruited by Dr Who to travel with him in the Tardis on a mission to explore what had become of Manchester United in the twenty-first century. As Jenkins points out, this subgenre of fan writing is discouraged by many in the fan community.[59]

9. *Emotional intensification* – the production of what are called 'hurt–comfort' stories in which favourite characters, for example, experience emotional crises.

10. *Eroticization* – stories which explore the erotic side of a character's life. Perhaps the best known of this subgenre of fan writing is 'slash' fiction, so called because it depicts same-sex relationships (as in Kirk/Spock, Bodie/Doyle, etc.).

In addition to fan fiction, fans make music videos in which images from favourite programmes are edited into new sequences to a soundtrack provided by a popular song; they make fan art; they produce fanzines; they engage in 'filking' (the writing and performing at conferences of songs – filk songs – about programmes, characters or fandom itself); and they organize campaigns to press television networks to bring back favourite programmes or to make changes in existing ones. As Jenkins points out, 'Fans are poachers who get to keep what they take and use their plundered goods as the foundations for the construction of an alternative cultural community'.[60]

In his discussion of filking, Jenkins draws attention to a common opposition within filk songs between fandom and 'Mundania' (the world in which non-fans – 'mundane readers' or 'mundanes' – live). The difference between the two worlds is not simply one of intensity of response, 'they are also contrasted in terms of the shallowness and shortsightedness of mundane thinking'.[61] 'Fans are defined in opposition to the values and norms of everyday life, as people who live more richly, feel more intensely, play more freely, and think more deeply than "mundanes"'.[62] 'Fandom constitutes . . . a space . . . defined by its refusal of mundane values and practices, its celebration of deeply held emotions and passionately embraced pleasures. Fandom's very existence represents a critique of conventional forms of consumer culture'.[63]

What Jenkins finds particularly empowering about fandom is its struggle to create 'a more participatory culture' from 'the very forces that transform many Americans into spectators'.[64]

> I am not claiming that there is anything particularly empowering about the texts fans embrace. I am, however, claiming that there is something empowering about what fans do with those texts in the process of assimilating them to the particulars of their lives. Fandom celebrates not exceptional texts but rather exceptional readings (though its interpretive practices makes it impossible to maintain a clear or precise distinction between the two).[65]

Like the classic cultural studies' model of subcultural reading, Jenkins' community of fandom struggles to resist the demands of the ordinary and the everyday. Whereas youth subcultures define themselves against parent and dominant cultures, the community of fandom sets itself in opposition to the everyday cultural passivities of 'Mundania'.

Lawrence Grossberg[66] is critical of the 'subcultural' model of fandom, in which 'fans constitute an élite fraction of the larger audience of passive consumers'.[67]

> Thus, the fan is always in constant conflict, not only with the various structures of power, but also with the vast audience of media consumers. But such an élitist view of fandom does little to illuminate the complex relations that exist between forms of popular culture and their audiences. While we may all agree that there is a difference between the fan and the consumer, we are

unlikely to understand the difference if we simply celebrate the former category and dismiss the latter one.[68]

In similar fashion, subcultural analysis has always tended to celebrate the extraordinary against the ordinary – a binary opposition between resistant 'style' and conformist 'fashion'. Subcultures, according to this model, represent youth in resistance, actively refusing to conform to the passive commercial tastes of the majority of youth. Once resistance has given way to incorporation, analysis stops, waiting for the next 'great refusal'. Gary Clarke rejects the 'dichotomy between subcultures and . . . the rest of society as being straight, incorporated'.[69] He also objects to the London-centredness of much subcultural theory and its suggestion that the appearance of a given youth subculture in the provinces is a telling sign of the subculture's incorporation.[70] Clarke points to an implicit cultural élitism structuring much of the classic work on youth subcultures.

> I would argue generally that the subcultural literature's focus on the stylistic deviance of a few contains (albeit implicitly) a similar treatment of the rest of the working class as unproblematically incorporated. This is evident, for example, in the distaste felt for youth deemed as outside subcultural activity – even though most 'straight' working-class youths enjoy the same music, styles, and activities as the subcultures – and in the disdain for such cults as glam, disco, and the ted revival, which lack 'authenticity'. Indeed, there seems to be an underlying contempt for 'mass culture' (which stimulates the interest in those who deviate from it) which stems from the work of the Marxism of the Frankfurt School and, within the English tradition, to the fear of mass culture expressed in *The Uses of Literacy*.[71]

If subcultural consumption is to remain an area of concern in cultural studies, Clarke suggests that future analysis 'should take the breakthrough of a style as its starting point', rather than as the defining moment of incorporation.[72] Better still, cultural studies should focus on 'the activities of all youths to locate continuities and discontinuities in culture and social relations and to discover the meaning these activities have for the youths themselves'.[73]

## The economic field

Despite his advocacy of the political economy approach to culture, McGuigan never offers examples of what he calls 'these more fundamental arrangements' so that we might compare them critically with the approaches of, say, Fiske and Willis. I suspect the reason is that they might look hopelessly reductive.[74] It is always much easier to suggest that there is the perfect methodology waiting in the wings ready to come on to steal the show; because without seeing the act it is difficult to be critical. But others have performed the act in public. Peter Golding and Graham Murdock, for instance, have offered a recent defence of its protocols and procedures:

> What distinguishes the critical political economy perspective . . . is precisely its focus on the interplay between the symbolic and economic dimensions of public communications [including popular culture]. It sets out to show how different ways of financing and organising cultural production have traceable consequences for the range of discourses and representations in the public domain and for audiences' *access* to them [my italics].[75]

The significant word here is 'access' (privileged over 'use' and 'meaning'). This reveals the limitations of the approach: good on the economic dimensions but weak on the symbolic. Golding and Murdock suggest that the work of theorists such as Willis and Fiske in its 'romantic celebration of subversive consumption is clearly at odds with cultural studies' long-standing concern with the way the mass media operate ideologically, to sustain and support prevailing relations of domination'.[76] What is particularly revealing about this claim is not the critique of Willis and Fiske, but the assumptions about the purposes of cultural studies. They seem to be suggesting that unless the focus is firmly and exclusively on domination and manipulation, cultural studies is failing in its task. There are only two positions: on the one hand, romantic celebration, and on the other, the recognition of ideological power – and only the second is a serious scholarly pursuit. Are all attempts to show people resisting ideological manipulation forms of romantic celebration? Is left pessimism and moral leftism the only guarantee of political and scholarly seriousness?

Critical political economy's idea of cultural analysis seems to involve little more than detailing access to, and availability of, cultural texts and practices. Nowhere do they actually advocate a consideration of what these texts and practices might mean (textually) or be made to mean in use (consumption). As Golding and Murdock point out, in contrast to recent work on audience activity within cultural studies, which concentrates on the negotiation of textual interpretations and media use in immediate social settings, critical political economy seeks to relate variations in people's responses to their overall location in the economic system.[77]

This seems to suggest that audience negotiations are fictitious, merely illusory moves in a game of economic power. Theorists within cultural studies, in a desire to avoid 'the *apparent* simplistic determinism . . . which sees audiences as the passive dupes of all powerful media' [my italics] are accused (this is a strategy adopted by McGuigan) of giving currency to 'an influential version of . . . free market philosophy'.[78] Their response to this is to evade the substantive point, and to refer again to questions of 'access'. While it is clearly important to locate the texts and practices of popular culture within the field of their economic determinations, it is clearly insufficient to do this and think you have also analyzed important questions of audience appropriation and use. It seems to me that neo-Gramscian hegemony theory still promises to do both, whereas critical political economy threatens, despite its admirable intentions, to collapse everything back into the economic.

It is Willis's attitude to the capitalist market that most offends McGuigan's political economy. He claims that the capitalist drive for profit produces contradictions which the symbolic creativity of the realm of common culture can exploit. But more than this, and more important than this, the capitalist drive for profit produces the very conditions for the production of the realm of common culture.

> No other agency has recognised this realm or supplied it with usable symbolic materials. And commercial entrepreneurship of the cultural field has discovered something real. For whatever self-serving reasons it was accomplished, we believe that this is an historical *recognition*. It counts and is irreversible. Commercial cultural forms have helped to produce an historical present from which we cannot now escape and in which there are many more materials – no matter what we think of them – available for necessary symbolic work than ever there were in the past. Out of these come forms not dreamt of in the commercial imagination and certainly not in the official one – forms which make up common culture.[79]

It is here that Willis opens himself to McGuigan's claim that he is simply echoing uncritically the rhetoric of consumer sovereignty.

Moreover, in his celebration of 'many more materials', he opens himself to the standard charge – more (quantity) always equals less (quality). I will consider the question of quality in a moment. But first his attitude to the market. Capitalism is not an ideologically monolithic system. For example, while one capitalist bemoans the activities of the latest subculture, another embraces it with economic enthusiasm. It is these contradictions in the capitalist market system which have produced the realm of common culture:

> Commerce and consumerism have helped to release a profane explosion of everyday symbolic life and activity. The genie of common culture is out of the bottle – let out by commercial carelessness. Not stuffing it back in, but seeing what wishes may be granted, should be the stuff of our imagination.[80]

This entails, what Willis knows will be an anathema for many, not least the advocates of political economy, the suggestion of 'the possibility of cultural emancipation working, at least in part, through ordinary, hitherto uncongenial economic mechanisms'.[81] It is never entirely clear what is intended by 'cultural emancipation', beyond, that is, the claim that it entails a break with the hegemonic exclusions of 'official culture'. But what is clear, and remains anathema to political economy, is that he sees the market, in part, because of its contradictions – 'supplying materials for its own critique'[82] – and despite its intentions and its distortions, as facilitating the symbolic creativity of the realm of common culture.

> People find on the market incentives and possibilities not simply for their own confinement but also for their own development and growth. Though turned inside out, alienated and working through exploitation at every turn, these incentives and possibilities promise more than any visible alternative. . . . Nor will it suffice any longer in the face of grounded aesthetics to say that modern 'consumer identities' simply repeat 'inscribed positions' within market provided texts and artifacts. Of course the market does not provide cultural empowerment in anything like a full sense. There are choices, but not choices over choices – the power to set the cultural agenda. Nevertheless the market offers a contradictory empowerment which has not been offered elsewhere. It may not be the best way to cultural emancipation for the majority, but *it may open up the way to a better way* [my italics].[83]

It is crude and simplistic to assume that the effects of consumption must mirror the intentions of production. As Terry

Lovell points out, the capitalist commodity has a double existence, as both use value and exchange value. Use value refers to 'the ability of the commodity to satisfy some human want'.[84] Such wants, says Marx, 'may spring from the stomach or from the fancy'.[85] The exchange value of a commodity is the amount of money realized when the commodity is sold in the market. Crucial to Willis's argument is the fact, as pointed out by Lovell, that 'the use value of a commodity cannot be known in advance of investigation of actual use of the commodity.'[86] The primary concern of capitalist production is exchange value leading to surplus value (profit). This does not mean of course that capitalism is uninterested in use value: without use value, commodities would not sell. But it does mean that the individual capitalist's search for surplus value can often be at the expense of the general ideological needs of the system as a whole. Marx was more aware than most of the contradictions in the capitalist system. Discussing bourgeois demands that workers should save in order better to endure the fluctuations of boom and slump, he points to the tension which exists between 'worker as producer' and 'worker as consumer':

> each capitalist does demand that his workers should save, but only *his* own, because they stand towards him as workers; but by no means the remaining *world of workers*, for these stand towards him as consumers. In spite of all 'pious' speeches he therefore searches for means to spur them on to consumption, to give his wares new charms, to inspire them with new needs by constant chatter etc. It is precisely this side of the relation of capital and labour which is an essential civilising moment, and on which the historic justification, but also the contemporary power of capital rests.[87]

Those on the moral and pessimistic left who attack the capitalist relations of consumption miss the point: it is the capitalist relations of production that justify its overthrow and not the consumer choice facilitated by the capitalist market. This also seems to be Willis's point. Moral leftists and left pessimists have allowed themselves to become trapped in an élitist and reactionary argument that claims more (quantity) always means less (quality). And as Lovell indicates, the commodities from which popular culture is made

> have different use values for the individuals who use and purchase them than they have for the capitalists who produce and sell them, and in turn, for capitalism as a whole. We may assume

**223**

that people do not purchase these cultural artifacts in *order* to expose themselves to bourgeois ideology . . . but to satisfy a variety of different wants which can only be guessed at in the absence of analysis and investigation. There is no guarantee that the use-value of the cultural object for its purchaser will even be compatible with its utility to capitalism as bourgeois ideology.[88]

It is important to distinguish between the power of the culture industries and the power of their influence. Too often the two are conflated, but they are not necessarily the same. The trouble with the political economy approach is that too often it is assumed that they are the same. Warner Bros. is undoubtedly part of a powerful multinational company, dealing in capitalist commodities. But once this is established, what next? Does it follow, for example, that all Warner Bros.' products are the bearers of capitalist ideology? Despite what R.E.M., for example, may say or think to the contrary, are they really purveyors of capitalist ideology? Are those who buy their records, pay to see them perform live, really in effect buying capitalist ideology; being duped by a capitalist multinational; being reproduced as capitalist subjects, ready to spend more and more money and consume more and more ideology? The problem with this approach is that it fails to acknowledge fully that capitalism produces commodities on the basis of their exchange value, whereas people tend to consume the commodities of capitalism on the basis of their use value. There are two economies running in parallel courses: the economy of use and the economy of exchange – we do not understand one by only interrogating the other.

The situation is further complicated by tensions between particular capitals and capitalism as a whole. Common class interests – unless specific restraints, censorship, etc., are imposed – usually take second place to the interests of particular capitals in search of surplus value:

> If surplus value can be extracted from the production of cultural commodities which challenge, or even subvert, the dominant ideology, then all other things being equal it is in the interests of particular capitals to invest in the production of such commodities. Unless collective class restraints are exercised, the individual capitalists' pursuit of surplus value may lead to forms of cultural production which are against the interests of capitalism as a whole.[89]

To explore this possibility would require specific focus on consumption as opposed to production. This is not to deny the claim of political economy that a full analysis must take into account technological and economic determinations. But it is to insist that if our focus is consumption then our focus must be consumption as it is experienced and not as it should be experienced given the relations of production.

To repeat the point made earlier, there are two economies of culture: production and consumption. For the purposes of detailed analysis they have to be kept artificially apart. We cannot understand consumption by collapsing it into production, nor will we understand production by reading it off consumption. Of course the difficulty is not keeping them apart, but bringing them into a relationship that can be meaningfully analyzed. However, if when studying popular culture our interest is the repertoire of products available for consumption, then production is our primary concern; whereas if we are interested in discovering the particular pleasures of a specific text or practice our primary focus would be on consumption. In both instances, our approach would be determined by the questions we seek to answer. Now it might be true that in an ideal research situation – given adequate time and funding – cultural analysis would remain incomplete until production and consumption had been dialectically linked; in the real world of study this is not always going to be the case. In the light of this, McGuigan's insistence that the only really valid approach to popular cultural analysis is that of the political economy of culture is not only untrue, but can result only in the reductive distortion and, ultimately, the stifling of cultural studies research.

## Hegemony revisited

Angela McRobbie's response to the so-called paradigm crisis in contemporary cultural studies is to argue for a return to neo-Gramscian hegemony theory. This is more or less my own position. McRobbie accepts that cultural studies has been radically transformed as debates about postmodernism and postmodernity have replaced the more familiar debates about ideology and hegemony. Cultural studies has responded in two ways. On the one hand, it has prompted a return to economic reductive forms of analysis; and on the other, it has given rise to an uncritical celebration of consumerism, in which consumption is understood *too* exclusively in terms of pleasure and meaning-making. McRobbie argues for a return to the concept of 'reproduction' to enable consumption to be seen in its broader context of political and social relations. One trend returns us to a reductive Marxism, while the other seems to be a move beyond Marxism altogether. In some ways, as she recognizes, this is a rerun of the structuralism/culturalism debate of the late 1970s, early 1980s, or the playing of one side of Marx's dialectic (we are made by history/we make history) against the other. She rejects a return 'to a crude and mechanical base–superstructure model, and also the dangers of pursuing a kind of cultural populism to a point at which anything which is consumed and is popular is also seen as oppositional'.[90] Instead, she calls for 'an extension of Gramscian cultural analysis';[91] and for a return to ethnographic cultural analysis which takes as its object of study 'the lived experience which breathes life into [the] . . . inanimate objects [of popular culture]'.[92] Such work would be situated in a context of reproduction. In short, McRobbie does what Hall did in the late 1970s and early 1980s: that is, proposes neo-Gramscian hegemony theory to hold a balance between questions of human agency ('active experience') and questions of social and economic structure ('reproduction').

Neo-Gramscian hegemony theory at its best insists that there is a dialectic between the processes of production and the activities of consumption. The consumer always confronts a text or practice in its material existence as a result of determinate conditions of production. But in the same way, the text or practice is confronted by a consumer who in effect *produces in use* the range of possible meaning(s) – these cannot just be read off from the materiality of the text or practice, or the means or relations of its production.

Although I still want to believe that hegemony theory is adequate to most of the tasks of cultural studies and the study of popular culture, I would suggest, at the risk of sounding hopelessly liberal (in the negative sense used by McGuigan), or hopelessly postmodernist (in the negative sense used by Jameson), or just hopelessly post-Marxist (again, in the negative sense), that rather than making claims and counter-claims about particular working traditions, we should instead celebrate the critical plurality of cultural studies – the different ways of working, the different contexts, the different conclusions – as equally valid (if differently weighted) contributions to the postdisciplinary field of cultural studies and the study of popular culture.

## The ideology of mass culture

We have to start from here and now, and acknowledge that we (all of us) live in a world dominated by multinational capitalism, and will do so for the foreseeable future ('pessimism of the intelligence, optimism of the will', as Gramsci said).[93] We need to see ourselves – all people, not just vanguard intellectuals – as active participants in culture: selecting, rejecting, making meanings, attributing value, resisting and, yes, being duped and manipulated. This does not mean that we forget about 'the politics of signification'. What we must do (and here I agree with Ang) is see that although pleasure is political, pleasure and politics can often be different. Liking *Father Ted* or *The X-Files* does not determine my politics, making me more leftwing or less leftwing. There is pleasure and there is politics: we can laugh at the distortions, the evasions, the disavowals, while still promoting a politics that says these are distortions, evasions, disavowals. We must teach each other to know, to politicize for, to recognize the difference between different versions of reality; and to know that each can require a different politics. This does not mean the end of a feminist or a socialist cultural politics, or the end of struggles around the representations race, class, gender or sexual preference but it *should* mean the final break with the 'culture and civilization' problematic, with its debilitating insistence that the consumption of culture is the judge and jury of the moral and political worth of an individual.

In many ways, this book has been about what Ang calls 'the ideology of mass culture'. Against this ideology, I have posed the patterns of pleasure in consumption and the consumption of pleasure, aware that I continually run the risk of advocating an uncritical cultural populism. Ultimately, I have argued that popular culture is what we make from the products and practices made available by the culture industries. To paraphrase what I said in the discussion of neo-Gramscian cultural studies, *making* popular culture ('production in use')[94] can be empowering to subordinate and resistant to dominant understandings of the world. But this is not to say that popular culture is always empowering and resistant.

To deny the passivity of consumption is not to deny that sometimes consumption is passive; to deny that the consumers of popular culture are not cultural dupes is not to deny that the culture industries seek to manipulate. But it is to deny that popular culture is little more than a degraded landscape of commercial and ideological manipulation, imposed from above in order to make profit and secure social control. Neo-Gramscian cultural studies insists that to decide these matters requires vigilance and attention to the details of the production, distribution and consumption of culture. These are not matters that can be decided once and for all (outside the contingencies of history and politics) with an élitist glance and a condescending sneer. Nor can they be read off from the moment of production (locating meaning, pleasure, ideological effect, the probability of incorporation, the possibility of resistance, in, variously, the intention, the means of production or the production itself): these are only aspects of the contexts for 'production in use'; and it is, ultimately, in 'production in use' that questions of meaning, pleasure, ideological effect, incorporation or resistance, can be (contingently) decided.

Such an argument will not satisfy those ideologues of mass culture whose voices seemed to grow louder, more insistent, during the period of writing this book. I am thinking of the British and American media panic about the threat to high culture's authority – the debate about 'political correctness' and multiculturalism. The canon is wielded like a knife to cut away at critical thinking. They dismiss with arrogance what most of us call culture. Saying popular culture (or more usually, mass culture) and high culture (or more usually, just culture) is just another way of saying 'them' and 'us'. They speak with the authority and support of a powerful discourse behind them. Those of us who reject this discourse – recognizing its thinking and unthinking élitism – find ourselves often with only the discursive support of (the often equally disabling) ideology of populism. The task for a radical cultural politics of popular culture is to steer a course which, without losing sight of the terrain mapped by these two ideologies, can nevertheless explore the terrain without resort to the disabling tendencies of, on the one side, a dismissive élitism, and, on the other, a disarming anti-intellectualism. Although this book has not made this voyage, I hope it has at least mapped the existing terrain in such a way as to help make this voyage a real possibility for other students of popular culture.

## Further reading

Simon During (ed), *The Cultural Studies Reader*, London: Routledge, 1993. A good selection of material from many of the leading figures in the field.

Ann Gray and Jim McGuigan (eds), *Studying Culture: An introductory reader*, London: Edward Arnold, 1993. A good selection of material from many of the leading figures in the field.

Lawrence Grossberg, Cary Nelson and Paula Treichler (eds), *Cultural Studies*, London: Routledge, 1992. The collection consists of forty essays (most followed by discussion). An excellent introduction to recent debates in cultural studies.

Paul Marris and Sue Thornham (eds), *Media Studies: A reader*, Edinburgh: Edinburgh University Press, 1996. An excellent introduction to developments in a discipline covering much the same terrain as cultural theory and popular culture.

David Morley and Kuan-Hsing Chen (eds), *Stuart Hall: Critical dialogues in cultural studies*, London: Routledge, 1995. This is a brilliant book. It brings together interviews and essays (on and by Stuart Hall). Together they weave an image of the past, present and possible future of cultural studies.

Jessica Munns and Gita Rajan, *A Cultural Studies Reader: History, theory, practice*, New York: Longman, 1995. Well organized, with a good selection of interesting essays.

John Storey (ed.), *What Is Cultural Studies?: A reader*, London: Edward Arnold, 1996. A collection of essays which in different ways attempt to answer the question, 'what is cultural studies?'

John Storey (ed.), *Cultural Theory and Popular Culture: A reader*, Hemel Hempstead: Harvester Wheatsheaf, 1994. This is the companion volume to *Cultural Theory and Popular Culture: An introduction*. It contains examples of most of the work discussed here.

# JOURNALS ON CULTURAL THEORY AND POPULAR CULTURE

The best way to keep up with debates within cultural studies is to read work published in journals. The following is a selection of academic journals which regularly carry articles on popular culture.

*Critical Studies in Mass Communication*
*Critical Quarterly*
*Cultural Studies*
*Feminist Review*
*European Journal of Communication*
*International Journal of Cultural and Media Studies*
*Journal of Popular Culture*
*Literature and History*
*Media, Culture and Society*
*New Formations*
*Screen*
*Southern Review*
*Textual Practice*
*Theory, Culture and Society*
*Women: A cultural review*
*Women's Studies*

# NOTES

## Preface

1. Walter E. Houghton, *The Victorian Frame of Mind 1830–1870*, New Haven: Yale University Press, 1957, p. xv.
2. See the companion volume to this book, *Cultural Theory and Popular Culture: A reader*, edited by John Storey, Hemel Hempstead: Harvester Wheatsheaf, 1994.

## Chapter 1   What is popular culture?

1. Tony Bennett, 'Popular culture: a teaching object' in *Screen Education* **34**, 1980, p. 18.
2. Ibid., p. 20.
3. Raymond Williams, *Keywords*, London: Fontana, 1983, p. 87.
4. Ibid., p. 90.
5. Ibid.
6. Ibid.
7. Graeme Turner, *British Cultural Studies: An introduction* (second edition), London: Routledge, 1996 p. 182.
8. James W. Carey, 'Overcoming resistance to cultural studies' in *What Is Cultural Studies: A reader*, edited by John Storey, London: Edward Arnold, 1996, p. 65.
9. Stuart Hall, 'Some paradigms in cultural studies' in *Annali* **3**, 1978, p. 23.
10. See Karl Marx and Frederick Engels, *The German Ideology* (student edition), edited and introduced by C. J. Arthur, London: Lawrence & Wishart, 1974.
11. Karl Marx, Preface and Introduction to *A Contribution to the Critique of Political Economy*, Peking: Foreign Languages Press, 1976, p. 3.

12. Tony Bennett, 'Popular culture: defining our terms' in *Popular Culture: Themes and issues 1*, Milton Keynes: Open University Press, 1982, p. 81.

13. Marx, Preface and Introduction to *A Critique of Political Economy*, p. 5.

14. Bertolt Brecht, *On Theatre*, translated by John Willett, London: Methuen, 1978, pp. 150–51.

15. Stuart Hall, 'The rediscovery of ideology: the return of the repressed in media studies' in *Subjectivity and Social Relations*, edited by Veronica Beechey and James Donald, Milton Keynes: Open University Press, 1985, p. 36.

16. See Stuart Hall, 'Notes on deconstructing "the Popular"', in *Cultural Theory and Popular Culture: A Reader*, edited by John Storey, Hemel Hempstead: Harvester Wheatsheaf, 1994.

17. Williams, *Keywords*, p. 237.

18. Bennett, 'Popular culture: a teaching object', pp. 20–21.

19. Pierre Bourdieu, *Distinction: A Social Critique of the Judgment of Taste*, translated by Richard Nice, Cambridge, MA: Harvard University Press, 1984, p. 5.

20. For a discussion of Shakespeare as popular culture in nineteenth century America, see Lawrence Levine, 'William Shakespeare and the American people: A study in cultural transformation' in *Rethinking Popular Culture*, edited by Chandra Mukerji and Michael Schudson, Berkeley: University of California Press, 1991.

21. See Bourdieu, p. 5.

22. See Williams, *Keywords*, pp. 236–8.

23. Hall, 'Notes on deconstructing "the popular"', pp. 461–2.

24. This is the principal theme of the 'production of culture' approach. See Paul DiMaggio, 'Cultural entrepreneurship in nineteenth-century Boston: The creation of an organizational base for high culture in America', in Chandra Mukerji and Michael Schudson, *Rethinking Popular Culture* Berkeley: University of California Press, and Diane Crane, *The Production of Culture*, London: Sage, 1992.

25. John Fiske, *Understanding Popular Culture*, London: Unwin Hyman, 1989, p. 31.

26. Simon Frith, *Sound Effects: Youth, leisure and the politics of rock*, London: Constable, 1983, p. 147.

27. Fiske, *Understanding Popular Culture*, p. 27.

28. Richard Maltby, Introduction to *Dreams for Sale: Popular culture in the 20th century*, edited by Richard Maltby, London: Harrap, 1989, p. 11.

29. Andrew Ross, *No Respect: Intellectuals and popular culture*, London: Routledge, 1989, p. 7.

30. See Duncan Webster, *Looka Yonder!*, London: Comedia, 1988.
31. Maltby, Introduction, p. 14.
32. Ibid.
33. Bennett, 'Popular culture: a teaching object', p. 27.
34. Antonio Gramsci, *Selections from Prison Notebooks*, edited and translated by Quintin Hoare and Geoffrey Nowell-Smith, London: Lawrence & Wishart, 1971, p. 57.
35. I call my approach neo-Gramscian in order to create some respectful theoretical and political distance between my own work and that of Antonio Gramsci. I am conscious of the fact that I am using an approach developed to analyze the general field of politics to understand the particular terrain of popular culture.
36. Gramsci, *Selections from Prison Notebooks*, p. 161.
37. Tony Bennett, 'Popular culture and the turn to Gramsci' in *Cultural Theory and Popular Culture: A reader*, edited by John Storey, Hemel Hempstead: Harvester Wheatsheaf, 1994, p. 226.
38. Chantal Mouffe, 'Hegemony and ideology in Gramsci' in *Culture, Ideology and Social Process*, edited by Tony Bennett, Colin Mercer and Janet Woollacott, 1981, London: Batsford Academic, p. 231.
39. Raymond Williams, 'Base and superstructure in Marxist cultural theory' in *Problems in Materialism and Culture*, London: Verso, 1980.
40. Stuart Hall, 'Encoding/decoding' in *Culture, Media, Language*, edited by Stuart Hall, Dorothy Hobson, Andrew Lowe and Paul Willis, London: Hutchinson, 1980. David Morley, *The Nationwide Audience*, London: BFI, 1980. For critical commentary see John Storey, *Cultural Studies and the Study of Popular Culture*, Edinburgh: Edinburgh University Press, 1996.
41. See Hall, 'Notes on deconstructing the popular'.
42. Tony Bennett, 'The politics of the popular' in *Popular Culture and Social Relations*, edited by Veronica Beechey and James Donald, Milton Keynes: Open University Press, p. 20.
43. Turner, *British Cultural Studies*, p. 6.
44. Lawrence Grossberg, *It's a Sin: Essays on postmodernism, politics and culture*, Sydney: Power Publications, 1988, p. 7.
45. Raymond Williams, *Culture and Society*, Harmondsworth: Penguin, 1963, p. 11.
46. R. J. Morris, *Class and Class Consciousness in the Industrial Revolution 1780–1850*, London: Macmillan, 1979, p. 22.
47. Bennett, 'Popular culture: defining our terms', p. 86.
48. Dick Hebdige, 'Banalarama, or can pop save us all?' in *New Statesman & Society*, 9 December 1988.
49. Geoffrey Nowell-Smith, 'Popular culture' in *New Formations* **2**, 1987, p. 80.

## Chapter 2    The 'culture and civilization' tradition

1. Matthew Arnold, *Culture and Anarchy*, London: Cambridge University Press, 1960, p. 6.
2. Ibid., p. 42.
3. Ibid., p. 46.
4. Ibid., p. 48.
5. Ibid., p. 89.
6. Ibid., p. 179.
7. Ibid., p. 31.
8. Ibid., p. 163.
9. Ibid., pp. 163–4.
10. Ibid., p. 163.
11. Ibid., p. 76.
12. Ibid., p. 69.
13. Ibid., p. 76.
14. Ibid., p. 193.
15. Ibid., pp. 80–81.
16. Ibid., p. 105.
17. Ibid.
18. Ibid., p. 107.
19. Ibid., p. 82.
20. Ibid., p. 76.
21. Ibid., p. 96.
22. Ibid., p. 209.
23. Matthew Arnold, *On Education*, Harmondsworth: Penguin, 1973, p. 39.
24. Matthew Arnold, *Letters 1848–1888*, volume I, London: Macmillan, 1896, p. 187.
25. Matthew Arnold, *Poetry and Prose*, London: Rupert Hart Davis, 1954, p. 343.
26. Arnold, *Culture and Anarchy*, p. 97.
27. See Raymond Williams, *Culture and Society*, Harmondsworth: Penguin, 1963.
28. Samuel Taylor Coleridge, *On the Constitution of the Church and State*, London: Dent, 1972, p. 33.
29. Ibid., p. 34.
30. Arnold, *Poetry and Prose*, p. 640.
31. Ibid., pp. 364–5.
32. Matthew Arnold, *Complete Prose Works*, volume III, Ann Arbor: University of Michigan Press, 1960–77, pp. 43–4.
33. Arnold, *Poetry and Prose*, p. 591.

34. F. R. Leavis, 'Mass civilisation and minority culture', in *Cultural Theory and Popular Culture: A reader*, edited by John Storey, Hemel Hempstead: Harvester Wheatsheaf, 1994, p. 12.
35. F. R. Leavis and Denys Thompson, *Culture and Environment*, Westport, CT: Greenwood Press, 1977, p. 3.
36. Ibid., p. 5.
37. Ibid., p. 3.
38. Ibid., p. 5.
39. Q. D. Leavis, *Fiction and the Reading Public*, London: Chatto & Windus, 1978, pp. 185 & 187.
40. Ibid., p. 191. John Docker refers to her as 'an old-style colonialist ethnographer, staring with distaste at the barbaric ways of strange and unknown people', *Postmodernism and Popular Culture: A cultural history*, Cambridge: Cambridge University Press, 1994, p. 25.
41. Ibid., p. 190.
42. Leavis and Thompson, *Culture and Environment*, p. 26.
43. F. R. Leavis, *For Continuity*, Cambridge: Minority Press, 1933, pp. 188–9.
44. Leavis, *Fiction and the Reading Public*, p. 270.
45. Ibid., p. 191.
46. Leavis and Thompson, *Culture and Environment*, p. 100.
47. Leavis, *Fiction and the Reading Public*, p. 152.
48. Ibid., p. 54.
49. Ibid., p. 74.
50. Leavis, 'Mass civilisation and minority culture', p. 14.
51. Leavis, *Fiction and the Reading Public*, p. 165.
52. Leavis and Thompson, *Culture and Environment*, p. 138.
53. Leavis, 'Mass civilisation and minority culture', p. 14.
54. Leavis and Thompson, *Culture and Environment*, p 4
55. Ibid., pp. 16–17.
56. Ibid., p. 40.
57. Ibid., p. 51.
58. Ibid., p. 114.
59. Ibid., p. 119.
60. Ibid., p. 121.
61. Ibid., p. 144.
62. Leavis, *For Continuity*, p. 216.
63. Leavis, *Fiction and the Reading Public*, p. 85.
64. Ibid., p. 264.
65. F. R. Leavis, *The Common Pursuit*, London: Hogarth, 1984, pp. 188–9 & 208.

66. It is not just that Leavis offers us an idealized account of the past, which he does; he actually idealizes Bourne's own account, failing to mention his criticisms of rural life.
67. Leavis and Thompson, *Culture and Environment*, pp. 1–2.
68. Ibid., p. 69.
69. Ibid., p. 99.
70. Ibid., p. 2.
71. Williams, *Culture and Society*, p. 253.
72. Leavis and Thompson, *Culture and Environment*, p. 97.
73. F. R. Leavis, *Nor Shall My Sword*, London: Chatto & Windus, 1972, p. 27.
74. Tony Bennett, 'Popular culture: themes and issues' in *Popular Culture* U203, Milton Keynes: Open University Press, 1982, pp. 5–6.
75. Andrew Ross, *No Respect: Intellectuals and popular culture*, London: Routledge, 1989, p. 42.
76. Ibid.
77. Ibid., p. 43.
78. Ibid.
79. Bernard Rosenberg, 'Mass culture in America' in *Mass Culture: The popular arts in America*, edited by Bernard Rosenberg and David Manning White, New York: Macmillan, 1957, p. 9.
80. David Manning White, 'Mass culture in America: another point of view' in *Mass Culture*, p. 13.
81. Ibid., p. 14.
82. Ibid.
83. Dwight Macdonald, 'A theory of mass culture' in *Cultural Theory and Popular Culture: A reader*, p. 30.
84. Ibid.
85. Ibid, p. 31.
86. Ibid.
87. Ibid.
88. Ibid., p. 34
89. Ibid., p. 36.
90. Ibid., p. 42.
91. Ernest van den Haag, 'Of happiness and despair we have no measure' in *Mass Culture*, p. 512.
92. Ibid., p. 521.
93. Ibid., p. 528.
94. Ibid., p. 529.
95. Ibid., pp. 532–5.
96. Ibid., p. 535.
97. Ibid., p. 536.

98. Edward Shils, 'Mass society and its culture' in *Literary Taste, Culture, and Mass Communication*, volume 1, edited by Peter Davison, Rolf Meyersohn and Edward Shils, Cambridge: Chadwyck Healey, 1978, p. 35.
99. Ibid., p. 36.
100. D. W. Brogan, 'The problem of high and mass culture' in *Literary Taste*, p. 191.
101. Ibid., p. 193.
102. Leslie Fiedler, 'The middle against both ends' in *Mass Culture*, p. 539.
103. Ibid.
104. Ibid., p. 540.
105. Ibid., p. 545.
106. Ibid., p. 547.
107. Edward Shils, 'Daydreams and nightmares' in *Literary Taste*, p. 206.
108. Ibid., p. 209.
109. Ibid.
110. Ibid., p. 218.
111. Ibid., p. 226.
112. Ross, *No Respect*, p. 58.
113. Melvin Tumin, 'Popular culture and the open society' in *Mass Culture*, p. 550.
114. Ibid.
115. For the 'common sense' inherited from the influence of the work of the 'culture and civilization' tradition see the 'quality' press.
116. Bennett, 'Popular culture: themes and issues', p. 6.
117. Ibid.
118. Ibid.
119. As Williams points out in *Culture and Society*, 'There are in fact no masses; there are only ways of seeing other people as masses' (p. 289).

## Chapter 3   Culturalism

1. Stuart Hall, 'Some paradigms in cultural studies' in *Annali* 3, 1978, p. 19.
2. See Stuart Hall, 'Cultural studies: two paradigms', in *What Is Cultural Studies: A reader*, edited by John Storey, London: Edward Arnold, 1996.
3. Richard Johnson, 'Three problematics: elements of a theory of working-class culture', in *Working Class Culture: Studies in history and theory*, edited by John Clarke *et al.*, London: Hutchinson, 1979.

4. Richard Hoggart, *The Uses of Literacy*, Harmondsworth: Penguin, 1990, p. 17.
5. Ibid., pp. 24 & 23.
6. Ibid., p. 32.
7. Ibid., p. 33.
8. Ibid., p. 238.
9. Ibid., p. 120.
10. Ibid., p. 340.
11. Ibid.
12. Ibid., p. 24.
13. Ibid., pp. 147–8.
14. Ibid., p. 151.
15. For an interesting discussion of this see Dave Harker, *Fakesong: The manufacture of British 'folksong' 1700 to the present day*, Milton Keynes: Open University Press, 1985.
16. Hoggart, *The Uses of Literacy*, p. 159.
17. Ibid., p. 162.
18. Raymond Williams, 'Fiction and the writing public', *Essays in Criticism* 7, 1957, pp. 426–7.
19. Raymond Williams, *The Long Revolution*, Harmondsworth: Penguin, 1965, pp. 377–8.
20. Hoggart, *The Uses of Literacy*, p. 169.
21. Ibid., p. 181.
22. Ibid.
23. Ibid., p. 193.
24. Ibid., p. 192.
25. Ibid., p. 193.
26. Ibid., pp. 196–7.
27. Ibid., p. 231.
28. Ibid., p. 237.
29. Ibid., p. 236.
30. Ibid., p. 235.
31. Ibid., p. 247.
32. Ibid.
33. Ibid., p. 248.
34. Ibid.
35. Ibid.
36. Ibid.
37. Ibid., pp. 248–9.
38. Ibid., p. 250.
39. Ibid., p. 316.
40. Ibid., p. 324.
41. Ibid.

42. Ibid., p. 325.
43. Ibid.
44. Ibid., p. 330.
45. Ibid., p. 340.
46. Ibid., p. 243.
47. Ibid., pp. 243–4.
48. Stuart Hall, 'Cultural studies and the Centre; some problematics and problems', in *Culture, Media, Language*, edited by Stuart Hall *et al.*, London: Hutchinson, 1980, p. 18.
49. See Alan O'Connor, *Raymond Williams: Writing, culture, politics*, Oxford: Basil Blackwell, 1989.
50. Williams, *The Long Revolution*, p. 57.
51. Ibid.
52. Ibid.
53. Raymond Williams, *Culture and Society*, Harmondsworth: Penguin, 1963, p. 17.
54. Williams, *The Long Revolution*, p. 57.
55. Ibid.
56. Ibid.
57. Ibid.
58. Ibid., p. 58.
59. Ibid.
60. Ibid., p. 59.
61. Ibid., p. 60.
62. Ibid., p. 63.
63. Ibid., p. 64.
64. Ibid.
65. Ibid., p. 65
66. Ibid.
67. Ibid., p. 66.
68. Ibid.
69. Ibid., p. 68.
70. Williams, *Culture and Society*, p. 308.
71. Ibid.
72. Ibid.
73. Ibid., p. 69.
74. Ibid.
75. Ibid., p. 70.
76. Ibid.
77. Ibid., p. 61.
78. Ibid., p. 313.
79. Ibid., p. 314.
80. Williams, 'Fiction and the writing public', pp. 424–5.

81. Ibid., p. 425.
82. Hall, 'Cultural studies and the Centre', p. 19.
83. E. P. Thompson, *The Making of the English Working Class*, Harmondsworth: Penguin, 1980, p. 8.
84. Ibid.
85. Ibid., pp. 8–9.
86. Ibid., p. 9.
87. Ibid., p. 10.
88. Ibid., p. 11.
89. Ibid., pp. 212–13.
90. Ibid., p. 213.
91. Ibid., p. 212.
92. Ibid., p. 914.
93. Hall, 'Cultural studies and the Centre', pp. 19–20.
94. E. P. Thompson, 'Interview' in *Radical History Review* **3**, 1976, p. 15.
95. Gregor McLellan, 'E. P. Thompson and the discipline of historical context' in *Making Histories: Studies in history writing and politics*, edited by Richard Johnson, London: Hutchinson, 1982, p. 107.
96. Thompson, *The Making of the English Working Class*, p. 12.
97. McLellan, 'E. P. Thompson and the discipline of historical context'.
98. Karl Marx, *The Eighteenth Brumaire of Louis Bonaparte*, Moscow: Progress Publishers, 1977, p. 10.
99. See Perry Anderson, *Arguments within English Marxism*, London: Verso, 1980.
100. See Raphael Samuel, *Peoples' History and Socialist Theory*, London: Routledge & Kegan Paul, 1981.
101. For further discussion of this point see R. S. Neale, 'E. P. Thompson: a history of culture and culturalist history' in *Creating Culture*, edited by Diane J. Austin Broos, London: Allen & Unwin, 1987.
102. Stuart Hall and Paddy Whannel, *The Popular Arts*, London, Hutchinson, 1964, p. 15.
103. Ibid.
104. Ibid., p. 23.
105. Ibid., p. 27.
106. Ibid., p. 28.
107. Ibid., p. 35.
108. Ibid., p. 36.
109. I remember at school a teacher who encouraged us to bring to music lessons our records by the Beatles, Dylan and the Stones. The class would always end the same way – he would try to convince us of the error of our musical taste.

110. Hall & Whannel, *The Popular Arts*, p. 37.
111. Ibid.
112. Ibid., p. 39.
113. Ibid., p. 38.
114. Ibid., p. 39.
115. Ibid., p. 46.
116. Ibid., p. 40.
117. Ibid., p. 47.
118. Ibid., p. 59.
119. Ibid., p. 66.
120. Ibid., p. 78.
121. Ibid.
122. Ibid., p. 269.
123. Ibid.
124. Ibid., p. 270.
125. Ibid., p. 276.
126. Ibid., p. 280.
127. Ibid., p. 281.
128. Ibid., p. 282.
129. Ibid., p. 311.
130. Ibid., pp. 311–12.
131. Ibid., p. 75.
132. Williams, *The Long Revolution*, p. 10.
133. Richard Hoggart, 'Schools of English and contemporary society' in *Speaking to Each Other*, volume II, edited by Richard Hoggart, London: Chatto and Windus, 1970, p. 258.
134. Michael Green, 'The Centre for Contemporary Cultural Studies' in *What Is Cultural Studies: A reader*, edited by John Storey, London: Edward Arnold, 1996, p. 49.
135. Hoggart, *The Uses of Literacy*, pp. 17–19.

## Chapter 4   Structuralism and post-structuralism

1. Terry Eagleton, *Literary Theory: An introduction*, Oxford: Basil Blackwell, 1983, p. 96.
2. Ferdinand de Saussure, *Course in General Linguistics*, London: Fontana, 1974, p. 120.
3. Roland Barthes, *Elements of Semiology*, London: Jonathan Cape, 1967, p. 14.
4. Claude Lévi-Strauss, *Structural Anthropology*, London: Allen Lane, 1968, p. 18.

5. Terence Hawkes, *Structuralism and Semiotics*, London: Methuen, 1977, p. 39.
6. Lévi-Strauss, *Structural Anthropology*, p. 209.
7. Ibid., pp. 224 & 229.
8. Will Wright, *Sixguns and Society: A structural study of the Western*, Berkeley: University of California Press, 1975, p. 17.
9. Ibid., p. 23.
10. Ibid., p. 49.
11. Ibid., p. 24.
12. See Vladimir Propp, *The Morphology of the Folktale*, Austin: Texas University Press, 1968.
13. Wright, *Sixguns and Society*, pp. 48–9.
14. Ibid., p. 165.
15. Guild Home Video, 1991.
16. Wright, *Sixguns and Society*, p. 15.
17. Ibid., pp. 186–7.
18. *Empire Magazine*, January 1992.
19. Roland Barthes, *Mythologies*, London: Paladin, 1973, p. 11.
20. Ibid., p. 9.
21. Ibid., p. 11.
22. Saussure, *Course in General Linguistics*, p. 16.
23. For analysis critical of Barthes's attitude to popular culture see Tony McNeil 'Roland Barthes: *Mythologies* (1957)', URL: http://orac.sund.ac.uk/~osOtmc/myth.htm.
24. Barthes, *Elements of Semiology*, pp. 89–91.
25. Barthes, *Mythologies*, pp. 125–6.
26. Barthes, *Mythologies*, p. 126.
27. Roland Barthes, 'The photographic message' in *Image–Music–Text*, London: Fontana, 1977, p. 26.
28. Ibid., pp. 134–5.
29. Ibid., p. 138.
30. Ibid., p. 142.
31. Ibid., p. 155.
32. Ibid.
33. Ibid., p. 156.
34. Barthes, 'The photographic message', p. 26.
35. Ibid., p. 27.
36. Ibid., p. 29.
37. Roland Barthes, 'Rhetoric of the image' in *Image–Music–Text*, p. 46.
38. Roland Barthes, 'The death of the author' in *Image–Music–Text*, p. 146.
39. Ibid., p. 157.

40. Jacques Derrida, *Speech and Phenomena*, Evanston: North Western University Press, 1973.
41. Jacques Derrida, *Writing and Difference*, London: Routledge & Kegan Paul, 1978, p. 25.
42. Jacques Derrida, *Positions*, London: Athlone Press, 1978, p. 41.
43. Jacques Derrida, *Of Grammatology*, Baltimore: Johns Hopkins University Press, 1976, p. 154.
44. Ibid., p. 144.
45. Ibid., p. 149.
46. Ibid., p. 163.
47. Ibid., p. 229.
48. Derrida, *Positions*, p. 41.
49. Derrida, *Of Grammatology*, pp. 158 & 163.
50. Eagleton, *Literary Theory*, p. 165.
51. Jacques Lacan, *The Four Fundamental Concepts of Psycho Analysis*, London: Hogarth, 1977, p. 218.
52. Jacques Lacan, *Ecrits: A selection*, London: Tavistock, 1977, p. 154.
53. Eagleton, *Literary Theory*, pp. 167, 168 & 185.
54. Quoted in Barry Smart, *Michel Foucault*, New York: Tavistock, 1985, p. 59.
55. Michel Foucault, *Discipline and Punish*, Harmondsworth: Penguin, 1979, p. 27.
56. Michel Foucault, *History of Sexuality*, Harmondsworth: Penguin, 1981 pp. 92–7.
57. Foucault, *Discipline and Punish*, p. 194.
58. Foucault, *History of Sexuality*, p. 11.
59. Ibid., pp. 22–3.
60. Edward Said, *Orientalism*, Harmondsworth: Penguin, 1985, p. 1.
61. Ibid., pp. 1–2.
62. Ibid., p. 3.
63. Ibid.

## Chapter 5   Marxism

1. Frederick Engels, *Ludwig Feuerbach and the End of Classical German Philosophy*, Peking: Foreign Languages Press, 1976, p. 65.
2. Fredric Jameson, *The Political Unconscious*, London: Methuen, 1981, p. 17.
3. Frederick Engels, 'Letter to Joseph Bloch', in *Cultural Theory and Popular Culture: A reader*, edited by John Storey, Hemel Hempstead: Harvester Wheatsheaf, 1994, p. 199.
4. Ibid., pp. 199–201.

5. Karl Marx and Frederick Engels, *The German Ideology* (student edition), edited and introduced by C. J. Arthur, London: Lawrence & Wishart, 1974, p. 64.

6. Ibid., pp. 65–6.

7. Karl Marx, Preface and introduction to *A Contribution to the Critique of Political Economy*, Peking: Foreign Languages Press, 1976, p. 4.

8. Theodor Adorno and Max Horkheimer, *Dialectic of Enlightenment*, New York: Herder and Herder, 1972, pp. 120–21.

9. Ibid., p. 125.

10. Theodor Adorno, 'How to look at television' in *The Culture Industry*, London: Routledge, 1991, pp. 143–4.

11. Bertolt Brecht, *On Theatre*, translated by John Willett, London: Methuen, 1978, p. 229.

12. Leo Löwenthal, *Literature, Popular Culture and Society*, Palo Alto, CA: Pacific Books, 1961, p. 11.

13. Ibid.

14. Herbert Marcuse, *One Dimensional Man*, London: Sphere, 1968, pp. 26–7.

15. Max Horkheimer, 'Art and mass culture' in *Literary Taste, Culture and Mass Communication*, volume 12, edited by Peter Davison, Rolf Meyersohn and Edward Shils, Cambridge: Chadwyck Healey, 1978, p. 5.

16. Herbert Marcuse, *Negations*, London: Allen Lane, 1968, p. 95.

17. Ibid., p. 96.

18. Ibid., p. 99.

19. Marcuse, *One Dimensional Man*, p. 58.

20. Ibid., p. 60.

21. Marcuse, *Negations*, pp. 118–21.

22. Ibid., p. 200.

23. Marcuse, *One Dimensional Man*, p. 61.

24. Horkheimer, 'Art and mass culture', p. 17.

25. Theodor Adorno, 'The schema of mass culture' in *The Culture Industry*, p. 79.

26. Marcuse, *One Dimensional Man*, p. 63.

27. Ibid., pp. 63–4.

28. Tony Bennett, 'Media theory and social theory' in *Mass Communications and Society DE 353*, Milton Keynes: Open University Press, 1977, p. 45.

29. Marcuse, *One Dimensional Man*, p. 64.

30. Adorno and Horkheimer, *Dialectic of Enlightenment*, p. 142.

31. Theodor Adorno, 'On popular music' in *Cultural Theory and Popular Culture: A reader*, edited by John Storey, Hemel Hempstead: Harvester Wheatsheaf, 1994, pp. 202–203.

32. Ibid., p. 207.
33. Ibid., p. 208.
34. Ibid., p. 211.
35. Ibid.
36. Ibid.
37. Ibid., p. 212.
38. For an interesting and sustained critique of Adorno on popular music see Richard Middleton, *Studying Popular Music*, Milton Keynes: Open University Press, 1990. For an equally interesting, and more sympathetic account, see Bernard Gendron, 'Theodor Adorno meets the Cadillacs' in *Studies in Entertainment: Critical approaches to mass culture*, edited by Tania Modleski, Bloomington: Indiana University Press, 1986.
39. Simon Frith, *Sound Effects: Youth, leisure and the politics of rock*, London: Constable, 1983, p. 147.
40. Ibid.
41. Quoted in Frith, *Sound Effects*, p. 147.
42. See John Storey, ' "Side saddle on the golden calf": moments of utopia in American pop music and pop music culture' in *An American Half Century: Postwar culture and politics in the USA*, edited by Michael Klein, London: Pluto Press, 1995.
43. Walter Benjamin, 'The work of art in the age of mechanical reproduction' in *Illuminations*, London: Fontana, 1973, p. 219.
44. Ibid., p. 222.
45. Ibid., p. 223.
46. Ibid., p. 226.
47. Ibid., p. 236.
48. Susan Willis, *A Primer for Daily Life*, London: Routledge, 1991, p. 10.
49. See *Aesthetics and Politics*, edited by New Left Review, London: Verso, 1977.
50. Frith, *Sound Effects*, p. 57.
51. J. M. Bernstein, introduction to *The Culture Industry*, 1978, p. 15.
52. Stuart Hall, 'Some paradigms in cultural studies' in *Annali 3*, 1978, p. 21.
53. Louis Althusser, *For Marx*, London: Allen Lane, 1969, p. 113.
54. Karl Marx, *Capital*, volume I, Harmondsworth: Penguin, 1976, p. 176.
55. Althusser, *For Marx*, p. 231.
56. Ibid., p. 166.
57. Ibid., p. 233.
58. Ibid., pp. 233–4.
59. Ibid., p. 67.

60. Louis Althusser and Etienne Balibar, *Reading Capital*, London: Verso 1979, p. 28.
61. Ibid.
62. Pierre Macherey, *A Theory of Literary Production*, London: Routledge & Kegan Paul, 1978, pp. 79–80.
63. Ibid., p. 78.
64. Ibid., p. 6.
65. Ibid., p. 87.
66. Ibid., p. 94.
67. Ibid., p. 130.
68. Ibid., p. 131.
69. Ibid., p. 60.
70. Ibid., p. 133.
71. Ibid., pp. 194–5.
72. Ibid., p. 230.
73. Ibid., p. 161.
74. Louis Althusser, *Lenin and Philosophy*, New York: Monthly Review Press, 1971, p. 222.
75. Ibid., p. 171.
76. See Robert Lapsley and Michael Westlake, *Film Theory: An introduction*, Manchester: Manchester University Press, 1988.
77. Judith Williamson, *Decoding Advertisements*, London: Marion Boyars.
78. See Gareth Stedman Jones, 'Working class culture and working class politics in London, 1870–1900: notes on the remaking of a working class' in *Cultural Theory and Popular Culture: A reader*, edited by John Storey, Hemel Hempstead: Harvester Wheatsheaf, 1994, pp. 76–87.
79. Antonio Gramsci, *Selections from Prison Notebooks*, edited and translated by Quintin Hoare and Geoffrey Nowell-Smith, London: Lawrence & Wishart, 1971, p. 5.
80. Ibid., p. 453.
81. See John Storey, 'Matthew Arnold: The politics of an organic intellectual' in *Literature and History* 11: 2, autumn 1985.
82. Ibid., pp. 149–50.
83. Dick Hebdige, *Subculture: The meaning of style*, London: Methuen, 1979, p. 96.
84. See John Storey, 'Rockin' hegemony: West Coast rock and Amerika's war in Vietnam' in *Cultural Theory and Popular Culture: A reader*, edited by John Storey, Hemel Hempstead: Harvester Wheatsheaf, 1994, pp. 330–40.
85. See Hall, 'The rediscovery of ideology: the return of the repressed in media studies', and 'On postmodernism and articulation: an interview with Stuart Hall', and Jennifer Daryl Slack, 'The theory and method of articulation in cultural studies' in *Stuart Hall:*

*Cultural dialogues in cultural studies,* edited by David Morley and Kuan-Hsing Chen, London: Routledge, 1996.

86. Valentin Volosinov, *Marxism and the Philosophy of Language,* New York: Seminar Press, 1973.
87. Hall, 'The rediscovery of ideology: the return of the repressed in media studies', p. 34.
88. Stuart Hall, 'Notes on deconstructing the popular' in *Cultural Theory and Popular Culture: A reader,* edited by John Storey, Hemel Hempstead: Harvester Wheatsheaf, 1994, p. 459.
89. Mikhail Bakhtin and Valentin Volosinov were almost certainly the same person.
90. Mikhail Bakhtin, *Problems of Dostoevsky's Poetics,* Manchester: Manchester University Press, 1984, p. 122.
91. Ibid., pp. 122–3.
92. Ibid., p. 123.
93. Ibid.
94. Ibid., p. 125.
95. Mikhail Bakhtin, *Rabelais and His World,* Bloomington, Indiana University Press, 1984.
96. Bakhtin, *Problems of Dostoevsky's Poetics,* pp. 129–30.
97. John Docker, *Postmodernism and Popular Culture: A cultural history,* Cambridge: Cambridge University Press, 1994, p. 185.
98. John Fiske, *Understanding Popular Culture,* London: Unwin Hyman, 1989, p. 85.
99. Ibid., p. 87.
100. Ibid., p. 85.
101. Fiske, *Television Culture,* London and New York: Routledge, 1987: pp. 248–9.
102. For example see Peter Stallybrass and Allon White, *The Politics and Poetics of Transgression,* Ithaca, NY: Cornell University Press, and Terry Eagleton, *Walter Benjamin,* London: Verso, 1981.
103. Fiske, *Television Culture,* p. 249.
104. Docker, *Postmodernism and Popular Culture,* p. 284.

## Chapter 6    Feminism

1. Elaine Showalter, Introduction to *Speaking of Gender,* edited by Elaine Showalter, London: Routledge, 1990, p. 1. Celia Lury remarks that 'it is my impression that current feminist cultural studies are repeatedly held back by the continued dominance of ungendered understandings of culture'. See Celia Lury, 'The rights and wrongs of culture: issues of theory and methodology', in

*Feminist Cultural Theory: Process and Production,* edited by Beverley Skeggs, Manchester: Manchester University Press, 1995.

2. Sylvia Walby, *Theorising Patriarchy,* Oxford: Blackwell, 1990, p. 1.
3. Rosemary Tong, *Feminist Thought: A comprehensive introduction,* London: Routledge, 1992, p. 1.
4. Michèle Barrett, 'Feminism and the definition of cultural politics' in *Feminism, Culture and Politics,* edited by Rosalind Brunt and Caroline Rowan, London: Lawrence & Wishart, 1982, p. 37.
5. Women's Study Group, Centre for Contemporary Cultural Studies, *Women Take Issue,* London: Hutchinson, 1978, p. 15.
6. Tania Modleski, *Loving With a Vengeance: Mass produced fantasies for women,* Hamden, CT: Archon Books, 1982, p. 14.
7. Ibid., p. 34.
8. Ibid., p. 14.
9. Ibid., p. 25.
10. Ibid., p. 47.
11. Ibid., p. 57.
12. Ibid., pp. 113–14.
13. Rosalind Coward, *Female Desire: Women's sexuality today,* London: Paladin, 1984, p. 14.
14. Ibid.
15. Ibid., p. 16.
16. Ibid.
17. Charlotte Lamb, originally in the *Guardian,* 13 September 1982, quoted in Coward, *Female Desire,* p. 190.
18. Coward, *Female Desire,* p. 190.
19. Ibid., pp. 191–2.
20. Ibid., p. 196.
21. Lorraine Gamman and Margaret Marshment, Introduction to *The Female Gaze: Women as viewers of popular culture,* edited by Lorraine Gamman and Margaret Marshment, London: The Women's Press, 1988, p. 1.
22. Ibid.
23. Ibid.
24. Ibid., p. 2.
25. Ibid.
26. Laura Mulvey, 'Visual pleasure and narrative cinema' in *Screen,* **16** (3), autumn 1975, p. 6.
27. Ibid., p. 7.
28. Ibid., p. 8.
29. Ibid.
30. Ibid., p. 10.
31. Ibid., p. 9.

32. Ibid.
33. Ibid., pp. 9–10.
34. Ibid., p. 10.
35. Ibid., p. 17.
36. Ibid., p. 11.
37. Ibid., pp. 11–12.
38. Ibid., p. 13.
39. Ibid.
40. Ibid., pp. 13–14.
41. Ibid., p. 14.
42. Ibid., p. 17.
43. Ibid., p. 18.
44. Ibid.
45. Ibid.
46. Jane M. Gaines, 'Review Article' in *Screen* **32** (1), spring 1991.
47. Antony Easthope and Kate McGowan (eds), *A Critical and Cultural Theory Reader*, Buckingham: Open University Press, 1992; and Jessica Munns and Gita Rajan (eds), *A Cultural Studies Reader: History, theory, practice*, London: Longman, 1995.
48. Mulvey, 'Visual pleasure and narrative cinema', pp. 7–8.
49. See Laura Kipnis, 'Feminism: the political conscience of postmodernism?' in *Universal Abandon: The politics of postmodernism*, edited by Andrew Ross, Minneapolis: University of Minnesota Press, 1986.
50. Gamman and Marshment, Introduction, p. 5.
51. Ibid.
52. For modifications in her position, see *Visual and Other Pleasures*, London: Macmillan, 1989.
53. Jackie Stacey, *Star Gazing: Hollywood and Female Spectatorship*, London: Routledge, 1994.
54. Ibid., p. 24.
55. Richard Dyer, 'Entertainment and utopia', in *Genre: the musical*, edited by Rick Altman, London: Routledge & Kegan Paul, 1981.
56. Stacey, *Star Gazing*, p. 99.
57. Ibid., p. 97.
58. Ibid., p. 187.
59. Ibid., p. 188.
60. Ibid., p. 198.
61. Ibid., p. 223.
62. Ibid., p. 238.
63. Ibid., p. 12.
64. Janice Radway, *Reading the Romance: Women, patriarchy, and popular literature*, London: Verso, 1987, p. 13.

65. Ibid., p. 53.
66. Janice Radway finds this figure implausible.
67. Radway, *Reading the Romance*, p. 83.
68. Nancy Chodorow, *The Reproduction of Mothering: Psychoanalysis and the sociology of gender*, Berkeley: University of California Press, 1978.
69. Radway, *Reading the Romance*, p. 84.
70. Ibid., p. 139.
71. Ibid., p. 140.
72. Ibid., p. 146.
73. Ibid., p. 149.
74. Ibid., p. 169.
75. Ibid., p. 184.
76. Ibid.
77. Ibid., pp. 199 & 198.
78. Ibid., p. 90.
79. Ibid., pp. 91 & 94.
80. Ibid., p. 97.
81. Ibid., p. 100.
82. Ibid., p. 61.
83. Ibid., p. 210.
84. Ibid.
85. Ibid.
86. Ibid., p. 217.
87 Ibid., pp. 221–2.
88. Ibid., p. 222.
89. Charlotte Brunsdon, 'Pedagogies of the feminine: feminist teaching and women's genres' in *Screen* **32** (4), winter 1991, p. 372.
90. Ien Ang, 'Feminist desire and female pleasure' in *Cultural Theory and Popular Culture: A reader*, edited by John Storey, Hemel Hempstead: Harvester Wheatsheaf, 1994, p. 517.
91. Ibid.
92. Ibid., p. 518.
93. Ibid., p. 519.
94. Ibid., p. 521.
95. Janice Radway, 'Romance and the work of fantasy: Struggles over feminine sexuality and subjectivity at the century's end', in *Viewing, Reading, Listening: Audiences and cultural reception*, edited by Jon Cruz and Justin Lewis, Boulder: Westview Press, 1994.
96. Alison Light, ' "Returning to Manderley" – Romance fiction, female sexuality and class', in Feminist Review **16**, 1984, pp. 7–25.
97. In similar fashion, it may be the case that reading Enid Blyton's *Secret Seven* books as a child prepared the ground for my commitment to socialism as an adult.

98. Radway, 'Romance and the work of fantasy', p. 20.
99. Quoted in Ien Ang, *Watching Dallas: Soap opera and the melodramatic imagination*, London: Methuen, 1985, p. 2.
100. Ang, *Watching Dallas*, p. 10.
101. Ibid., p. 9.
102. Ibid., p. 12.
103. Ibid.
104. See ibid., pp. 34–8.
105. See ibid., pp. 38–41.
106. Ibid., p. 42.
107. Ibid., p. 43.
108. ibid., p. 46.
109. Ibid., p. 49.
110. Ibid.
111. See Tony Bennett, 'Text, readers, reading formations' in *Literature and History* 9 (2), autumn 1983, and John Storey, 'Text, readers, reading formations: *My Poll and My Partner Joe* in Manchester in 1841' in *Literature and History* 1 (2), autumn 1992.
112. Peter Brooks, *The Melodramatic Imagination*, New Haven: Yale University Press, 1976.
113. Ang, *Watching Dallas*, p. 82.
114. Ibid., p. 83.
115. Ibid., p. 15.
116. Ibid., pp. 95–6.
117. Ibid., p. 96.
118. Ibid., p. 97.
119. Ibid., p. 98.
120. Ibid., p. 100.
121. Ibid., p. 101.
122. Ibid., p. 103.
123. Ibid., p. 105.
124. Ibid., p. 106.
125. Ibid., p. 109.
126. Ibid., pp. 109–10.
127. Ibid.
128. Ibid., p. 113.
129. Ibid., p. 115.
130. Ibid.
131. Ibid., pp. 118–19.
132. Ibid., p. 133.
133. Ibid., p. 135.
134. Ibid.
135. Ibid., pp. 135–6.

136. Dana Polan, 'Complexity and contradiction in mass culture analysis: on Ien Ang *Watching Dallas*' in *Camera Obscura* **16**, winter 1988, p. 198.
137. Ibid., p. 202.
138. Janice Winship, *Inside Women's Magazines*, London: Pandora, 1987, p. xiii.
139. Ibid.
140. Ibid.
141. Ibid., pp. xiii–xiv.
142. Ibid., p. 8.
143. Ibid., p. 39.
144. Ibid., p. 56.
145. Ibid., pp. 56–7.
146. Ibid., p. 67.
147. Ibid., p. 70.
148. Ibid., p. 76.
149. Ibid., p. 77.
150. Ibid., p. 80.
151. Ibid.
152. Ibid., p. 140.
153. Ibid., p. 149.
154. Ibid.
155. Ibid. Winship repeats this definition, more or less, in 'The impossibility of best: enterprise meets domesticity in the practical women's magazines of the 1980s' in *Cultural Studies* **5** (2), May 1991. See also '"A girl needs to get street wise": magazines for the 1980s' in *Feminist Review* **21**, 1985.
156. Quoted in Showalter, *Speaking of Gender*, p. 7.
157. Antony Easthope, *What a Man's Gotta Do: The masculine myth in popular culture*, London: Paladin, 1986, p. 1.
158. Ibid., p. 167.
159. Joyce Canaan and Christine Griffin, 'The new men's studies: part of the problem or part of the solution' in *Men, Masculinities and Social Theory*, edited by Jeff Hearn and David Morgan, London: Unwin Hyman, pp. 207–208.
160. bell hooks, *Talking Back: Thinking feminist, thinking Black*, London: Sheba Feminist Publishers, 1989, p. 12.
161. Quoted in Modleski, *Loving with a Vengeance*, p. 25.

## Chapter 7   Postmodernism

1. Dick Hebdige, *Hiding in the Light*, London: Comedia, 1988, pp. 181–2.
2. See Steven Best and Douglas Kellner, *Postmodern Theory: Critical investigations*, London: Macmillan, 1991.
3. See Susan Sontag, *Against Interpretation*, New York: Deli, 1966, and Leslie Fiedler, *The Collected Essays of Leslie Fiedler*, volume 2, New York: Stein and Day, 1971.
4. Sontag, *Against Interpretation*, p. 296.
5. Ibid., p. 299.
6. Ibid., p. 302.
7. Ibid., p. 303.
8. Fredric Jameson, 'Postmodernism, or the cultural logic of late capitalism' in New Left Review **146**, 1984, p. 56.
9. Fredric Jameson, 'The politics of theory: ideological positions in the Postmodernism debate' in *The Ideologies of Theory Essays*, volume 2, London: Routledge, 1988, p. 104.
10. Andreas Huyssen, *After the Great Divide: Modernism, mass culture and postmodernism*, London: Macmillan, 1986, p. viii.
11. Ibid., p. 57.
12. Hal Foster, Introduction to *Postmodern Culture*, edited by Hal Foster, London: Pluto, 1985, pp. xi–xii.
13. Best and Kellner, *Postmodern Theory*, p. 15.
14. Dick Hebdige says the term was coined by Lawrence Alloway.
15. As Hall says, there is a sense in which postmodernism 'is about how the world dreams itself to be "American"', 'On postmodernism and articulation an interview with Stuart Hall' in *Stuart Hall: Cultural dialogues in cultural studies*, edited by David Morley and Huan-Hsing Chen, London: Routledge, 1996.
16. Quoted in Simon Frith and Howard Horne, *Art into Pop*, London: Methuen, 1987, p. 104.
17. Quoted in Frith and Horne, *Art into Pop*, p. 109.
18. Ibid., p. 109.
19. Ibid., p. 120.
20. Huyssen, *After the Great Divide*, p. 188.
21. Ibid., p. 195.
22. Ibid.
23. Jean-François Lyotard, *The Postmodern Condition: A report on knowledge*, Manchester: Manchester University Press, 1984, p. xxiv.
24. Steven Connor, *Postmodernist Culture: An introduction to theories of the contemporary*, Oxford: Basil Blackwell, 1989, p. 28.
25. Lyotard, *The Postmodern Condition*, p. 46.

26. Ibid., p. 48.
27. Ibid., p. 51.
28. For a more positive view of the possibilities for a postmodern pedagogy see Henry A. Giroux and Peter McLaren (eds) *Between Borders: Pedagogy and the politics of cultural studies*, London: Routledge, 1994.
29. Nancy Fraser and Linda Nicholson, 'Social criticism without philosophy: an encounter between feminism and postmodernism' in *Universal Abandon: The politics of postmodernism*, edited by Andrew Ross, Minneapolis: University of Minnesota Press, 1988, p. 87.
30. Lyotard, *The Postmodern Condition*, p. 79.
31. Ibid., p. 79.
32. Quoted in Connor, *Postmodernist Culture*, p. 41.
33. Michel Foucault, *Power/Knowledge*, New York: Pantheon Books, 1980, p. 62.
34. Iain Chambers, *Popular Culture: The metropolitan experience*, London: Routledge, 1988, p. 216.
35. Angela McRobbie, *Postmodernism and Popular Culture*, London: Routledge, 1994, p. 23.
36. Kobena Mercer, *Welcome to the Jungle: New positions in black cultural studies*, London: Routledge, 1994, p. 2.
37. Best and Kellner, *Postmodern Theory*, p. 109.
38. Ibid., p. 111.
39. Connor, *Postmodernist Culture*, p. 51.
40. Jean Baudrillard, *For a Critique of the Political Economy of the Sign*, St Louis: Telos Press, 1981, p. 185.
41. Jean Baudrillard, *Simulations*, New York: Semiotext(e),1983, p. 2.
42. Ibid., p. 55.
43. Quoted in Frith and Horne, *Art into Pop*, p. 7.
44. Ibid., p. 182.
45. John Fiske, *Media Matters: Everyday culture and media change*, Minnesota: University of Minnesota Press, 1994, p. xv.
46. Ibid., p. xxii.
47. Baudrillard, *Simulations*, p. 23.
48. Ibid., p. 25.
49. Ibid.
50. Ibid., p. 30.
51. Ibid., p. 36.
52. Ibid., pp. 28–9.
53. Ibid., pp. 12–13.
54. Lawrence Grossberg, *It's a Sin: Essays on postmodernism, politics and culture*, Sydney: Power Publications, 1988, p. 175.

55. John Docker, *Postmodernism and Popular Culture: A cultural history*, Cambridge: Cambridge University Press, 1994, p. 105.
56. Jameson, 'The politics of theory', p. 111.
57. Fredric Jameson, 'Postmodernism and consumer society', p. 112.
58. Jameson, 'The politics of theory', p. 112.
59. Ibid.
60. Jameson, 'Postmodernism and consumer society', p. 112.
61. Ibid., p. 113.
62. Ernest Mandel, *Late Capitalism*, London: Verso, 1978.
63. Jameson, 'Postmodernism, or the cultural logic of late capitalism', p. 78.
64. Ibid.
65. See Raymond Williams, 'Base and superstructure in Marxist cultural theory' in *Problems in Materialism and Culture*, London: Verso, 1980.
66. Jameson, 'Postmodernism, or the cultural logic of late capitalism', p. 55.
67. Ibid., p. 56.
68. Jameson, 'The politics of theory', p. 105.
69. Jameson, 'Postmodernism, or the cultural logic of late capitalism', p. 65.
70. Ibid., p. 64.
71. Jameson, 'Postmodernism and consumer society', p. 115.
72. Ibid., p. 116.
73. Jameson, 'Postmodernism, or the cultural logic of late capitalism', p. 60.
74. Ibid., p. 61.
75. See Grossberg, *It's a Sin*, pp. 178–81.
76. Grossberg, *It's a Sin*, p. 174.
77. Jameson, 'Postmodernism, or the cultural logic of late capitalism', p. 67.
78. Jameson, 'Postmodernism and consumer society', p. 116.
79. Jameson, 'Postmodernism, or the cultural logic of late capitalism', pp. 65–6.
80. Ibid., p. 67.
81. Ibid.
82. Jameson, 'Postmodernism and consumer society', p. 120.
83. Ibid., p. 125.
84. Jameson, 'Postmodernism, or the cultural logic of late capitalism', p. 85.
85. Ibid., p. 56.
86. Ibid., p. 85.
87. Ibid.

88. Ibid., p. 89.
89. McRobbie, *Postmodernism and Popular Culture*, p. 13.
90. Ibid., p. 15.
91. Ibid.
92. Frith and Horne, *Art into Pop*, p. 5.
93. Connor, *Postmodernist Culture*, p. 186.
94. See Jameson, 'Postmodernism, or the cultural logic of late capitalism'.
95. Andrew Goodwin, 'Popular music and postmodern theory', in *Cultural Studies* 5 (2), 1991. See Andrew Goodwin, 'Popular music and postmodern theory' in *Cultural Theory and Popular Culture: A reader*, edited by John Storey, Hemel Hempstead; Harvester Wheatsheaf, 1994, and Andrew Goodwin, *Dancing in the Distraction Factory: Music Television and Popular Culture*, London: Routledge, 1993.
96. Williams, 'Base and superstructure in Marxist cultural theory'.
97. Goodwin, 'Popular music and postmodern theory', p. 173.
98. Ibid., p. 175
99. Cornel West, 'Interview' in *Cultural Theory and Popular Culture: A Reader*, p. 402.
100. McRobbie, *Postmodernism and Popular Culture*.
101. Fred Pfeil, ' "Makin' flippy floppy": postmodernism and the baby boom PMC' in *The Year Left*, edited by Mike Davis, London: Verso, 1985, and 'Postmodernism as a "structure of feeling" ' in *Marxism and the Interpretation of Culture*, edited by Cary Nelson and Lawrence Grossberg, London: Macmillan, 1988.
102. Goodwin, 'Popular music and postmodern theory', p. 175.
103. Frith and Horne, *Art into Pop*, p. 58.
104. Quoted in Roy Boyne and Ali Rattansi (eds), *Postmodernism and Society*, London: Macmillan, 1990, p. 105.
105. Goodwin, 'Popular music and postmodern theory', p. 185.
106. Ibid., p. 178.
107. Jim Collins, 'Postmodernism and television' in *Channels of Discourse, Reassembled*, edited by Robert C. Allen, London: Routledge, 1992.
108. Charles Jencks in Collins, 'Postmodernism and television' p. 338.
109. Collins, 'Postmodernism and television', p. 337.
110. Ibid., p. 338.
111. Ibid., p. 341.
112. Ibid., p. 345.
113. Ibid.
114. Ibid.
115. Ibid., p. 347.
116. Ibid., pp. 347–8.

117. Ibid., p. 348.
118. See Antony Easthope, *Literary into Cultural Studies*, London: Routledge, 1991, and Steven Connor, *Theory and Cultural Value*, Oxford: Blackwell, 1992. See also the debate on value between Antony Easthope and Steven Connor in *Textual Practice* 4 (3) 1990 and 5 (3) 1991. See also John Frow, *Cultural Studies and Value*, New York: Oxford University Press, 1995.
119. See Jane Thompkins, *Sensational Designs: The cultural work of American fiction*, 1790–1860, New York: Oxford University Press, 1985, and Barbara Herrnstein Smith, *Contingencies of Value*, Cambridge MA: Harvard University Press, 1988.
120. See Pierre Bourdieu, *Distinction: A social critique of the judgement of taste*, translated by Richard Nice, Cambridge, MA: Harvard University Press, 1984.
121. John Fekete, 'Introductory notes for a postmodern value agenda' in *Life After Postmodernism*, edited by John Fekete, New York: St Martin's Press, 1987, p. 17.
122. Sontag, *Against Interpretation*, p. 304.
123. Frith and Home, *Art into Pop*, p. 169.

## Chapter 8 The politics of the popular

1. Jim McGuigan, *Cultural Populism*, London: Routledge, 1992, p. 4.
2. Ibid., p. 5.
3. Ibid., pp. 40–41.
4. Ibid., p. 76.
5. Ibid.
6. Ibid., p. 79.
7. Ibid., p. 159.
8. Ibid., p. 171. For a similar claim see the Introduction to *Reading into Cultural Studies*, edited by Martin Barker and Anne Beezer, London: Routledge, 1992.
9. Ibid., p. 85.
10. Ibid., p. 72.
11. Ibid., p. 75.
12. John Fiske, *Television Culture*, London: Routledge, 1987, p. 309.
13. Ibid.
14. Ibid., p. 311.
15. Ibid.
16. Ibid., p. 313.
17. Ibid.
18. Ibid.

19. Ibid., p. 316.
20. Ibid., p. 320.
21. Ibid., p. 316.
22. Ibid.
23. John Fiske, *Understanding Popular Culture*, London: Unwin Hyman, 1989, p. 8.
24. Ibid., pp.20–21.
25. McGuigan, *Cultural Populism*, p. 75.
26. Nicholas Garnham and Raymond Williams, 'Pierre Bourdieu and the sociology of culture: an introduction' in *Media, Culture and Society* **2** (3), 1980, p. 215.
27. Ibid., p. 219.
28. Ibid., p. 220.
29. Pierre Bourdieu, *Distinction*, p. 5.
30. Ibid., p. 30.
31. Ibid., p. 6.
32. Ibid., p. 7.
33. Ibid., p. 31.
34. Ibid., p. 32.
35. Ibid.
36. Ibid., p. 57.
37. Ibid., p. 68.
38. Paul Willis, *Common Culture*, Buckingham: Open University Press, 1990, p. 3.
39. Ibid., p. 21.
40. Ibid., p. 22.
41. Ibid., p. 24.
42. Ibid., p. 135.
43. Ibid., p. 21.
44. Michel de Certeau, *The Practice of Everyday Life*, Berkeley: University of California, 1984. See also de Certeau, 'The practice of everyday life', in *Cultural Theory and Popular Culture: A reader*, edited by John Storey, Hemel Hempstead: Harvester Wheatsheaf, 1994.
45. de Certeau, *The Practice of Everyday Life*, pp. xii–xiii.
46. Ibid., p. xiii.
47. Ibid., p. 174.
48. Joli Jenson, 'Fandom as pathology', in *The Adoring Audience*, edited by Lisa Lewis, London: Routledge, 1992.
49. Ibid., p. 9.
50. Ibid.

51. Jenson argues convincingly that it is possible to be a fan of James Joyce in much the same way as it is possible to be a fan of Barry Manilow; 'Fandom as pathology', pp. 19–20.
52. Henry Jenkins, *Textual Poachers*, New York: Routledge, 1992.
53. Ibid., p. 5.
54. Ibid., p. 62.
55. Ibid., p. 63.
56. Roland Barthes, *S/Z*, London: Jonathan Cape, 1975.
57. Jenkins, *Textual Poachers*, p. 86.
58. Ibid., pp. 162–77.
59. Ibid., pp. 171–2.
60. Ibid., p. 223.
61. Ibid., p. 264.
62. Ibid., p. 268.
63. Ibid., p. 283.
64. Ibid., p. 284.
65. Ibid.
66. Lawrence Grossberg, 'Is there a fan in the house?', in *The Adoring Audience*, pp. 50–65.
67. Ibid., p. 52.
68. Ibid.
69. Gary Clarke, 'Defending Ski-jumpers: a critique of theories of youth subcultures', in *On Record*, edited by Simon Frith and Andrew Goodwin, New York: Pantheon, 1990, p. 84.
70. Ibid., p. 86.
71. Ibid., p. 90.
72. Ibid., p. 92.
73. Ibid., p. 95.
74. For an informed and polemical debate between cultural studies and the political economy of culture, see *Critical Studies in Mass Communication* **12**, 1995.
75. Peter Golding and Graham Murdock, 'Culture, communications and political economy' in *Mass Media and Society*, edited by James Curran and Michael Gurevitch, London: Edward Arnold, 1991, p. 15.
76. Ibid., p. 17.
77. Ibid., p. 27.
78. Ibid., p. 28.
79. Willis, *Common Culture*, p. 19.
80. Ibid., p. 27.
81. Ibid., p. 131.
82. Ibid., p. 139.
83. Ibid., p. 160.

84. Terry Lovell, *Pictures of Reality, Aesthetics, Politics and Pleasure*, London: British Film Institute, 1983, p. 57.
85. Ibid., p. 57.
86. Ibid.
87. Karl Marx, *Grundrisse*, Harmondsworth: Penguin, 1973, p. 287.
88. Lovell, *Pictures of Reality*, p. 60.
89. Ibid., p. 61.
90. Angela McRobbie, *Postmodernism and Popular Culture*, p. 39.
91. Ibid.
92. Ibid., p. 27
93. Antonio Gramsci, *Selections from Prison Notebooks*, edited and translated by Quintin Hoare and Geoffrey Nowell-Smith, London: Lawrence & Wishart, 1971 p. 175.
94. Marx makes the point that 'a product only obtains its last finish in consumption. . . . For example, a dress becomes a real dress only in the act of being worn; a house which is uninhabited is in fact no real house; in other words, a product, as distinct from a mere natural object, proves itself as such, becomes a product, only in consumption', Preface and Introduction to *A Critique of Political Economy*, Peking: Foreign Languages Press, 1976, p. 19. This is the difference between a book and a text; the first is produced by a publisher, the second is produced by a reader.

# INDEX

acid perspectivism, 187
*Adam Bede*, 51
Adopt-a-Building project, 179
Adorno, T.W., 105, 108, 110, 111, 112, 113, 114
advertising, 31–2, 163
aesthetic gaze, 210
'After the Ball is Over', 49
Alloway, Lawrence, 172
already said, 192
Althusser, Louis, 5, 71, 73, 115, 117, 122, 123, 126
Althusserianism, 115, 116
American Counterculture, 35, 112, 128, 173
Americanization, 11, 12
amplification, 86
anchorage, 87
*Angel Heart*, 186
Ang, Ien, 152, 153, 155, 156, 157, 158, 159, 160, 161, 205, 227
*Apocalypse Now*, 98, 178
Arnold, Malcolm, 63, 64
Arnold, Matthew, 10, 19, 22, 24, 25, 26, 27, 28, 29, 54, 59, 105, 106, 114, 125, 170, 172
articulation, 14, 15, 128, 156, 180
aura, 112, 113
axiology, 196

Babylon Zoo, 16
Bach, J.S., 109
*Back to the Future I* and *II*, 186
Bakhtin, Mikhail, 130, 131, 132, 133
Barrett, Michele, 136
Barthes, Roland, 73, 75, 81, 82, 83, 84, 85, 87, 89, 216

base-superstructure, 101 102, 104, 115, 116, 226
Baudelaire, Charles, 109
Baudrillard, Jean, 170, 177, 178, 180, 181, 182, 200
Beatles, The, 112, 173, 189, 190, 199
Beethoven, Ludwig van, 63, 65, 69, 111
Bell, Daniel, 172
Benjamin, Walter, 105, 112, 177
Bennett, Tony, 1, 14, 18, 34, 43, 109
Bernstein, J.M., 114
Best, Steven, 177
binary oppositions, 6, 77, 78, 79, 80, 91, 131, 133, 143, 158, 176, 219
Blake, Peter, 173
Block, Joseph, 103
*Blue Velvet*, 186
Bogart, Humphrey, 52
Bourdieu, Pierre, 8, 159, 197, 198, 205, 209, 211, 212
Bourne, George, 33
Brando, Marlon, 179
brass bands, 53
Brecht, Bertolt, 5, 106, 170
bricolage, 126, 194
British cultural studies, 3, 42, 71, 206
British underground scene, 173
Brogan, D.W., 40
Brooks, Peter, 155
Brunsdon, Charlotte, 136, 152
Bryars, Gavin, 198
Burke, Edmund, 59

Canaan, Joyce, 166
*Capital*, 115
capitalism, 13, 17, 21, 36, 102, 104, 106, 107, 108, 110, 111, 112, 115, 123, 124, 127, 133, 135,

capitalism (*continued*)
  136, 139, 156, 169, 172, 183,
  184, 186, 187, 188, 196, 206,
  207, 208, 221, 222, 223, 224,
  227
Carey, James, 3
Carlyle, Thomas, 18
carnival, 130, 131, 132, 133
carnivalesque, 130, 132, 133, 134
Cartland, Barbara, 153, 192
Centre for Contemporary Cultural
  Studies, 45, 46, 68, 70, 136
Certeau, Michel de, 16, 214
Chambers, Iain, 176, 186, 200
*Change in the Village*, 33
Chaplin, Charlie, 66, 113
Charles, Ray, 64
Chartism, 22
Chodorow, Nancy, 147, 148, 150
Christmas, 2, 5, 12, 19
cine-psychoanalysis, 146
City Arts workshops, 179
Clarke, Gary, 219
Clash, The, 13, 16, 190
class, 3, 8, 9, 14, 18, 21, 22, 24, 25, 26,
  37, 40, 42, 50, 57, 69, 87, 97,
  102, 103, 117, 122, 124, 125,
  126, 127, 131, 133, 164, 170,
  171, 173, 177, 183, 192, 194,
  208, 209, 214, 215, 224, 227
classical music, 68, 111
Coleridge, Samuel Taylor, 27
Collins, Jim, 193, 194, 195
*Collins Pocket Dictionary of the English
  Language*, 90
Connor, Steven, 176, 189
connotation, 6, 82, 83, 85, 86, 87, 89,
  154, 155
Conservative Party, 6, 14, 83, 125
consumption, 46, 111, 112, 113, 114,
  122, 123, 126, 127, 129, 143,
  144, 145, 147, 151, 160, 162,
  163, 184, 192, 193, 198, 203,
  204, 206, 212, 213, 214, 220,
  223, 225, 226, 227, 228
*Cosmopolitan*, 165
Coward, Rosalind, 137, 138
cultural capital, 155, 209, 211
cultural codes, 84
cultural competence, 89
cultural economy, 206, 207, 208
cultural field, 205, 209, 210,
  214

cultural politics, 136, 139, 160, 161,
  188, 228
*Cultural Populism*, 203
cultural populism, 203, 204, 205, 206,
  226, 227
cultural studies, 3, 17, 32, 45, 46, 49,
  54, 70, 82, 93, 115, 116, 122,
  123, 126, 128, 129, 143, 196,
  203, 206, 214, 215, 218, 219,
  220, 221, 225, 226, 227
culturalism, 18, 45, 49, 54, 55, 62, 63,
  70, 71, 127, 226
culture, 2, 3, 4, 6, 7, 8, 13, 17, 21, 22,
  23, 25, 29, 30, 32, 34, 41, 46,
  47, 54, 56, 59, 60, 61, 63, 67,
  71, 75, 87, 94, 101, 102, 103,
  106, 107, 108, 110, 112, 126,
  129, 134, 136, 145, 159, 161,
  166, 171, 177, 182, 188, 192,
  193, 197, 203, 209, 227, 228
  affirmative, 104, 107
  authentic, 105, 106, 108, 109, 110,
    111
  autonomous, 104
  the best that has been thought and
    said, 10, 23, 26, 30, 34, 54,
    69, 172, 204
  brutal, 41
  brutal–populist, 41
  common, 21, 30, 33, 59, 212, 221,
    222
  as court of human appeal, 54
  documentary record, 54, 57
  dominant, 1
  folk, 1, 11, 12, 18, 37, 39, 183
  high, 7–8, 8, 9, 10, 12, 18, 19, 36, 37,
    38, 39, 43, 58, 64, 65, 92,
    107, 114, 161, 170, 171, 173,
    176, 182, 188, 193, 208, 228
  ideal, 54
  industries, 16, 53, 126, 127, 129,
    159, 202, 206, 207, 224, 227,
    228
  industry, The, 105, 106, 107, 108,
    109, 110
  ironical-aristocratic sensibility, 41
  mass, 1, 13, 16, 18, 30, 34, 35, 36, 38,
    39, 40, 41, 42, 43, 47, 48, 50,
    51, 53, 64, 67, 105, 107, 108,
    109, 110, 113, 114, 132, 156,
    157, 161, 171, 173, 193, 219,
    228
  particular way of life, 2, 55, 56, 172

process of intellectual, spiritual and
 aesthetic development, 2
as selective tradition, 10, 57, 69
social definition, 55
superior or refined, 41
texts and practices of intellectual
 and artistic activity, 2
*Culture and Anarchy*, 22, 25
'culture and civilization' tradition, 18,
 22, 42, 43, 45, 114, 127, 137,
 227
*Culture and Environment*, 29, 30, 31, 33
*Culture and Society*, 17, 45, 54, 57, 58

*Daily Mirror*, 9
*Daily Telegraph*, 86
*Dallas*, 153, 154, 155, 156, 157, 158,
 159, 165, 207
*Dances with Wolves*, 80, 81, 92
Dante Alighieri, 38
darts, 53
Davis, Miles, 64
*Dead Man Walking*, 148
'death of the author, The', 90
decentred text, 119
decreation, 34
*Decoding Advertisements*, 122
deconstructive reading, 92
democracy, 29, 36, 41
denotation, 82, 86, 87, 89, 154, 155
Department of Education and Science,
 88
Derrida, Jacques, 90, 91, 92
desire, 94, 95, 96, 163
determination in the last instance, 115,
 116
Dickens, Charles, 8, 64, 66, 91
*différance*, 90, 91
*Discipline and Punish*, 97
discourse(s), 15, 91, 96, 97, 98, 99
Disneyland, 180, 181
Disraeli, Benjamin, 22
distinction, 8, 10, 198
Docker, John, 132, 133
*Dr Who*, 217
dominant/emergent/residual, 15, 183,
 190
dominoes, 53
Don Quixote, 116
'Dorothy's diary of romance reading',
 146
double coding, 192
Dvorak, Antonin, 110

Dyer, Richard, 143, 144

Eagleton, Terry, 73, 167
Earle, Steve, 178
Easthope, Antony, 166
*East Lynne*, 51
Eco, Umberto, 192
economic field, 205
*Elements of Semiology*, 82
Eliot, T.S., 170, 198
*Empire Magazine*, 89
Engels, Frederick, 4, 103, 104
escapism, 12, 143, 144, 150, 155
*Essential Pavarotti I* and *II*, 9
ethnographic cultural analysis, 226
exchange value, 156, 223, 224

Faith, Adam, 63, 64
false consciousness, 106, 139
fan culture, 157, 158, 161, 215, 216
 character dislocation, 217
 cross overs, 217
 emotional intensification, 217
 eroticization, 217
 expanding the series timeline, 216
 genre shifting, 217
 moral realignment, 217
 personalization, 217
 refocalization, 216–17, 217
 recontextualization, 216
*Father Ted*, 227
Fekete, John, 199
*Female Desire*, 137, 143
*Female Gaze, The*, 139
female gaze, the, 137–38
femininity, 145, 162, 163
feminism, 4, 15, 136, 138, 139, 143,
 152, 153, 154, 160, 161, 174,
 205
feminisms
 dual-systems theory, 135
 existentialist, 136
 liberal, 135, 136
 Marxist, 135, 136
 postmodern, 136
 psychoanalytic, 136
 radical, 135, 136
 socialist, 136
*Fiction and the Reading Public*, 29,
 33
Fiedler, Leslie, 40, 41, 42, 170, 172
filking, 217, 218
film noir, 8, 14, 142

film studies, 143
financial economy, 206, 207, 208
Fiske, John, 11, 16, 132, 133, 179, 206, 207, 208, 209, 220
football, 188
For a Critique of the Political Economy of the Sign, 177
forces of production, 102
fort-da game, 94
Foster, Hal, 171
Foucault, Michel, 16, 73, 96, 97, 98, 176
Four Tops, The, 188, 197
Frankfurt School, 11, 104, 105, 110, 114, 126, 137, 183, 185, 188, 219
Freakpower, 16
Free, 16
French imperialism, 85, 92, 93, 118, 121
French Revolution, 18, 60, 83, 84
Freud, Sigmund, 39, 89, 94, 109, 117, 120, 140, 181
Frith, Simon, 112, 114, 179, 189, 200

Gaines, Jane, 142
Gammon, Lorraine, 139
Gasset, Ortega y, 211
gender, 14, 87, 127, 133, 134, 177, 194, 205, 214, 227
German Ideology, The, 103
Godard, Jean-Luc, 199
Golding, Peter, 220
Goodwin, Andrew, 189, 190, 191, 192, 193
Goon Show, The, 66
Gorecki, Henryk, 188
Gosse, Edmund, 29
Gramsci, Antonio, 13, 14, 16, 70, 71, 123, 124, 125, 126, 127, 177, 227
Green, Michael, 70
Greenberg, Clement, 64
Griffin, Christine, 166
Grossberg, Lawrence, 17, 182, 185, 186, 200, 218
grounded aesthetics, 212, 213, 222
Guevara, Che, 109

Haag, Ernest van den, 38, 39
Hall, Stuart, 3, 5, 10, 15, 45, 46, 53, 61, 63, 64, 66, 67, 68, 69, 70, 71, 115, 128, 129, 226

Hamilton, Richard, 172, 173
Harlequin Romances, 136, 137
Hassan, Ihab, 172
Hawkes, Terence, 73
Heart of Darkness, 98
Hebdige, Dick, 19, 126, 169, 174
Hegel, G.W.F., 109
hegemony, 13, 14, 15, 123, 124, 125, 126, 127, 128, 203, 204, 206, 208, 221, 225, 226
hermeneutic code, 216
hermeneutics of suspicion, 181
Herman's Hermits, 193
Hill Street Blues, 207
Hirsch, Paul, 112
history from below, 61, 62
History of Sexuality, The, 97
'History Workshop', 62
Hitler, Adolf, 104
Hobson, Dorothy, 136
Hoggart, Richard, 35, 45, 46, 47, 48, 49, 50, 51, 52, 53, 59, 62, 63, 65, 70, 71
Hollies, The, 16
Hollywood's Vietnam, 99
hooks, bell, 166
Horkheimer, Max, 105, 106, 108
Horne, Howard, 179, 189, 200
horoscopes, 137
Houghton, Walter, xi
Hovis bread, 110
Howe, Irving, 172
Huyssen, A., 171, 172, 173
hyperrealism, 178, 180, 181

identity, 67, 148, 149, 153, 159, 207
ideological forms, 5, 104, 151
Ideological State Apparatuses, 122, 126
ideology, 12, 14, 83, 101, 115, 116, 117, 120, 121, 123, 132, 133, 151, 156, 157, 181, 186, 206, 208, 224, 225
of art, 211
as distortion, 3
as effacement of contradictions, 120, 121
as imaginary relation, 117
of mass culture, 156, 157, 158, 159, 160, 161, 203, 227
as material practice, 5, 122, 164
as myth, 6, 83, 84, 89
of natural taste, 212
patriarchal, 5

ideology (*continued*)
  of populism, 159
  of romance, 96
  as systematic body of ideas, 3
imaginary, the, 93, 95, 96
imperial narratives, 98, 99
incorporation, 13, 14, 15, 127, 130, 219
Independent Group, The, 172
industrialization, 17, 18, 21, 26, 33, 34, 41, 66
Industrial Revolution, 17, 30, 58, 60, 61
*Inside Women's Magazines*, 161, 162
intellectuals, 17, 35, 40, 42, 49, 125, 126, 173, 176, 177, 186, 191, 204, 210, 227
internal distanciation, 120
internal hyperinstitutionalization, 212
interpellation, 122, 123, 156, 164
interpretative fallacy, 118
intertextuality, 90, 185, 191, 194
Island Records, 127

Jam, The, 13
Jameson, Fredric, 101, 171, 174, 182, 183, 186, 187, 188, 189, 191, 200
jazz, 64, 66, 67, 68
Jefferson Airplane, 128
Jencks, Charles, 192
Jenkins, Henry, 215, 216, 218
Jenson, Joli, 214, 215
*Johnny Guitar*, 80
'Johnny Too Bad', 178
Johns, Jasper, 199
Johnson, Richard, 45, 69
Joyce, James, 170

King, Ben E., 16

Labour Party, 3, 6, 124
Lacan, Jacques, 94, 95, 140, 187
lack, 93, 94, 95
*LA Law*, 179
Lang, Jack, 153
langue, 75, 76, 77, 89
*L'Année Dernière à Marienbad*, 64
Lawrence, D.H., 47, 64
Leavis, F.R., 28, 29, 30, 31, 32, 33, 34, 39, 53, 59
Leavis, Q.D., 29, 30, 31, 33, 65
Leavisism, 28, 29, 30, 31, 33, 34, 35, 41, 43, 45, 46, 49, 51, 53, 54, 58,

59, 61, 63, 64, 65, 69, 70, 71, 105, 106, 114
left-Leavisism, 45, 46, 65
'Le Pont', 109
Levi jeans, 13, 16
Levin, Harry, 172
Levi-Strauss, Claude, 73, 77, 78
Liberace, 64
Light, Alison, 153
Liverpool F.C., 76
Lloyd, Marie, 66, 104
L'objet petit à, 93
London Institute of Contemporary Art, 172
*Long Revolution, The*, 45, 54, 59, 61, 70
Lovell, Terry, 223
*Loving With a Vengeance*, 136, 153
Lowenthal, Leo, 105, 106
Lynch, David, 194, 195
Lyotard, Jean-François, 174, 175, 176, 181, 182

MacCabe, Colin, 154
Macdonald, Dwight, 37, 40
McGuigan, Jim, 203, 206, 209, 219, 221, 225
Macherey, Pierre, 118
McLellan, Gregor, 62
McRobbie, Angela, 136, 177, 186, 189, 191, 225, 226
made message communication, 213
*Making of the English Working Class, The*, 22, 60, 62
male gaze, the, 139, 140, 141
Maltby, Richard, 12
Manchester United, 76, 217
Mandel, Ernest, 183
Marcuse, Herbert, 105, 106, 108, 110
Marshment, Margaret, 139
Marx, Karl, 4, 62, 101, 103, 104, 108, 109, 115, 117, 118, 137, 156, 181, 188, 223, 226
Marxism, 46, 101, 105, 114, 115, 116, 117, 167, 169, 174, 177, 182, 219, 226
masculinity, 148, 166
*Mass Civilisation and Minority Culture*, 29, 30
*Mass Culture: The Popular Arts in America*, 36
mass entertainment, 46, 47, 50, 67
materialist conception of history, 101
Matisse, Henri, 109

meaning, 74, 75, 76, 77, 83, 84, 87, 89,
90, 91, 92, 94, 113, 114, 119,
123, 126, 129, 130, 136, 139,
145, 146, 151, 161, 181, 185,
194, 199, 200, 205, 207, 208,
212, 216, 219, 220, 226, 228
men's studies, 165
melodrama, 104
melodramatic imagination, 155, 156
Mercer, Kobena, 177
metanarratives, 174, 175, 181
Christianity, 174
culture, 176
God, 181
liberalism, 174
Marxism, 174
nature, 181
science, 175, 181
working class, 181
'Middle Against Both Ends, The', 40
Miller Lite, 16
Milton Berle, 39
mirror phase, the, 93, 140
misrecognition, 93, 123, 140, 141
mode of production, 101, 102
modernism, 133, 134, 170, 171, 174,
176, 182, 184, 187, 189, 191,
199, 204
Modleski, Tania, 136, 137, 153
moment of plenitude, 93, 94, 95
Morley, David, 15
Morris, William, 65
Mother Courage, 106
Mouffe, Chantal, 14
MTV, 192
multiculturalism, 228
Mulvey, Laura, 142, 143
Mundania, 218
Murdock, Graham, 220
music hall, 66
My Poll and My Partner Joe, 104
myth, 77, 78, 82, 84, 85, 89, 98, 99
mythemes, 77
Mythologies, 81, 82
'Myth Today', 82

narcissism, 140
National Union of Teachers, 63
'Nessun Dorma (None Shall Sleep)', 9
New Left Review, 115
new revisionism, 205, 206
new sensibility, 170, 174, 199
New World Symphony, 110

Nietzsche, Friedrich, 97
Northumbrian Police Force, 179
nostalgia film, 186
Nowell-Smith, Geoffrey, 19
nurturing male, 147, 148, 149

O'Connor, Alan, 54
oedipus complex, 95, 138, 148
One Dimensional Man, 106
'On Popular Music', 110
organic community, 34, 53, 65, 66
orientalism, 98, 99
overdetermination, 115

paradigmatic axis, 74, 90
paradigm crisis in cultural studies, 203,
225
Paris Match, 83, 84
Paris Texas, 96
parody, 184, 191
parole, 75, 76, 77, 89
pastiche, 184, 185, 186, 191
patriarchy, 135, 136, 138, 149, 151, 166
Pavarotti, Luciano, 9, 188, 198
Peggy Sue Got Married, 186
Pfeil, Fred, 192
'photographic message, The', 84
Picasso, Pablo, 170
Plato, 109
pleasure, 130, 137, 139, 140, 141, 152,
154, 155, 156, 157, 158, 160,
161, 162, 163, 200, 205, 206,
207, 208, 226, 227, 228
Polan, Dana, 160, 161
political correctness, 228
political economy of culture, 203, 204,
205, 207, 219, 220, 221, 222,
224, 225
polysemy, 83, 195, 196
pop art, 172, 173
pop music, 13, 64, 68, 69, 110, 111,
112, 114, 189, 190, 192
emotional type of listener, 111
pseudo-individualization, 110, 111,
112
rhythmically obedient type of
listener, 111
as social cement, 111, 112
socio-psychological function, 111
pop music culture, 67, 69, 70, 192
popular, 7, 10
popular aesthetic, the, 50, 159, 211
popular art, 66, 67, 68, 69

*Popular Arts, The,* 46, 63, 64, 67
popular cinema, 139, 140, 141, 142
popular culture, 1, 2, 3, 5, 6, 7, 8, 9,
    10, 11, 12, 13, 14, 15, 19, 21,
    22, 23, 25, 26, 27, 34, 35, 36,
    39, 41, 42, 43, 45, 46, 49, 50,
    53, 54, 58, 59, 61, 63, 64, 66,
    67, 70, 71, 77, 81, 92, 101, 104,
    105, 110, 114, 116, 118, 122,
    123, 126, 127, 130, 132, 136,
    139, 154, 156, 159, 161, 171,
    172, 173, 175, 183, 188, 189,
    193, 199, 200, 202, 205, 206,
    208, 209, 210, 215, 220 221,
    223, 225, 226, 227, 228
    absent/present other, 1, 18–19
    and Americanization, 11, 12
    as 'anarchy', 19
    and hegemony theory, 14–16
    and industrialization and
        urbanization, 17–18
    as mass culture, 10, 11
    and 'the people', 14
    and postmodernism, 16–17
    as public fantasy, 12
    as quantitative index, 7
    as residual category, 8
'Popular culture and personal
    responsibility' (NUT
    conference), 63
popular discrimination, 64, 147, 149,
    206
popular fiction, 19, 30, 31, 51, 166
Porter, Cole, 65
post-feminism, 165
*Postmodern Condition, The,* 174, 176
*Postmodern MTV,* 192
postmodernism, 17, 44, 170, 171, 172,
    204, 205, 226
    collapse of distinction between high
        and popular culture, 16,
        172, 175, 185, 188, 199
    film, 186
    pop music, 170, 189–93
    television, 170, 193–6
'Postmodernism and consumer
    society', 182
'Postmodernism, or the cultural logic
    of late capitalism', 182–3
post-structuralism, 2, 12, 90, 93, 96,
    185
power, 97, 196, 197, 198, 200, 208, 210,
    218, 224

power-knowledge, 96, 97, 98, 99
*Preface and Introduction to A Critique of
    Political Economy,* 101
primary signification, 82
problematic, the, 117
production in use, 129, 213, 226, 227
psychedelic art, 174
psychoanalysis, 93, 105, 139, 143, 144
Puccini, Giacomo, 9
*Pulp Fiction,* 187

race, 14, 87, 127, 133, 164, 194, 214,
    227
racism, 127, 128, 191, 205, 206
radical eclecticism, 194
Radway, Janice, 146, 147, 148, 149,
    150, 151, 152
*Raiders of the Lost Ark,* 186
*Raise the Titanic,* 207
*Rambo,* 181, 207
Rantzen, Ester, 164
rap, 191
Rastafarian culture, 127
Rauschenberg, Robert, 170
RCA Records, 128
*Reading Capital,* 117
reading formation, 155, 156, 192, 195
reading position, 15, 156
*Reading the Romance,* 150, 152, 153
realism, 154, 183, 190
    classic, 154
    emotional, 68, 154, 155
    empiricist, 154
    grotesque, 132, 133
Redding, Otis, 198
relations of production, 102
relay, 86
REM, 224
Repressive State Apparatus (RSA), 126
resistance, 13, 14, 15, 125, 126, 127,
    145, 151, 167, 205, 206, 207,
    208, 219, 228
rituals of truth, 97, 99
*Robin Hood, Prince of Thieves,* 186
Rock Against Racism, 112
Rockwell, John, 173
Rolling Stones, 189, 190, 193
romance,
    failed, 148, 149
    ideal, 147, 148
romance fiction, 31, 137, 138
romance reading, 146, 147, 148, 149,
    150, 151, 152

Rosenberg, Bernard, 36
Ross, Andrew, 11, 35, 42
Rousseau, Jean-Jacques, 91, 92
*Rumble Fish*, 186
Ruthless Rap Assassins, 191

Said, Edward, 98
sampling, 190, 191
Saussure, Ferdinand de, 73, 74, 76, 81, 89, 90
schizophrenia, 187
Schlesinger, Philip, 206
'Schools of English and Contemporary Society', 70
Schwenger, Peter, 166
scopophilia, 140, 141, 142
*Screen*, 114
scriptural economy, 214
seaside holiday, 2, 5, 12, 14, 19
secondary signification, 82
*Secret Diary of Laura Palmer, The*, 194
Seldes, Gilbert, 38
semiology, 82, 85
semiotic guerrilla warfare, 207
sent message communication, 213
*Sergeant Pepper's Lonely Hearts Club Band*, 173
Shakespeare, William, 8, 32, 36, 37, 64, 69
*Shane*, 79
Sharp, Cecil, 49
Shelley, Percy Bysshc, 109
Sherman, Cindy, 188
Shils, Edward, 39, 40, 41
Showalter, Elaine, 135, 167
showing, 120
signification, 81, 83, 87
signifier/signified/sign, 73, 74, 82, 85, 89, 90, 91, 95
Simpson, O.J., 180
simulation(s), 177, 178, 180, 181, 187, 193
Sinatra, Frank, 64
*Sixguns and Society*, 78
Smith, Adam, 117, 118
*Socialist Review*, 84
*Socialist Worker*, 86
Sontag, Susan, 170, 172, 199
Southcott, Joanna, 61
*South Pacific*, 64
*Spare Rib*, 162, 165
*Sports Illustrated*, 38
Stacey, Jackie, 143, 144, 146

standardization, 28, 111
*Star Gazing*, 143
*Star Wars*, 186, 217
Steiner, George, 172
Steve Miller Band, 16
*Sticky Fingers*, 173
strategy, 214
Stravinsky, Igor, 171
structuralism, 2, 12, 62, 71, 73, 74, 75, 76, 77, 90, 92, 93, 95, 96, 127, 226
structure in dominance, 115
structure of feeling, 56, 57, 71, 192
subject/subjectivity, 15, 93, 94, 95, 122, 123, 138, 141, 156, 164, 196, 224
substitute gratifications, 39
substitute-living, 34
*Sun, The*, 9
supplement, the, 91
Supremes, The, 170
surplus value, 223, 224
symbolic, the, 94, 95
symptomatic reading, 117, 118, 121, 122
syntagmatic axis, 74, 89

tactics, 214
Talking Heads, 190
Tarzan, 98, 99
taste, 29, 38, 50, 65, 69, 160, 161, 173, 192, 193, 197, 198, 210, 211, 212
*Taxi Driver*, 118
telling, 120
text, 90
*Textual Poachers*, 215
*Theory of Literary Production, A*, 118
'Theory of Mass Culture, A', 37
Thompson, Denys, 29
Thompson, E.P., 22, 45, 46, 60, 61, 70, 71, 104
*Times, The*, 109
Tin Pan Alley, 49
to-be-looked-at-ness, 141
Tong, Rosemary, 136
*Top of the Pops*, 198
tragic structure of feeling, 155, 156
True Romance, 187
Tumin, Melvin, 42
Turner, Graeme, 2
*Twin Peaks*, 194, 195, 196

U2, 178

unconscious, 95, 96
unconscious of the text, 120
urbanization, 17, 18, 21, 66
use value, 156, 223, 224
*Uses of Literacy, The*, 45, 46, 49, 59, 219
utopian sensibility, 143, 144

value, 63, 65, 68, 107, 113, 173, 176,
    177, 196, 197, 198, 199, 213,
    227
Verne, Jules, 118, 121, 122
Vietnam War, 35, 84, 99, 128, 174, 181
violent hierarchy, 91
'Visual pleasure and narrative cinema',
    139
*Viva*, 153
*Vogue*, 189
Volosinov, V.N., 128

Walby, Sylvia, 135
waning of affect, 185
*War Cry, The*, 73
*War and Peace*, 73
Warhol, Andy, 173
Warner Brothers, 224
*Watching Dallas*, 152, 153, 160
Watergate, 181
Wellington, Duke of, 26
West, Cornel, 191
Western, the,
    classic, 78, 79, 80
    narrative functions, 78–9, 80, 92
    professional, 78, 79, 80, 81
    transition theme, 78, 79, 80, 81
    vengeance, 78, 80
Whannel, Paddy, 45, 46, 63, 64, 66, 68,
    69, 70, 71

*What a Man's Gotta Do*, 166
*Wheelwright's Shop, The*, 33
White, David Manning, 36
'white album', The, 173
Williams, Raymond, 2, 15, 17, 35, 45,
    46, 49, 54, 56, 57, 58, 59, 62,
    63, 65, 70, 71, 183, 190
Williamson, Judith, 122
Willis, Paul, 16, 205, 212, 213, 220,
    221, 222, 223
Willis, Susan, 114
Winship, Janice, 136, 161, 163, 164, 165
*Woman's Own*, 162, 165
women's magazines, 137, 161–5
Women's Study Group, 136
*Women Take Issue*, 136
'Work of Art in the Age of Mechanical
    Reproduction, The', 112
working class, 12, 21, 22, 23, 26, 28, 47,
    49, 52, 53, 58, 60, 61, 62, 114,
    129, 143, 177, 181, 191, 219
working-class culture, 13, 18, 21, 23,
    24, 26, 47, 48, 49, 50, 53, 58,
    59, 60
working men's clubs, 53
*Working Papers in Cultural Studies*,
    115
Wrangler jeans, 16
wrestling on TV, 132, 133
Wright, Will, 78, 79, 80, 81, 92
Wrigley's Spearmint Gum, 16

*X-Files, The*, 227

Young, G.M., 61
youth cultures, 2, 19, 52, 67, 112, 126,
    214, 218